The Human Tradition in

CHARLES W. CALHOUN
Series Editor
Department of History, East Carolina Un.

The nineteenth-century English author Thomas Carlyle once remarked that "the history of the world is but the biography of great men." This approach to the study of the human past had existed for centuries before Carlyle wrote, and it continued to hold sway among many scholars well into the twentieth century. In more recent times, however, historians have recognized and examined the impact of large, seemingly impersonal forces in the evolution of human history—social and economic developments such as industrialization and urbanization as well as political movements such as nationalism, militarism, and socialism. Yet even as modern scholars seek to explain these wider currents, they have come more and more to realize that such phenomena represent the composite result of countless actions and decisions by untold numbers of individual actors. On another occasion, Carlyle said that "history is the essence of innumerable biographies." In this conception of the past, Carlyle came closer to modern notions that see the lives of all kinds of people, high and low, powerful and weak, known and unknown, as part of the mosaic of human history, each contributing in a large or small way to the unfolding of the human tradition.

This latter idea forms the foundation for this series of books on the human tradition in America. Each volume is devoted to a particular period or topic in American history and each consists of minibiographies of persons whose lives shed light on that period or topic. Well-known figures are not altogether absent, but more often the chapters explore a variety of individuals who may be less conspicuous but whose stories, nonetheless, offer us a window on some aspect of the nation's past.

By bringing the study of history down to the level of the individual, these sketches reveal not only the diversity of the American people and the complexity of their interaction but also some of the commonalities of sentiment and experience that Americans have shared in the evolution of their culture. Our hope is that these explorations of the lives of "real people" will give readers a deeper understanding of the human tradition in America.

Volumes in the Human Tradition in America series:

Ian K. Steele and Nancy L. Rhoden, eds., *The Human Tradition in Colonial America* (1999). Cloth ISBN 0-8420-2697-5 Paper ISBN 0-8420-2700-9

Nancy L. Rhoden and Ian K. Steele, eds., *The Human Tradition in the American Revolution* (2000). Cloth ISBN 0-8420-2747-5 Paper ISBN 0-8420-2748-3

Ballard C. Campbell, ed., *The Human Tradition in the Gilded Age and Progressive Era* (2000). Cloth ISBN 0-8420-2734-3 Paper ISBN 0-8420-2735-1

Steven E. Woodworth, ed., *The Human Tradition in the Civil War and Reconstruction* (2000). Cloth ISBN 0-8420-2726-2 Paper ISBN 0-8420-2727-0

David L. Anderson, ed., *The Human Tradition in the Vietnam Era* (2000). Cloth ISBN 0-8420-2762-9   Paper ISBN 0-8420-2763-7

Kriste Lindenmeyer, ed., *Ordinary Women, Extraordinary Lives: Women in American History* (2000). Cloth ISBN 0-8420-2752-1 Paper ISBN 0-8420-2754-8

Michael A. Morrison, ed., *The Human Tradition in Antebellum America* (2000). Cloth ISBN 0-8420-2834-X Paper ISBN 0-8420-2835-8

Malcolm Muir Jr., ed., *The Human Tradition in the World War II Era* (2001). Cloth ISBN 0-8420-2785-8   Paper ISBN 0-8420-2786-6

Ty Cashion and Jesús F. de la Teja, eds., *The Human Tradition in Texas* (2001). Cloth ISBN 0-8420-2905-2   Paper ISBN 0-8420-2906-0

Benson Tong and Regan A. Lutz, eds., *The Human Tradition in the American West* (2002). Cloth ISBN 0-8420-2860-9 Paper ISBN 0-8420-2861-7

Charles W. Calhoun, ed., *The Human Tradition in America from the Colonial Era through Reconstruction* (2002). Cloth ISBN 0-8420-5030-2   Paper ISBN 0-8420-5031-0

Donald W. Whisenhunt, ed., *The Human Tradition in America between the Wars, 1920–1945* (2002). Cloth ISBN 0-8420-5011-6   Paper ISBN 0-8420-5012-4

Roger Biles, ed., *The Human Tradition in Urban America* (2002). Cloth ISBN 0-8420-2992-3   Paper ISBN 0-8420-2993-1

Clark Davis and David Igler, eds., *The Human Tradition in California* (2002). Cloth ISBN 0-8420-5026-4 Paper ISBN 0-8420-5027-2

THE HUMAN TRADITION IN
URBAN AMERICA

THE HUMAN TRADITION IN
URBAN
AMERICA

No. 13
Human Tradition in America

Edited by
Roger Biles

A Scholarly Resources Inc. Imprint
Wilmington, Delaware

© 2002 by Scholarly Resources Inc.
All rights reserved
First published 2002
Printed and bound in the United States of America

Scholarly Resources Inc.
104 Greenhill Avenue
Wilmington, DE 19805-1897
www.scholarly.com

Library of Congress Cataloging-in-Publication Data

The human tradition in urban America / edited by Roger Biles.
    p. cm. — (The human tradition in America ; no. 13)
    Includes bibliographical references and index.
    ISBN 0-8420-2992-3 (cloth : alk. paper) — ISBN 0-8420-2993-1
(paper : alk. paper)
    1. United States—Biography. 2. Urbanization—United States—
History. 3. City and town life—United States—History. 4. Cities and
towns—United States—History. I. Biles, Roger, 1950–   II. Series.

CT214 .H86 2002
920.073—dc21   2002024525

∞ The paper used in this publication meets the minimum requirements
of the American National Standard for permanence of paper for printed
library materials, Z39.48, 1984.

About the Editor

Roger Biles received his Ph.D. degree from the University of Illinois at Chicago and is currently professor of history at East Carolina University, Greenville, North Carolina. He is the author of several books, including *Richard J. Daley: Politics, Race, and the Governing of Chicago* (1995), and the coeditor of *From Tenements to the Taylor Homes: In Search of an Urban Housing Policy in Twentieth-Century America* (2000).

Contents

Introduction

Roger Biles

From the beginning of New World settlement, cities have exerted a significant influence on the development of the United States. Although quite small in the preindustrial era, cities served as centers of defense, trade, government, and culture for surrounding areas. Acting as the hubs of emerging trade and transportation networks, these communities served vitally important functions in the development of a national economy. With the coming of industrialization, the impressive size of the rapidly growing metropolitan areas bespoke their growing importance in an increasingly complex society. Sprawling metropolitan areas, composed of cities and suburbs, dominated American life by the close of the nineteenth century. For a host of economic, social, and cultural reasons, rural folk and immigrants moved to urban areas in increasing numbers throughout American history. The shortcomings of urban life notwithstanding, the overwhelming percentage of Americans chose to reside in urban and suburban settings. As the essays in this volume illustrate, the ways in which they chose to live their lives and the improvements they sought to impose on their urban environments tell us much about the history of the nation.

Urban life in North America actually predated the establishment of the British colonies along the Atlantic coastline. Long before Europeans arrived in the New World, Native Americans lived in settlements containing populations ranging from fifty to several thousand inhabitants. On the eastern banks of the Mississippi River near St. Louis, Missouri, for example, the Indian community of Cahokia covered six square miles with a population estimated at 35,000. Native American pueblos of varying sizes honeycombed the American Southwest long before the Spanish conquistadors arrived in search of gold and glory. The extensive Spanish network of communities, called an "empire of towns" by the geographer D. W. Meinig, stretched from St. Augustine to Santa Fe. To support their incursions into the continent's rich interior, the French established fortified settlements at places such as Montreal, Quebec, Detroit, St. Louis, and Fort Duquesne (Pittsburgh), while creating an administrative center for their lower Mississippi holdings at New Orleans.[1]

Beginning with their earliest attempts to establish a mercantile empire in Virginia and New England, the British encouraged the founding of cities. After an initial concentration of population in cities, however, a period of dispersion ensued. In 1700 an estimated 7.7 percent of the British population in the New World lived in five port cities—Boston, Massachusetts; Newport, Rhode Island; New York City, New York; Philadelphia, Pennsylvania; and Charleston, South Carolina—but by 1760 the percentage had fallen to 4.5. Even as the number of communities increased throughout the growing colonies, more pioneers ventured out into the surrounding countryside than returned to the cities. In a pattern frequently repeated in the early decades of American history, cities acted as spearheads of the developing frontier.

Cities played the pivotal role in the colonists' decision to seek independence from Britain, supplying the ideas and leadership to forge a revolution. Merchants in ports along the Atlantic coast chafed under colonial rule and led the opposition to the series of tax laws imposed by the British Parliament after 1763. Politicians in Boston, New York City, and Newport led protests—often in the form of mob violence—that contributed to the deepening imperial crisis. The Boston Massacre of 1770 highlighted the existence of a prolonged urban guerilla warfare between urban dissidents and colonial officials. In short, historians have noted, the restive populations of the colonial cities helped to create a nascent sense of nationalism and led the way to revolution while the balance of the population, 95 percent of which resided in rural areas, followed along.

The new nation remained predominantly rural after the American Revolution, and urban growth rates vacillated in the early nineteenth century. While the nation's population increased 84 percent from 1790 to 1810, the urban population rose 160 percent. During those years, British attacks on American maritime commerce, as well as the turmoil surrounding the French Revolution and the rise of Napoleon, disrupted U.S. trade networks with European nations. The War of 1812 exacerbated America's economic plight and, as the nation's seaport cities languished, disgruntled urban spokesmen called for secession. Between 1810 and 1820 the urban proportion of the population actually declined; by 1820 only 7.2 percent of Americans resided in urban places.

From 1820 to 1870 the nation experienced an unprecedented period of urban growth. The urban population grew three times as fast as the national population during each of those decades, and by 1870 one-fourth of all Americans lived in cities. Only twelve cities had populations exceeding 10,000 in 1820, whereas 101 cities did so by 1870, and eight of those communities boasted populations of more than 100,000. Although cities in the Northeast remained the largest—Philadelphia reported a population of one-half million, and the combined populations of New York City and Brooklyn surpassed one million—the nation's urban population had become more widely distributed. In 1840 the five largest cities contained nearly half of the nation's urban population, but by 1860 those communities claimed just 38 percent of the total.

The rapidly rising population in the cities paralleled the opening of the trans-Appalachian frontier. In the late eighteenth and early nineteenth centuries, settlers traversed the Appalachian Mountains along narrow roadways or floated westward down the Ohio River and its tributaries. The arrival of the steamboat on the internal waterways accelerated the movement of people and freight and, in the words of the historian Patricia Mooney Melvin, "telescoped at least a half-century's development into a single generation." As farms produced bountiful yields in the Old Northwest and steamboat traffic grew apace, cities along the Ohio and Mississippi Rivers thrived. Pittsburgh, Lexington, Louisville, Cincinnati, and St. Louis laid imperial claim to vast hinterlands just as seaport cities had done generations before. Following the opening of the Erie Canal, communities along the Great Lakes attracted a host of land speculators followed by thousands of new residents. Soon Buffalo, Cleveland, Detroit, Chicago, and Milwaukee experienced phenomenal growth and eclipsed the cities of the Mississippi and Ohio River valleys. A burgeoning railroad network quickly surpassed the steamboats and reinforced the growth of midwestern cities. Meanwhile, the discovery of gold in distant California resulted in the remarkable growth of San Francisco from an insignificant port with fewer than 1,000 residents in 1848 to a bustling boomtown of 56,800 inhabitants in 1860.[2]

In the antebellum years, cities grew at extraordinary rates everywhere but in the stubbornly rural South. Charleston, South Carolina, which ranked as the nation's fifth largest city as late as 1810, slipped into a period of prolonged decline thereafter and had dropped off of the list of the twenty largest cities by 1860. Indeed, only New Orleans could be described as a major southern city by the time of the Civil War. The region's subservience to the cultivation of cotton and tobacco, though an immediate source of considerable prosperity, worked against urban development. The simple growth of staple crops with no need for marketing arrangements and plantation owners' development of processing facilities on their own property made the need for cities less urgent. Inextricably tied to the countryside, the South's cities became junior partners in the developing national urban economy. As the historians David R. Goldfield and Blaine A. Brownell concluded, "Southern cities served more as adjuncts of the northeastern regional economy than as cogs in an independent regional urban system."[3]

Following the Civil War, rapid industrialization produced another period of striking urban growth. By 1890, according to the U.S. Bureau of the Census, manufacturing had surpassed commerce as the primary source of urban wealth. Cities along the eastern seaboard specialized in the production of shoes and clothing, with the preponderance of the garment industry wedged into Manhattan's tenements. Metallurgy and other forms of heavy industry predominated in such cities as Pittsburgh, Detroit, Cleveland, and Milwaukee. Steel mills dotted the Chicago landscape as well, but the Windy City's meteoric rise owed even more to its meatpacking and lumber industries. With a rapidity that European observers found remarkable, American cities became the pacesetters in industrial productivity.

Cavernous factories required a massive and growing labor force, and workers from European countries arrived in the United States by the millions. A series of devastating crop failures in the 1840s sparked massive waves of emigration from Ireland, Germany, and Scandinavia, but those numbers seemed modest in comparison with the mass migration of the postbellum era. Between 1870 and 1890, fully 8 million immigrants arrived in America, most of them settling in the cities; another 8.75 million arrived between 1900 and 1910. While the number of German and Irish immigrants remained high, limited economic opportunities, repressive political regimes, and improved transportation in southern and eastern Europe led millions of Jews, Italians, Poles, Slavs, Czechs, and Greeks to seek the promise of a new life in America. Although some American cities continued to grow principally through rural-to-urban migration and their populations remained relatively homogeneous, the ethnic composition of most large urban places increasingly showed the impact of the huge and diverse immigration from Europe. By 1920, three-fourths of the nation's foreign-born lived in cities, and the impact of immigration resounded most clearly in large industrial cities. In 1900 first- and second-generation immigrants comprised 75 percent of the population of Buffalo, New York; in 1890 immigrants and their offspring accounted for nearly 90 percent of Milwaukee's population. As such statistics revealed, the effect of immigration on America's polyglot cities was both unmistakable and indelible.

To reformers of the late nineteenth and early twentieth centuries, the rapid growth of a heterogeneous population, the development of an exploitative factory system, and the noticeable deterioration of urban living conditions made the teeming industrial cities the nation's greatest problem. Such uncontrolled urban growth seemed to threaten the physical and emotional well-being of millions of people, and progressives conducted a variety of crusades to eradicate urban evils. The woeful performance of municipal governments led to proposals for new forms of governance such as city managers or city commissions, as well as crusades against the saloons where political bosses hatched their nefarious schemes for graft and influence-peddling. To improve the conditions of the poor and to combat the baleful influences of saloons, brothels, and gambling dens, adherents of the Social Gospel movement opened missions and summoned inner-city churches to devote more attention to the relief of human suffering in this world than to salvation in the afterlife. To improve the lot of the masses crammed into tenements, housing reformers fought for new housing codes and regulations. To temper the frenzied pace of urban life, reformers called for the creation of parks, playgrounds, gymnasiums, and other places for rest and recreation. In all, a disparate group of reformers endeavored to ameliorate living conditions worsened by inexorable urban growth.

In 1920 the census reported that, for the first time in American history, a majority of the nation's citizens resided in urban areas. Yet even as the country eventually became an urban nation, close observers noted that population deconcentration was indeed outpacing centripetal forces in metropolitan areas. Americans had been seeking more salubrious living conditions on the outskirts of urban areas since colonial times, but the pace of suburbanization quickened in the nineteenth century with improvements in surface transportation and the development of balloon-frame wooden construction techniques for home building. With the advent of the automobile in the twentieth century, middle-class Americans found it even easier to escape overcrowding, smoke, grime, and the other unpleasantness of urban life. Real estate developers preached the suburban gospel in newspapers, advertising circulars, and brochures, while suburban chambers of commerce and other boosters trumpeted the clean air and lush greenery of their communities. In 1920 two-thirds of the nation's metropolitan population resided in central cities; by 1940 the figure had dropped to 62.7 percent.

In many ways, some no doubt unintended, the federal government supported suburbanization. Federal road building early in the twentieth century proved a boon to commuters, and a batch of New Deal programs in the 1930s made suburban living a much more attractive option to the middle and working classes. With President Franklin D. Roosevelt's blessing, the Resettlement Administration built a number of subsistence homestead communities across the nation as well as three greenbelt towns just outside of large cities, but these decentralization projects elicited a decidedly modest population redistribution. More important, such New Deal agencies as the Home Owners Loan Corporation (HOLC) and the Federal Housing Administration (FHA) revolutionized home ownership patterns in the country by employing the federal government to insure mortgages. By increasing the affordability of home loans, the FHA encouraged Americans to buy rather than rent, and by making much more money available for new construction than for home improvement, the agency underwrote the building of countless suburban tracts. Allowing borrowers to deduct mortgage interest and property taxes on their federal income tax returns, the Internal Revenue Service did the same.

As the rush to suburbia continued, America's inner cities became home to increasing African American populations. Beginning in the late nineteenth century, rural blacks migrated to cities in the North and the South. Between 1910 and 1920 an estimated 500,000 African Americans left the South and resettled principally in the industrial cities of the Northeast and Midwest. This so-called Great Migration owed both to the severity of conditions in the South and the attractions of urban destinations. The decimation of cotton fields by the boll weevil drove thousands of black sharecroppers and tenant farmers off the land at the same time that the advent of Jim Crow laws poisoned the southern racial climate. Relegated to second-class citizenship, systematically disfranchised, and increasingly segregated in all areas of public life, African Americans also feared for their safety as the number of lynchings rose alarmingly in the South. At the same time, the burgeoning industrial growth in the North that attracted so many immigrants from Europe offered the prospect of steady work and high wages to African Americans as well. Labor recruiters, big-city daily newspapers, relatives, and friends depicted northern industrial cities as beacons of economic opportunity and salubrious race relations. The *Chicago Defender*, one of the leading black newspapers in the country, told its southern readers that "to die from the bite of frost is far more glorious than at the hands of a mob" and urged them "to leave the benighted land [of the South]." In substantial numbers, they did.[4]

The same factors that triggered the Great Migration after World War I launched an even more intense northward movement of African Americans in the wake of World War II. In both the 1940s and 1950s an estimated 1.5 million blacks departed the South and settled in the inner-city neighborhoods of midwestern, northeastern, and western cities. By 1960 two-thirds of the African Americans living outside of the South resided in the twelve largest U.S. cities. Whereas 75 percent of blacks had lived in the countryside in 1910, 72 percent lived in cities in 1960. In roughly the first half of the twentieth century, isolated black urban neighborhoods of modest sizes had metamorphosed into sprawling ghettos, and the faces of America's largest cities looked altogether different as more affluent white populations contemporaneously relocated in the suburbs.

After World War II, developers converted farmland into housing subdivisions, and the economic activities long situated in big-city downtowns likewise spilled into the suburbs. Manufacturers deserted their multistory urban factories for the greater convenience of spacious, one-story structures more conducive to assembly line production and more accessible to trucks. With abundant land available for employee parking, suburban workplaces offered a number of advantages to industrialists, and industrial parks sprang up on the fringes of metropolitan areas. With residents and jobs decentralized, retail establishments similarly forsook the downtown sites they had occupied for generations and relocated in suburban locations. In the 1940s and 1950s suburbanites enjoyed the convenience of buying at nearby shopping centers and in the 1960s and 1970s at enclosed malls anchored by major department stores. Once an activity identified with the central city, shopping became an essentially suburban pastime.

Alarmed at the precipitous loss of tax dollars and retail customers, embattled central cities fought back in an attempt to halt the forces of decentralization. In hopes of restoring central business districts as the hubs of metropolitan areas, city leaders sought help from the federal government. Just as networks of streetcar lines had once funneled workers and shoppers into city centers, inner-city officials posited, high-speed expressways could perform the same function with automobiles.

Generously funded by the federal government in the 1950s and 1960s, these superhighways indeed made downtowns more readily accessible but failed to halt the cities' depopulation. Urban renewal programs, again largely underwritten in Washington, DC, replaced blighted central city neighborhoods with gleaming high-rise office buildings and hotels but did little to attract suburban families. Extensive freeway networks serving entire metropolitan areas provided suburbanites with easy access to shopping malls, restaurants, and cinema multiplexes. Downtown building booms and talk of an urban renaissance could not reverse the deconcentration of population.

In post–World War II America, rapid suburbanization coincided with the spectacular growth of cities in the Sunbelt areas of the South and Southwest. Sunbelt cities boomed because of mobilization for World War II and continued to grow in the postwar decades. In 1950 slightly less than half of the people in the South resided in cities, but by 1970 nearly two-thirds did. Communities in southern and western states accounted for 62 percent of metropolitan growth in the 1960s and a phenomenal 96 percent in the 1970s. Six cities in California, Texas, and Arizona—Los Angeles, San Diego, Houston, Dallas, San Antonio, and Phoenix—climbed into the list of the nation's ten largest cities, while smaller Sunbelt communities from Miami to Las Vegas to Anaheim recorded even more dramatic growth rates. (Conversely, northeastern and midwestern cities steadily lost population; by the 1990s, St. Louis ranked forty-third, Pittsburgh forty-fifth, Cincinnati forty-sixth, and Minneapolis forty-seventh in population among U.S. cities.) Warm weather, inviting tax laws, and the opportunity for year-round outdoor recreation attracted retirees, high-tech industries, and the military-industrial complex. Along with the huge influx of population to the southern and western states came an increase in problems like crime, traffic, and pollution that had long plagued the cities in the Northeast and Midwest. By the end of the twentieth century, inhabitants of the Sunbelt as well as the Frostbelt continued to struggle with the challenges of urban life.

As this brief overview of American urban life suggests, large, impersonal forces have strongly influenced community growth and development. Still, in discussing sweeping population changes, mass migrations, technological breakthroughs, and reform movements, the student of history should not lose sight of individual people who resided in the urban areas. We can understand urban history better through the experiences of "real people" who coped with changes and accommodated themselves to life in the cities in a myriad of ways. The historian Perry

Duis notes that millions of city dwellers made individual decisions that collectively helped to shape the contours of urban life; the individuals' responses were "solitary," yet "one of thousands or millions of individual stitches in the social fabric." At the same time, as some of the biographies in this book reveal, the actions of some individuals resounded in ways that helped redefine urban life. Men and women have attempted to improve their own lives in cities as well as the lives of others who lived in urban environments—and frequently with remarkable success. Not surprisingly, the thirteen biographies in this collection remind us that the human tradition has been vitally important in America's cities just as it has been everywhere in the nation.[5]

Notes

1. D. W. Meinig, *The Shaping of America: A Geographical Perspective on 500 Years of History*, 3 vols. (New Haven: Yale University Press, 1986), 1:14 (quotation).

2. Patricia Mooney Melvin, "Steamboats West: The Legacy of a Transportation Revolution," *The Old Northwest* 7 (Winter 1981–82): 340 (quotation).

3. David R. Goldfield and Blaine A. Brownell, *Urban America: A History*, 2d ed. (Boston: Houghton Mifflin, 1990), 109 (quotation).

4. Allan H. Spear, *Black Chicago: The Making of a Northern Ghetto, 1890–1920* (Chicago: University of Chicago Press, 1967), 137 (quotations).

5. Perry R. Duis, *Challenging Chicago: Coping with Everyday Life, 1837–1920* (Urbana: University of Illinois Press, 1998), xii (quotations).

1

Jeremiah Dummer
From Puritan Son to Worldly Gentleman

Phyllis Whitman Hunter

The cities of colonial America dotted the Atlantic coast from Boston to Savannah like pearls on a string. Early settlers gathered together and founded cities to safeguard their families and possessions in an alien and foreboding environment. From the beginning of British settlement in the New World, urban places served as the necessary trading centers for an extractive economy. As outposts of the British Empire, those communities served as trade entrepôts, marketplaces for the collection of raw materials, and bureaucratic centers within the existing mercantile system. Colonial cities grew along with a flourishing maritime commerce underwritten and administered by British imperial institutions. Products like fish, furs, lumber, rice, tobacco, indigo, tar, and other agricultural crops departed on ships bound for Europe, Africa, and the West Indies, while arriving vessels brought manufactured goods, sugar, slaves, and other commodities in short supply in North America. Recognizing the importance of cities to the economic development of the colonies, British investors and merchant companies promoted urbanization.

Most residents of colonial seaport communities had been city dwellers in the Old World and naturally sought to replicate European conditions in their new homes. The wilderness environment dictated much of the character of colonial cities, but the transplanted Europeans struggled valiantly to preserve the urban forms and functions they brought with them. Continued interactions across the Atlantic Ocean, based upon firm economic ties and sustained family relationships, ensured that American colonial cities would not develop in isolation. The particularities of place gave colonial communities their own character, but shared traditions and common Enlightenment ideas in the years before the American Revolution bound citizens of the British Empire together in many ways. Eighteenth-century travelers saw significant differences between Boston and London but also perceived strikingly similar institutions and customs in the two urban places—as illustrated by Jeremiah Dummer's tale of two cities.

Phyllis Whitman Hunter received a Ph.D. degree from the College of William and Mary, Williamsburg, Virginia, and currently teaches history at the University of North Carolina at Greensboro. She is the author of *Purchasing Identity in the Atlantic World: Massachusetts Merchants, 1670–1780* (2001).

In London, on July 15, 1709, Jeremiah Dummer began a spiritual diary. He noted how carefully he kept account of his worldly estate, yet "how careless" he remained in the "vastly superior concern of the Soul." Dummer vowed to keep a record of his spiritual struggles and of God's mercies. In spite of his promise, almost a month went by before his next entry. The delay, he admitted with chagrin, resulted from "the many avocations in this city." In these two entries, Dummer encapsulated the cultural change that transformed Anglo-American urban society during the years between 1660 and 1760.[1]

Jeremiah Dummer's life illustrates the intimate connection between England and the thirteen American colonies during the late seventeenth century and the first half of the eighteenth century. Born in America and educated for the ministry at Harvard, Dummer spent much of his adult life in London, representing several New England colonies at Parliament and Court. Residing in two important urban centers of the Atlantic world, Dummer brings to life for us the tensions of provincial status in America and the pleasures and dangers of residence in metropolitan London. Jeremiah Dummer lived through the transformation of Anglo-America from a seventeenth-century world dominated by religious intensity and inherited privilege to a society fostering urban areas characterized by a "polite and commercial" culture.[2] His personal struggles perfectly illustrate the cultural contradictions inherent in New England's Puritan society built on a desire for religious community and a need for commercial expansion. Like many in his hometown of Boston, Dummer endeavored to balance his spiritual and secular interests as the world moved forward into a new age of affluence, consumption, display, and social pursuits.

Early Life

The Dummer family claimed the rank of minor gentry in England, where they owned and operated a grist mill. Gentry status, practical knowledge, and available funds aided their rise to the highest levels of social and political life in early America. In Massachusetts Bay, Jeremiah's grandfather and great uncle joined several other entrepreneurial gentlemen in settling Newbury, Massachusetts, along the Parker River. They devised a scheme for importing cattle, constructed grist mills, and acquired substantial landholdings. Grandfather Richard Dummer, a strong supporter of the Puritan church, also became one of the wealthiest men in the colony and served in the prestigious position of treasurer of the Massachusetts Bay Colony.

Jeremiah's father (Jeremiah Dummer Sr.) was apprenticed to John Hull, a leading goldsmith and merchant in Boston. Hull maintained an overseas shipping business, sending cattle, farm products, and timber to the West Indies and importing clothing and small manufactured goods from England. He succeeded to the post of colony treasurer. Dummer Sr. completed his apprenticeship and chose to remain in Boston. He rose to prominence by following Hull's pattern of combining goldsmithing and mercantile ventures. Goldsmiths occupied a special position in seventeenth-century England and America; they were artisans, crafting beautiful serving pieces and jewelry, primarily in silver, but they also operated as bankers, using their knowledge of precious metals to assess the value of coins and to lend money. Through investing in shipbuilding (goldsmith Dummer owned shares in at least eleven vessels) and transatlantic trade with other merchants from Boston and Salem, Dummer Sr. built up his wealth and his political importance as well. He served in Boston's highest office of selectman and for many years as a member of the council, the upper house of the Massachusetts legislative body. He participated in civic affairs as a justice of the peace, an overseer of the poor, a member of the board of the Society for the Propagation of the Bible in New England, and a trustee of Harvard College. When Jeremiah Sr. died in 1718 he owned several properties in Boston and Newbury and thousands of acres of undeveloped land in central Massachusetts and on Casco Bay in Maine. Young Jeremiah thus descended from a long line of financially successful gentlemen who provided important service to the colony of Massachusetts. His older brother William took over his grandfather's estate in Newbury while Jeremy (as he was called when a boy) trained for the ministry at Harvard, completing his studies there in 1696.

The Boston of Jeremy's youth, home to 5,000 to 6,000 people, had the air of a bustling market town. The buildings lining Boston's streets resembled the Tudor Stuart-styled half-timbered houses that can still be found in medieval villages all over England. New Englanders followed traditional English building methods, constructing heavy post-and-beam, multigabled houses with small diamond-paned windows, low ceilings, and a projecting second story. Tourists can still view this early style at the House of the Seven Gables in Salem, Massachusetts.

Unpaved, winding streets led through various neighborhoods of the town. The edge of the city was fringed in docks and wharves on two sides. On the other two sides lay open land not suitable for farming. Townspeople used the space as common land to graze cattle and also for burying grounds, small orchards, gardens, and rope walks—long outdoor ranges where workers twisted strands of hemp into rope as they walked. At this time, Boston was virtually an island, connected to the mainland by a small neck of land only a few feet across. From time to time, Boston was completely cut off when the neck was buried underwater by the high tides of ferocious storms.

Shipping, shipbuilding, and fishing were the most important industries and the mainstay of the town's economy. Goods from the countryside flowed into Boston via the Road to the Neck. Fish, caught in plentiful quantities off the coast of Massachusetts, fueled trade with the West Indies and Europe. Boston merchants sent farm products, timber, and cattle to support the West Indian sugar planters and refuse fish— the poor-quality fish not acceptable in the European market—to feed slaves working the plantations. Traders shipped the better whitefish, preserved by drying or packing in salt, to Spain and Portugal, providing an important source of protein to the Europeans and an important source of profit to themselves.

A few blocks from the water's edge, the Town House and the First Church clustered around a small square marking the center of town and joining the two bulwarks of early Boston: religious faith and overseas trade. An English visitor, John Josselyn, described the town as it appeared shortly before Jeremiah Dummer Jr.'s birth. The houses stand "close together on each side of the streets as in London . . . with many fair shops." Josselyn viewed the town as "rich and very populous, and much frequented by strangers," among them merchants and seamen from other ports in the colonies, England, and Europe. Visitors and local traders congregated at the Town House and the nearby Exchange Tavern to conduct business and seal the contract over ale or wine.[3]

The town also drew people from the surrounding countryside and smaller ports to buy and sell farm products and purchase goods, especially cloth and small metal items such as nails, pulleys, tools, and buckles. The more prosperous country dwellers also acquired elaborate silver pieces like those fashioned by Dummer's father. Leading citizens from the surrounding region flocked to Boston to attend court sessions or participate in the General Court, the legislative body of the colony.

Constables, watchmen, and tithingmen walked the streets to keep order at night and to make sure all families attended the lengthy Sunday services and Thursday "lectures." Puritan ministers such as Increase Mather would hold forth, sometimes for hours on end, while many in their congregation took notes to be studied and prayed over later. Fathers were instructed to lead families in prayer every morning and evening and to make certain that all their children could read the Bible. The result was that New England had the highest literacy rate in the English-speaking world. Yet overall, the town and surrounding communities retained the air of medieval villages even as booming economic growth and long-distance trade propelled Bostonians, like their London counterparts, forward into the modern world.

We know little about Jeremy's boyhood in Boston. As a member of a prominent family, he probably attended Boston Latin School in preparation for college. He entered Harvard ranked first in the class of 1699, based on a combination of family social status and individual academic ability. Many considered him to be the most brilliant scholar of his generation. The dual nature of Dummer's personality that emerges so clearly in his diary of 1709 to 1711 appeared at Harvard, where this fine student also gained a reputation for mischief. College records indicate that he broke windows and incurred fines for various infractions. During one exploit, he managed to fall off his horse into the Charles River at midnight. It must have been quite a party!

Dummer's classmate Jonathan Belcher, a future governor of Massachusetts, may have joined in the revelry, for he, too, was assessed a fine for broken windows. Both young men had a reputation for spending money lavishly. After finishing Harvard, the two classmates traveled to England and Europe, Dummer to study for advanced degrees at Leiden and Utrecht in the Netherlands and Belcher to tour the continent, visiting his friend in Utrecht and staying at the court of the future English royal family in Hanover, Germany. When sojourners from Massachusetts such as Dummer and Belcher arrived in London, they would go first to the New England Coffeehouse to meet fellow colonists who had also crossed the Atlantic. There they would mingle with English merchants who carried on business with America. The London traders often provided introductions to other English gentlemen, who would entertain the visiting Americans. From the coffeehouse, groups would gather for dinner and a night on the town that might include attending a play or concert, stopping at a social club for a game of chance, or spending several hours at a tavern. Any and all of these events included liberal quantities of wine. In Anglo-America the gentry drank wine while commoners imbibed locally brewed ale.

When the two travelers returned to Boston, they had a difficult time finding their place in a small provincial city, accustomed as they had become to continental learning and aristocratic living. Boston refused to welcome Jeremy Dummer when he appeared after several years bearing published academic papers and an M.A. and Ph.D. from European universities. Some, including influential Puritan minister Increase Mather, valued his knowledge. Mather immediately sought a place for Dummer on the Harvard faculty. But others seemed wary of his obvious erudition, his European connections, and his cosmopolitan polish. Several of the local leaders expressed doubt about the value of his advanced degrees. Samuel Sewall, a prominent Puritan figure soon to become chief justice of the colony, said about Dummer's qualifications, "as to your Title of Dr. of Philosophy; seeing the very ancient and illustrious Universities of England, Scotland and Ireland know nothing of it; I am of the Opinion that it would be best for you not to value your self upon it, as to take place any otherwise than as if you had only taken the Degree of Master [the highest degree offered at Harvard]."[4] Dummer's controversial appointment at Harvard never materialized.

Dummer preached before several congregations in hopes of being offered a pulpit but there, too, he came up short. His friend Jonathan Belcher also seemed ill-equipped for any profession on the colonial scene. Belcher halfheartedly joined his father in merchant ventures until he was able to fashion a career as a colonial official. After a few discouraging years during which Jeremy saw "all his faults are publish't with additions," he returned in 1708 to London. There his advanced learning and polished bearing would prove to be assets rather than liabilities.[5]

Finding a Career in London

In London, Jeremy was able to choose among several possible careers. He had been offered the pulpit of the English Church in Amsterdam. Many friends, recognizing his talent at disputations, suggested he become a lawyer. His Bostonian supporters thought that he might make a fine assistant to Sir William Ashurst, then representing Massachusetts's interests to the Royal Court, the King's ministers, and Parliament. Jeremy also received feelers about working for the Tory party led by Henry St. John Bolingbroke. Dummer chose to ally himself with the Tories, apparently undertaking some kind of secret negotiations.

In 1710, Dummer became the agent for Massachusetts in spite of Governor Dudley's objections. When supporters in Boston had nominated Dummer for agent the previous year, Dudley had refused to consent. Samuel Sewall recorded the Governor as saying that he would be "drawn asunder with wild Horses before" he would "accept the [Dummer's] agency." Several months later, Sewall reported that Governor Dudley was "now more calm" and Dummer was voted in as agent.[6] Agent Dummer continued to have enemies in Massachusetts, sometimes as a result of political maneuverings between the Massachusetts house and the upper council (together called the General Court) or between the General Court and the royally appointed governor. And sometimes, one suspects, Dummer's European panache and undeniable brilliance aroused jealousy and suspicion among the locals.

Dummer sought to find his place in an England that was in transition. The power of aristocrats and the landed gentry was declining in the face of a rising moneyed class—families who acquired wealth through trade and investments rather than inheritance. Tory conservatives like Bolingbroke wanted to preserve the old order that valued family lineage and landed property. They vehemently objected to the growing influence of capital and mobile property that could be acquired quickly and could vault uneducated and unrefined individuals into prominence and power. In contrast, Dummer's polish attracted the attention of the Tory leader, who sought men of virtue and learning. No doubt Bolingbroke admired Dummer's European degrees and learned discourse as a refreshing change from the stockjobbers and corrupt officials—men of "low talents" and "still lower habits"—who thronged the halls of Westminster and crowded into London's Royal Exchange, the Bank of England, and the coffeehouses of Exchange Alley.[7] During the reign of Queen Anne (1702–1714) the Tories held power. As Bolingbroke rose in importance, so, too, did Dummer's prospects for political advancement.

Bolingbroke was an appealing figure for someone like Dummer. Both men were erudite and ambitious. Bolingbroke held high positions in the government, being appointed Secretary of War at age twenty-six and later de facto prime minister. He also created a circle of supporters that included the most famous figures of England's Augustan age. He founded the Brothers Club for gentlemen of learning and wit, whose members included Jonathan Swift, Alexander Pope, and John Gay. We do not know if Dummer also attended the Brothers Club but we do know that he dined out frequently, played cards often, heard lectures on anatomy at the Surgeons Hall, and seemed to take full advantage of the city's diversions. London must have been dazzling to a young man of twenty-eight, coming from a culture still dominated by Puritan suspicions of Anglicans, of pleasure, and of luxury.

London and the Urban Renaissance

During the decades that Dummer spent in London (c. 1710–1740), a burgeoning trade with Asia controlled by the powerful East India Company and increasing markets for colonial raw materials, especially sugar and tobacco, fueled the rise of a "polite and commercial" class in England. The docks and warehouses of London overflowed with tea and silks from India, porcelain from China, coffee from the Middle East, spices from Indonesia, sugar from the West Indies, and tobacco from Virginia and the Carolinas. As many as 1,800 ships at a time crowded into the Pool, the main harbor on the Thames River, bringing exotic goods and mundane commodities to the 500,000 inhabitants of London and its surroundings. The streets were thronged with thousands from all stations of life: people hawking goods, rolling barrels, racing coaches, and delivering parcels swarmed the streets while the gentry made their way among the hordes to attend meetings and entertainments. Visitors exclaimed about a pall of smoke that lay over the city, a product of coal-burning fires that warmed houses and fueled urban industries like smelting, baking, tanning, soap boiling, glass blowing, sugar distilling, iron forging, and brewing—all necessary to support the growing population. London brewhouses, for example, produced over six million barrels of porter and small beer annually.

An urban renaissance transformed the appearance of the city during Dummer's residence. Newly designed houses adopted a disciplined regularity with matched sash windows—just coming into use—arrayed symmetrically across plain brick or stone facades, contrasting clearly with the half-timbered, jumbled appearance of most seventeenth-century dwellings. New public buildings in the same style (called Georgian) arose to accommodate favored leisure pursuits including dancing, card playing, attending concerts, and gathering in clubs. Georgian architecture spread to provincial cities in England and America via the pattern books of architects like Colen Campbell, who published his designs in 1715. A fascination for exotic imported goods prompted a heightened interest in the appearance of things and contributed to the importance of personal display. Well-to-do Londoners loved to promenade through parks, saunter before shop windows, and parade through the steps of an elaborate dance, always conscious of their fashionable appearance and genteel manners.

To accommodate the need to see and be seen, savvy entrepreneurs built extensive pleasure gardens. Vauxhall Gardens, constructed during the Restoration (1660s) and rebuilt in 1732, offered a place for people to stroll, listen to wandering musicians, dance, and watch fireworks. The 12-acre gardens, geometrically landscaped around a 900-foot grand walk, contained covered boxes for the gentry. The remodeled pleasure palace opened with a masquerade ball and drew one thousand people nightly to its grounds. In 1760 the proprietors constructed a grand salon lined with history paintings celebrating Britain's imperial achievements. Vauxhall also became known as a place for sexual misadventure where, in the smaller, more sheltered walkways, gentlemen (and ladies) of breeding could mix with the common sort. Under the protection of a mask, they might breach polite norms with ease. We do not know for certain that Jeremiah Dummer attended Vauxhall, but its attractions must have appealed to a young man far from home.

Coffeehouses and gentlemen's clubs catered to business gatherings and to pleasurable conversation. Around the Royal Exchange, coffeehouses attracted stockjobbers (Jonathan's Coffeehouse) and merchants. One of the first marine insurance companies was formed at Lloyd's Coffeehouse. Tories met at the Cocoa Tree near the promenade in Pall Mall, Whigs met at St. James's Coffeehouse, and the Augustan wits met at Wills. Newspapers and conversation about the news became important draws for coffeehouses, where warm and stimulating beverages enhanced the pleasures of reading and conversation. By 1730, London had several important newspapers including the *Evening Post*, the *London Journal*, and (established in 1727) Bolingbroke's opposition paper, the *Craftsman*, all available for coffeehouse reading.

A French observer described a gentleman's day in London: "He gets up at ten or eleven and has breakfast (always with tea). He then makes a tour of the town for about four hours until 5 o'clock, which is the dinner hour: at 9 o'clock in the evening he meets his friends in a tavern or a club and there the night is passed in play and drink." Another observer remarked on the one essential stop on the tour of town when, "About Twelve the *Beau-Monde* assembles in several Chocolate and Coffee Houses . . . all these so near one another, that in less than an Hour you see the Company of them all." He also noted the "Turn in the Park" in the afternoon and the habit of playing cards or talking politics at the clubs after dinner.[8] We know from his diary that Dummer spent many an evening talking frivolously and playing cards. Given his obligations as agent, he most likely spent some time in the morning corresponding and drafting pamphlets and his afternoons prowling Westminster to promote New England's interests to anyone willing to listen. Social occasions and the affability they promoted were essential to successful lobbying, and that was Dummer's job—lobbying for Massachusetts, Connecticut, and New Hampshire.

The Diary

Shortly after arriving in England, Dummer began a spiritual diary that revealed his ambivalence about the pleasures of London and his longing for the lifestyle he left behind in New England, "a land of great light and purity." The diary, carried on sporadically for two years, charts Dummer's inner struggle to live up to the Puritan ideals that remained a powerful but no longer controlling force in his life. Again and again he promises to foreswear the lavish and "corrupt" enjoyments of the city—card playing, dallying with women, and competing for esteem among courtiers and gentlemen. Again and again he fails. His anguish pours forth in what must have been a very private document while, in his public life, he intrigues to gain power and position in political circles. Dummer began the diary by considering "how very accurate I & others endeavor to be in stating in our books of merchandize an account of profit & loss by which we may at any time know whether we improve or decline in our Worldly Estate." Yet he marveled at "how careless most men are & my self especially in the vastly superior concern of the Soul." To redress this imbalance, Dummer vowed to "keep a diary wherein to enter all the mercys of God." In addition, he pledged to record "all the afflictive evils & tryals" and "all my temptations."[9]

A month later, in August 1709, Dummer wrote his second diary entry, explaining the delay by noting, "The many avocations in this city & my unsettled condition here have hitherto prevented my beginning these memorials." Already, worldly temptations had deterred him from his spiritual duty. Confessing that "this day I bewailed before God my abominable corrupt nature," he penned a long list of "vicious habits" that included "a light and frothy spirit," "pride," "ambition," "envy," "hypocrisy," "uncharitableness," and "especially my covetousness, sensuality, & carnal concupiscence." In an agony of guilt, Dummer admitted that "these are the depraved habits that render me a foul & loathsome object in the eyes of God." As he humbled himself before God, his tears "flowed plentifully." Ten days later Dummer is in his chamber, reading passages on the life of Jesus and reflecting on Jesus' humility in washing his disciples' feet. Dummer prays for the Lord to "wash my impure soul from all its uncleanness." He continues in several more entries to plead for humility and virtue. By mid-September, Dummer is again confessing to frivolous pursuits. He writes, "I have divers times of late been engaged at cards, which I could not well avoid, it being customary in this City to use that diversion after dinner." Echoing the Puritan disdain for card playing that involves the loss of money and of precious time, Dummer resolves to "wholly lay aside that pastime" and to spend his leisure in "useful conversation" and other profitable diversions. Recognizing his fondness for gambling at card games, he hopes this diary entry "may be a reproach to me" if "my foolish and treacherous heart should betray me again"—as it did repeatedly.[10]

Skilled and Faithful Agent

Although Dummer continually fell short of his personal goals for sober living, he performed effectively as agent for Massachusetts and the other New England colonies that employed him. Engaged first by Massachusetts in 1710, Dummer's close connections with the leading Tory and de facto minister in the last years of Queen Anne's reign gave him the access and influence he needed to present the colonies' actions in the best light possible. He composed and published two important pamphlets to advocate for his clients. The first was in defense of Massachusetts's actions in a failed expedition to conquer French Catholic outposts in Canada. The second pamphlet, *The Defense of the New England Charters*, written in 1715, circulated in manuscript for several years among ministers and politicians in Westminster and Boston. It was published in London in 1721, and several decades later John Adams and James Otis used it in framing the argument on behalf of American rights just prior to the revolution.

Frequently, Dummer's writings and learned discourse prevented or moderated the government's efforts to tighten control over the colonies, especially Massachusetts—always a thorn in the British side. On the other hand, Dummer was often able to warn the colonial assemblies when they were in danger of overstepping the bounds and incurring censure from the king or the Board of Trade and Plantations that supervised and regulated colonial matters. Occasionally, Dummer's defense of his client colonies grew too vehement; at one point he was banned from the Board of Trade and Plantations for "ill language publically administered."[11]

The death of Queen Anne and the installation of the Hanoverian King George I changed the political climate in England. Dummer's patron,

Tory leader Bolingbroke, fled to France fearing retribution from the Whigs, who now ran the government; the Whig parliament actually pushed through an act of impeachment against him. While Bolingbroke associated with French philosophes and aristocrats, Dummer nimbly navigated the transition from Tory to Whig. His friend Jonathan Belcher, who arrived in London in 1714, may have helped Dummer find allies in the new administration. Belcher had been a favorite of the new king's mother when he visited the court in Hanover, Germany.

Belcher and Dummer made a powerful pair. In despair over the future of Massachusetts under newly appointed Governor Elizeus Burgess, a former army officer reported to be profane and greedy and considered wholly unsuitable by many colonists, the two men raised £1,000 between them to bribe Burgess to relinquish his position. Belcher raised his half from his father's merchant associates, and Dummer borrowed from his assets in South Sea Company stock. In place of Burgess, they convinced the British government to appoint Samuel Shute to the Massachusetts governorship. Belcher and Dummer also secured the lieutenant governor's position for Dummer's brother William. The two friends must have felt proud: they had saved the colony from an inept placeman and enhanced their reputations with many in England and New England.

In spite of what could be viewed as a superior performance, Dummer continued to be castigated by the popular faction in the Massachusetts house. Led by Elisha Cooke, they called unsuccessfully for Dummer's removal as agent, claiming that his close ties to the former Tory government would prejudice his advocacy. They circulated reports that Dummer donned disguises for nighttime visits to noted Tory Lord Oxford, where he was richly reimbursed for his undercover activities. A nasty rumor spread that Dummer had taken advantage of an English gentleman, Sir Alexander Brand, "as if he made the Knight drunk, and pick'd his pocket of 26 Guineas and brought in two Lewd Women into the Cross-Keys [tavern]." Samuel Sewall defended Dummer, saying if Brand was truly drunk, "how could he tell who pick'd his Pocket?" and suggesting that the two women "pressed close" so that it looked like Dummer had invited them. A few days later, a letter arrived from England that "much explod[ed] the story," vindicating Dummer and supporting Sewall's interpretation. Even so, given what Dummer himself reported a few years earlier in his diary when he bewailed his "covetousness, sensuality & carnal concupiscence," the story may have been at least half true.[12]

Boston's Urban Renaissance

While Dummer used his learning and his persuasive powers on behalf of Massachusetts and enjoyed the pleasure palaces of London and its environs, his hometown of Boston experienced many changes as well. In 1711 a fire swept through much of Boston, causing misery but also creating a space for the well-to-do to begin to refashion the town in a style adopted by the urban elite in London and in port cities and market towns in England such as Bristol, York, and Chester.

Although London was truly sui generis, a city unto itself, the customs, social life, and architecture found there influenced the urban centers of British America. Like London, most colonial cities were ports—Salem, Boston, Newport, New York, Philadelphia, Charleston, Savannah. (Buffalo, Rochester, Cincinnati, Chicago, and other large inland cities did not develop until better modes of transportation such as steamships, canals, and railroads made the interior of the country more accessible in the nineteenth century.) Closely linked to England through trade, print, and politics, colonial towns turned east to London and the provincial ports that lay across the Atlantic. Forsaking earlier styles, Bostonians built two-story brick houses with sash windows ranged across symmetrical facades. Boston merchants pooled their funds to extend King Street, the main street from the waterfront to the Town House, well out into the harbor, creating Long Wharf. Brick warehouses covered one side of the wharf and lined the street beside it called Merchant's Row. The Bunch of Grapes Tavern and the Crown Coffeehouse provided meeting places for local traders and merchants from overseas, much like the coffeehouses around London's Royal Exchange. The tall steeples of Anglican churches pierced the skyline, and the mansion houses of wealthy merchants included extensive landscaped gardens and summerhouses.

Genteel leisure activities appeared in colonial towns as well. In Boston a biweekly subscription assembly began not long after the famous York Assembly Rooms in England had opened. During the winter season of 1733, Peter Pelham gave notice "to the Gentlemen and Ladies Subscribers and others," that biweekly assemblies would be held in "Mr. Pelham's great Room" through the winter season.[13] For several decades as the town expanded, the merchant elite continued to sponsor public buildings and churches. The rebuilding of Boston culminated in 1742 with the construction of Faneuil Hall, paid for by wealthy merchant

Peter Faneuil. Donated as a market hall for the town, the multiwindowed, red brick building was capped by a cupola sporting a grasshopper weathervane just like the one atop the Royal Exchange in London.

Jeremiah Dummer would barely have recognized his boyhood home, and his fellow colonists may barely have recognized him. Suffering from an unspecified illness, he had relinquished or been dismissed from his agencies for Massachusetts and Connecticut by the early 1730s. He retired to a suburban village southeast of London, where he died in 1739. The *Gentleman's Magazine*, a fashionable English periodical, noted that "he had elegant Taste both in Men and Books, and was a Person of excellent Learning, solid Judgement, and polite Conversation, without the least Tincture of Political or Religious Bigotry."[14] But Dummer's reputation in Massachusetts continued to be uneven. Later accounts suggest that, toward the end of his life, he became "a Libertine and kept a Seraglio of Misses around him." One colonial gentleman who visited Dummer in 1738 related that he "went to wait upon him at his Seat in Plaistow on a Sunday after Church and found him with his Ladies sitting round a Table after dinner drinking Raspberry Punch." As the visitor entered the room, he observed "a confusion in Mr. Dummer's countenance and the Girls fled out of the Door like Sheep—almost over one another's back."[15] Yet in his will, Dummer trusted that God would not "afflict me in another World for some follys I have committed in this." He continued his loyalty to his homeland, asking his executors to "invite to my funeral all such New England gentlemen as shall be in London" and to give them each a "twenty shilling ring." He also sent his brother William £20 "to distribute among the poor Indian Squaws that may come a begging at his door in the country."[16] He ended his life much as he had ended his spiritual diary many years before, unable to forgo his "diversions" nor forget his dependence on God's mercy.

Notes

1. Jeremiah Dummer, July 15, 1709, London, "Diary of Jeremiah Dummer" (1681–1739), Massachusetts Historical Society, Boston, Massachusetts.

2. The phrase "polite and commercial" is from Paul Langford, *A Polite and Commercial People: England, 1727–1783* (Oxford: Clarendon Press, 1989).

3. John Josselyn, *An Account of Two Voyages to New-England* (London, 1674). Quoted in Walter Muir Whitehill, *Boston: A Topographical History*, 2d ed. (Cambridge: Harvard University Press, 1968), 15.

4. Samuel Sewall, Letter-Book I, 302. Quoted in Clifford K. Shipton, *New England Life in the 18th Century: Representative Biographies from Sibley's Harvard Graduates* (Cambridge: Harvard University Press, 1963), 63.

5. Dummer, quoted in Shipton, *New England Life in the 18th Century*, 63.

6. Samuel Sewall, *The Diary of Samuel Sewall 1674–1729*, 2 vols., ed. M. Halsey Thomas (New York: Farrar, Straus and Giroux, 1973), 2:644.

7. Isaac Kramnick, *Bolingbroke and His Circle: The Politics of Nostalgia in the Age of Walpole* (Ithaca: Cornell University Press, 1968), 76.

8. La Rochefoucauld, quoted in Roy Porter, *London: A Social History* (Cambridge: Harvard University Press, 1995), 169; John Macky, quoted in ibid., 170.

9. Dummer, "Diary."

10. Ibid.

11. Sewall, *Diary*, 2:815–16.

12. Ibid., 2:815.

13. *Boston Gazette*, January 8, 1733.

14. *Gentleman's Magazine* 9 (1739): 273. Quoted in Shipton, *New England Life in the 18th Century*, 72.

15. Shipton, *New England Life in the 18th Century*, 72, note 49.

16. Quoted in Clifford K. Shipton, *Biographical Sketches of Those Who Attended Harvard College . . .* , 14 vols. (Cambridge: Harvard University Press, 1993–1975), 4:466; "Will of Jeremiah Dummer," *New England Historical and Genealogical Register* 41 (1739): 57–58.

Suggested Readings

Jeremiah Dummer left a diary of his early years in London (1709–1711). The manuscript, "Diary of Jeremiah Dummer" (1681–1739), is available at the Massachusetts Historical Society, Boston, Massachusetts. Scattered letters can be found in manuscript collections at the Massachusetts Historical Society and the American Antiquarian Society, Worcester, Massachusetts. There are no full biographies of Jeremiah Dummer as the agent for Massachusetts. Clifford K. Shipton has a biographical sketch of Dummer in *Biographical Sketches of Those Who Attended Harvard College . . .* , 14 vols. (Cambridge: Harvard University Press, 1933–1975), reprinted in *New England Life in the 18th Century: Representative Biographies from Sibley's Harvard Graduates* (Cambridge: Harvard University Press, 1963). Michael Batinski has written a biography of *Jonathan Belcher, Colonial Governor* (Lexington: University Press of Kentucky, 1996). Belcher was a Harvard classmate of Dummer's and a cosmopolitan Bostonian who also traveled abroad as a young man. Batinski's work sheds light on life at Harvard and in Boston during Dummer's era. In *Bolingbroke and His Circle: The Politics of Nostalgia in the Age of Walpole* (Ithaca: Cornell University Press, 1968), Isaac Kramnick discusses the political debates that Dummer found himself embroiled in during his years in London. The developing townscape and architecture of Boston are chronicled best in Walter Muir Whitehill, *Boston: A Topographical History*, 2d ed. (Cambridge: Harvard University Press,

1968). To understand the Boston of Dummer's father and grandfather, read Darrett Rutman, *Winthrop's Boston: Portrait of a Puritan Town, 1630–1649* (Chapel Hill: University of North Carolina Press, 1965). A traditional history focusing on events and politics can be found in G. B. Warden, *Boston, 1689–1776* (Boston: Little, Brown and Company, 1970). The workings and important role of coffeehouses and taverns in Boston are explored in David W. Conroy, *In Public Houses: Drink and the Revolution of Authority in Colonial Massachusetts* (Chapel Hill: University of North Carolina Press, 1995). Several histories published in the nineteenth century cover events in this period, especially Justin Winsor et al., *The Memorial History of Boston: Including Suffolk County, Massachusetts, 1630–1880*, 3 vols. (Boston: Ticknor, 1868–1874).

The best primary sources available are M. Halsey Thomas, ed., *The Diary of Samuel Sewall, 1674–1729*, 2 vols. (New York: Farrar, Straus and Giroux, 1973), and Cotton Mather, *The Diary of Cotton Mather*, 2 vols. (Boston: Massachusetts Historical Society, 1911–12). Both men were contemporaries of Dummer and offered him grudging respect. Their diaries open a window into Puritan sensibilities and the growing influence of Georgian gentility in early eighteenth-century Boston. Boston newspapers from the period included the *Boston News Letter*, the *Boston Gazette* (founded 1719), and the *New England Courant* (begun by James Franklin in 1723). Like Bolingbroke's *Craftsman*, the *Courant* pilloried the newly gentrified mercantile classes in satirical sketches including the Silence Do Good essays written by Benjamin Franklin.

For a comparison of Boston, New York, and Philadelphia, Gary Nash's, *The Urban Crucible: Social Change, Political Consciousness, and the Origins of the American Revolution* (Cambridge: Harvard University Press, 1979), is invaluable. Ian K. Steele, *The English Atlantic, 1675–1740: An Exploration of Communication and Community* (New York: Oxford University Press, 1986); and Phyllis Whitman Hunter, *Purchasing Identity in the Atlantic World: Massachusetts Merchants, 1670–1780* (Ithaca: Cornell University Press, 2001), both stress the close connections between England and America in communication and cultural transformation.

Daniel Defoe's many works offer some of the best insights into eighteenth-century London, especially *A Tour Thro' the Whole Island of Great Britain* (London: G. Strahan, 1724; reprint, London: Penguin Books, 1971). Histories of the city include Roy Porter, *London: A Social History* (Cambridge: Harvard University Press, 1995); and George Rudé, *Hanoverian London, 1714–1808* (Berkeley: University of California Press, 1971). On the development of English towns from a somewhat broader perspective, see Mark Girouard, *The English Town: A History of Urban Life* (New Haven: Yale University Press, 1990). The leading source on architecture in London and elsewhere in Britain remains John Newenham Summerson, *Architecture in Britain, 1530 to 1830*, 9th ed. (New Haven: Yale University Press, 1993). Paul Langford, in *A Polite and Commercial People: England, 1727–1783* (Oxford: Clarendon Press, 1989), charts the rise of what he terms "a polite and commercial society" in England. In *The English Urban Renaissance: Culture and Society in the Provincial Town,*

1660–1770 (Oxford: Clarendon Press, 1990), Peter Borsay tracks the spread of Georgian social pursuits and the attendant rebuilding of provincial towns across the realm. For cultural interpretations of the eighteenth-century city, see Miles Ogborn, *Spaces of Modernity: London's Geographies, 1680–1780* (New York: Guilford Press, 1998); and Richard Sennett, *The Conscience of the Eye: The Design and Social Life of Cities* (New York: Alfred A. Knopf, 1990).

Literary studies, beginning with Raymond Williams, *The Country and the City* (New York: Oxford University Press, 1971), and including J. Paul Hunter, *Before Novels: The Cultural Contexts of Eighteenth-Century English Fiction* (New York: W. W. Norton, 1990), and Michael McKeon, *The Origins of the English Novel, 1600–1740* (Baltimore: Johns Hopkins University Press, 1987), offer important insights into the tension between the urban and the pastoral in English literature and into the role of London as the center of print culture for the English-speaking world during the seventeenth and eighteenth centuries.

2

Andrew Jackson Downing
Promoter of City Parks and Suburbs

David Schuyler

In the early nineteenth century, Americans struggled to reconcile the growth of cities with the images they cherished of a virtuous agrarian republic. Appalled at the crime, poverty, and filth that they saw in European cities, they dreaded the replication of Old World conditions in the American Eden. "I view large cities," Thomas Jefferson cautioned, "as pestilential to the morals, the health, and the liberties of man." Reluctantly testifying to the cultural benefits of urban life and acknowledging the city's undeniable magnetism, Jefferson, Henry David Thoreau, and others still lauded the health and happiness attendant to rural life. How could the vice, immorality, and distemper in the city be minimized while preserving its economic opportunity and artistic richness? How could bucolic amenities be transplanted in the forbidding urban landscape?

In several ways horticulturists, landscape architects, and reformers sought to inject the civilizing influence of nature into the burgeoning cities. Following the establishment of Boston's Mount Auburn Cemetery in 1831 and Philadelphia's Laurel Hill Cemetery in 1836, a host of cities founded "rural" cemeteries that provided city residents with rustic retreats for quiet contemplation and repose. Soon urban leaders called for the creation of open public spaces to be used for recreation as well as quiet relaxation. In New York City landscape architect Andrew Jackson Downing and poet William Cullen Bryant, among others, successfully urged the development of more than six hundred acres in the heart of Manhattan Island for a public park; Frederick Law Olmsted and Calvert Vaux completed the landscaping of Central Park and thereby established the prototype for other American cities. Downing further sought the refinement of urban life through the construction of graciously landscaped communities surrounding cities. Noting that new steam railroads made commuting possible for urban workers, he urged suburban development as an anodyne to the cramped living conditions prevalent in cities. Model suburbs, he believed, could avoid the dreary sameness of urban gridirons by platting irregular-shaped lots on curving streets following the contours of the landscape. Before he died tragically at the age of thirty-six, Downing laid the foundation for suburban aesthetics that predominated in America thereafter. Similarly, later generations of reformers battled to minimize the distances between urban dwellers and the sustaining countryside by carving out green islands amid acres of concrete.

A professor of American Studies at Franklin and Marshall College, Lancaster, Pennsylvania, David Schuyler is the coeditor of several volumes of the Frederick Law Olmstead Papers. He is also the author of *The New Urban Landscape: The Redefinition of City Form in Nineteenth-Century America* (1986), and *Apostle of Taste: Andrew Jackson Downing, 1815–1852* (1996).

Andrew Jackson Downing was a nurseryman, landscape gardener, and prolific author whose writings shaped middle-class taste in the United States in the two decades prior to the Civil War. In four widely read books and his monthly journal, the *Horticulturist,* Downing advised his readers on appropriate styles of residential architecture, the treatment of grounds, and household furnishings. At a time when classical styles in building and formality in garden design were dominant, Downing promoted Gothic, Italianate, and bracketed cottages and villas and the modern or naturalistic style of landscape gardening. Each of Downing's books proved enormously influential: the popular novelist Catharine Sedgwick found Downing's writings to be universally admired and told a friend that "nobody, whether he be rich or poor, builds a house or lays out a garden without consulting Downing's works." His career was closely identified with rural and village improvements, agricultural education, and the development of fruit growing. Indeed, in the early twentieth century a prominent landscape architect, Wilhelm Miller, pointed out that through his writings and his example, Downing had "affected country life in its every aspect." Important as was Downing's influence on the design of country houses and rural villages, equally significant was his role as a form giver for the mid-nineteenth-century metropolis. Late in life he became an advocate for comprehensively designed suburban communities and the most articulate spokesman for large urban parks.[1]

Downing was born in the village of Newburgh, New York, in 1815. At that time, Newburgh was a small community of 2,370 residents on the west bank of the Hudson River, its commercial economy dependent on transporting the produce of a rich agricultural countryside to urban markets. Samuel Downing, a wheelwright, had migrated from Lexington, Massachusetts, to settle in Newburgh around 1800. Surely the volume of wagon and carriage traffic entering the town from nearby farms and villages would have provided ample work for a wheelwright. By 1810 the elder Downing had started a commercial nursery on the family property in Newburgh, and his youngest son, Andrew, would grow up on the nursery grounds and make horticulture and landscape gardening his life's work.[2]

The middle decades of the nineteenth century were years of wrenching transition for agriculture in the Hudson Valley. Canals and railroads brought the larger farms and fertile soils of the trans-Appalachian West into competition with agriculturists in the East, forcing many farmers in the Hudson Valley to abandon a traditional way of life and others to shift from growing grains to producing dairy and fruits. The dramatic growth of New York City created unprecedented demand for milk, butter, fresh fruit, and vegetables, which also supported the smaller-scale economies of market villages such as Newburgh. At the same time, a number of prosperous New Yorkers established country seats on the banks of the Hudson and began creating elaborate pleasure grounds as well as gardens and orchards. Horticulture became a genteel avocation, and in providing trees and advice to a wealthy clientele, Downing and other nurserymen would begin to establish landscape architecture as an art profession.[3]

Upon finishing schooling at the age of sixteen, Downing joined his brother Charles in managing the family's nursery business. During the next decade, this ambitious youth worked hard to establish himself professionally, married well, and built an imposing Gothic Revival house overlooking the Hudson. He also wrote dozens of articles for horticultural magazines and read extensively in the history and theory of landscape design. Perhaps as early as 1836 he had begun writing a book on the use of trees in gardening, which evolved into a much more ambitious text published in 1841 as *A Treatise on the Theory and Practice of Landscape Gardening*. This book sparked a revolution in American taste: dismissing the classical revival styles in architecture and the formal or geometric garden, Downing introduced readers to the Beautiful and the Picturesque, aesthetic categories that reflected the international romantic movement in literature and art. Downing made no secret of his preference for the romantic over the classical style. Indeed, he posited a progression of taste from a formal, ordered landscape garden, which was favored when primitive nature or wilderness predominated, and described the settlers' reliance on the formal garden as evidence of "a meagre taste, and a lower state of the art, or a lower perception of beauty in the individual." Downing clearly hoped that the reader would follow his argument to its logical conclusion: that as the eastern United States moved beyond the stage of a newly settled area, taste should likewise evolve from the ancient or geometric to what he termed the "present more advanced state of Landscape Gardening," the modern or natural style. His analysis of history, then, was more than an overview of changing taste in the landscape; it served as justification for the style of gardening he championed. Although most of the book was devoted to descriptions of trees, advice on laying out grounds, and discourses on the ornamental uses of water and statuary, Downing also included a philosophical discussion of taste and a chapter devoted to rural architecture. Gracefully written and handsomely illustrated, the *Treatise* became an immediate success: it went through four editions during the next twelve years and sold approximately 9,000 copies.[4]

The following year, Downing published *Cottage Residences*, a series of designs for houses of modest size that he hoped would "contribute something to the improvement of the domestic architecture and the rural taste of our country." This was arguably the first of the new genre in publishing known as house pattern books. Earlier builders' guides presented views of facades, details explaining construction techniques, and a brief text addressed to the contractor or artisan. The house pattern book, by contrast, depicted the home in its landscaped setting, plans of the grounds, and ornamental details, along with an explanatory text to assist the reader in choosing a residence in keeping with his or her needs and circumstances. Each of the ten chapters of *Cottage Residences* presented a design for a dwelling in such avant-garde styles as a bracketed farm house, a board-and-batten cottage, an English or rural Gothic cottage, and an Italianate villa. Most were small in scale and represented the kinds of homes Downing considered appropriate to an emerging middle class. As was true of the *Treatise*, *Cottage Residences* also reached a large audience: several of its designs were reprinted in agricultural or horticultural periodicals in succeeding years, and numerous extant houses still bear testament to the influence of Downing's ideas.[5]

Downing's renown as an author brought invitations to visit properties and design their grounds, and in June 1842 he began advertising his services as a professional landscape gardener. But more enduring than the houses and gardens he designed were the books and articles he wrote. He published a significantly enlarged edition of the *Treatise* in 1844 as well as a new printing of *Cottage Residences*, and the following year completed his classic *Fruits and Fruit Trees of America*, a 594-page treatise that attempted to systematize pomological knowledge in the United States. *Fruits* earned its author numerous honors from abroad and became a publishing sensation, running through five large printings in 1845 and numerous others in succeeding years.[6]

Downing continued his efforts to influence American taste as editor of the *Horticulturist*, a monthly that commenced publication in July 1846. As he had done in the *Treatise*, Downing used the *Horticulturist* to educate the public taste and promote his vision of a refined society. He attempted to persuade readers that they should devote the energies once spent transforming the wilderness into more civilized pursuits, and particularly "the refinements and enjoyments which belong to a country life, and a country home." He denounced the free-roaming pigs that menaced the streets of countless towns, urged the formation of village improvement societies, and provided designs for sensible yet tasteful rural buildings. Rural economy was as important as matters of taste: because he realized that farmers were wastefully extracting nutrients from the soil and in older settled areas were experiencing declines in productivity, Downing became a powerful advocate of publicly supported agricultural education.[7]

In the *Horticulturist*, Downing continued his crusade to influence the progress of architecture in the United States, and many of the designs first published there were incorporated in *The Architecture of Country Houses* (1850). As was true of Downing's earlier books, *Architecture of Country Houses* instructed readers in the social and cultural significance of architecture and the types of dwellings suitable to different classes in society and various locations. Downing also included chapters on the design of interiors and furnishings. He advised readers on how to decorate simple cottages, the most economical and durable wall paints, wallpapers, even curtains and prints suitable for hanging in cottages, as well as architectonic features for parlors, libraries, and dining rooms in more substantial houses. Given the few photographs of interiors prior to 1850, these chapters of *Architecture of Country Houses* are an invaluable source of information on middle- and upper-class taste in domestic design.[8]

Although Downing spent his entire life in a village and addressed most of his advice on houses and landscapes to those people who lived in rural areas, his was a world that was rapidly transforming itself. The growth of cities, the beginnings of industrialization, and the tremendous mobility of the American people all challenged traditional ideas of social order, as did the emergence of political and social democracy. Downing decried the "spirit of unrest" he observed in too many of his fellow citizens. "Unable to take root anywhere," he wrote of the typical migrating Americans, "he leads, socially and physically, the uncertain life of a tree transplanted from place to place, and shifted to a different soil every season." Downing's first book, the *Treatise on Landscape Gardening*, promoted a conservative worldview, an attachment to place, at a time of tremendous social change. In subsequent books, Downing articulated the importance of well-designed houses as bastions of stability. The home was a "powerful means of civilization," he wrote in the preface to *Architecture of Country Houses*, a reflection of the nation's progress from barbarism to a more advanced state of social organization. Downing went so far as to attribute a "moral influence" to the home, a counterweight to the "feverish unrest" so characteristic of the United States. In promoting the reform of domestic architecture, Downing also defined the optimal location for the family home, the middle landscape, a symbolic space standing between the frantic pace, squalid conditions, and sordid temptations of the evil city on one hand, and the barbarism of the frontier on the other.[9]

The middle landscape became, in Downing's conceptualization, the suburban community. He attributed the emergence of the suburb to a matrix of factors, including a belief in the moral superiority of rural over urban life, cultural values that celebrated the single-family home on its own plot of land, transportation innovations, and greater economies in the cost of living in small-town or rural America. Downing both reflected and extended the prevailing cultural attitudes toward country and city: he approvingly quoted Alexander Pope's famous remark that God made the country but man the town, and criticized the practice of building cities "as though there was a frightful scarcity of space" in the New World. In appearance as well as disposition a country gentleman, he believed that the only reason to live in a city was to make enough money to retire to a house with extensive grounds some distance from the metropolis. Nevertheless, Downing conceded that cities were a fact of life in nineteenth-century America and sought to reconcile the seemingly divergent realms of urban and rural existence.[10]

The key to this reconciliation was new transportation technologies. In 1848, Downing applauded the "rapid multiplication of pretty cottages and villas in many parts of North America," and while he used the terms "country house" and "suburban cottage" interchangeably, he was actually describing the beginnings of suburbanization. A new way of life, tied to the city but located far from the congestion of the metropolis, was being made possible by horse-drawn street railways and the railroad networks that were extending outward from major cities. Although the railroads were originally built for commerce, Downing insisted that they "cannot wholly escape doing some duty for the Beautiful as well as the useful" by making land on the periphery of cities suitable for metropolitan homes. "Hundreds and thousands," he wrote, "formerly obliged to live in the crowded streets of cities, now find themselves able to enjoy a country cottage, several miles distant—the old notions of time and space being half annihilated." The development of suburbs was a positive good that enabled families to enjoy natural surroundings while maintaining proximity to urban jobs, friends, and cultural attractions.[11]

Downing quickly discovered that the emergence of the commuter suburb brought problems as well as the promise of a more spacious metropolitan landscape, particularly when real estate promoters and transportation companies laid out rectangular streets and advertised lots for sale in what they described as ideal communities. The plat of the village of Dearman (now Irvington, New York) exemplified what Downing considered the worst kind of suburban development. Located on a large, hilly tract overlooking the Hudson River twenty miles north of New York City, the site was connected to the metropolis by the Hudson River Railroad, the Albany Post Road, and frequent steamboat excursions. Dearman possessed all the requisites for advantageous development in the modern or natural style of landscape gardening that Downing favored. Given the topography of the site, curvilinear streets and irregularly shaped lots following the contours of the land would not only have enhanced Dearman's attractiveness as a location for suburban homes but would have reduced the cost of grading and filling the property. The real estate promoters, Cole and Chilton, instead imposed a rectangular gridiron on the site, with a central avenue, seventy feet wide, running east from the river, directly up a steep hill, intersected by eight narrower streets running north and south. They then subdivided the tract into uniform lots of fifty by one hundred feet.[12]

Downing had special cause for concern with the Dearman plan. Although the developmental scheme violated every precept of landscape theory he had promulgated in the preceding decade, Cole and Chilton attempted to capitalize on Downing's cultural authority by placing engravings from *Cottage Residences* in the upper left and right corners of the subdivision map published prior to the sale of lots at auction. Downing must have been enraged, and with this misrepresentation as incentive, offered a devastating critique of the speculative suburban community. That essay, "Our Country Villages," also established the general outlines of the suburban ideal in mid-nineteenth-century America.[13]

Because of the rapid development of communities throughout the United States, Downing argued, "the plan and arrangement of new towns ought to be a matter of national importance." He cited the example of recently platted suburbs along the Hudson River that claimed to combine "the advantages of the country with easy railroad access" to the city. In a veiled reference to Dearman, Downing wrote that fifty-foot lots and rows of houses along shaded streets amounted to "the sum total of the rural beauty, convenience and comfort of the latest plan for a rural village in the Union." Alas, in forsaking the city the purchaser sacrificed urban amenities yet found himself in a place "with houses on all sides, almost as closely placed as in the city, which he has endeavored to fly from."[14]

If the suburb were to be a handsomely landscaped community where families escaped the "turmoil of cities," Downing believed that it had to offer more than "mere rows of houses upon streets crossing each other at right angles, and bordered with shade trees." He conceded that either by choice or necessity "people must live in towns and villages," but could not accept that they should live in a place such as Dearman, which was devoid of the attractions he considered essential to residential life. The most important requirement of a comprehensively designed suburban community was the provision of a "large open space, common, or park, situated in the middle of the village." This area, jointly owned by all lot holders, should be at least twenty acres in extent and "should be well planted with groups of trees, and kept as a lawn." Such a park, Downing explained, would be the "nucleus or *heart of the village*, and give it an essentially rural character." He then recommended that wide, tree-lined avenues and the "best cottages and residences" front the park, much as the largest dwellings in New England towns faced the common, and that throughout the remainder of the village proprietors secure "sufficient space, view, circulation of air, and broad, well-planted avenues of shade-trees."[15]

Important as they were, platting curving streets, building houses, and reserving a park were but the first steps in developing a true community. After a few years, Downing predicted, residents "would not be contented with the mere meadow and trees" and would decide to make the park into "pleasure-grounds." Using funds obtained from a small assessment paid by each family, the park could be planted with handsome trees and shrubs as well as beds of flowers and orchards. One advantage of such an arrangement, Downing explained, was that families that possessed "neither the means, time, nor inclination to devote to the culture of private pleasure-grounds, could thus enjoy those which belonged to all." Still later, residents would decide that they wanted additional amenities, and so would construct rustic seats and arbors, organize summer concerts on the lawns, and provide refreshments to all those in attendance.[16]

Here was Downing's ideal of a suburban community, a private space that enshrined the "power and virtue of the *individual home*" and at the same time promoted communal activities. Private dwellings provided the optimal surroundings for nurture, while the park and its various entertainments offered positive "mental and moral influences" for all members of the community. A home in such a suburb enabled a family to reside free from the congestion, disease, and "immoral influences" of the city, to enjoy the beneficent surroundings of nature while remaining a part of the metropolitan landscape. The suburb itself was one of the many institutions Downing hoped would contribute to the realization of his ideal of "a virtuous and educated republic."[17]

Most of the houses Downing designed were substantial dwellings for prosperous clients. He did provide several plans for modest cottages in the *Horticulturist* and *Architecture of Country Houses*, and, as his friend Nathaniel Parker Willis noted, devoted considerable effort to dignifying the "homes of The Many," but these were generally simple board-and-batten dwellings he deemed appropriate for industrious workers and their families who lived in rural areas. Downing had hoped that the suburb would be a community that included families from all economic levels and walks of life. Because of the instability of job tenure, however, most working-class residents of cities lived within a mile of their places of work, which tended to cluster near other establishments in the city. Moreover, while the 5-cent fare of an omnibus or horse-drawn streetcar might seem modest, the cost of travel from a distant home to work and back again represented 10 percent of a laborer's daily pay.[18]

During the two decades prior to the Civil War, the United States experienced the fastest rate of increase in urban population in its history. The sheer speed and scale of this growth—the product both of immigration from abroad and the cityward migration of native-born residents seeking work in industrial and commercial centers—transformed metropolitan America. As his career unfolded, Downing witnessed firsthand the growth of cities. The tiny village of his youth had become home to 8,933 residents in 1840 and increased by 28 percent, to 11,415, over the next decade. Population growth was the result of prosperity brought about by industrialization. The largest factory, the Newburgh Steam Cotton Works, had been organized in 1845 by several of the city's wealthy merchants. The imposing new five-and-one-half-story cotton mill stood adjacent to the Hudson just three blocks from Downing's grounds. More than 300 people, principally unskilled women, worked in the mill, while a number of iron foundries and other works located nearby provided employment for men.[19]

Downing was deeply ambivalent about the emergence of industrialism in Newburgh. While he welcomed the prosperity the new factories brought to the community and surely benefited from the opportunity to design houses and landscapes for clients who could afford his services, he worried that poorly-paid laborers were forced to live in densely-crowded neighborhoods, in modest brick and frame houses erected on lots too small for a garden. Downing also witnessed the results of urban growth and the increase in poverty and squalor on his frequent trips to New York City, Albany, and Boston. He feared that the growth of urban areas—in population, density and scale of buildings, and sheer expanse of built space—portended the development of a rigidly stratified society he considered a threat to the nation's republican institutions. One tangible solution to the lack of open space in cities would be the development of urban parks.[20]

In October 1848, Downing published an editorial in the *Horticulturist* entitled "A Talk about Public Parks and Gardens." The text took the form of a dialogue between the editor and an American who had just returned from Europe. What most surprised the tourist were the opportunities for public recreation he encountered in Germany, which far surpassed anything then available in American cities. Parks on the continent promoted a "*social freedom*, and an easy and agreeable intercourse of all classes." In Munich's English Garden, as well as in the parks constructed on the site of the former ramparts of Frankfurt, kings and commoners alike enjoyed recreational facilities built and maintained at public expense. While in the parks, citizens gained "health, good spirits, social enjoyment, and a frank and cordial bearing towards their neighbors, that is totally unknown either in England or America." Downing found in the park a solution to the congestion of cities and the increasing stratification of American society—a republican institution that brought all classes of residents together to enjoy healthful recreation.[21]

Two years later, Downing had the opportunity to visit England, home of his ancestors and the place that inspired the aesthetic he pro-

moted in landscape and architectural design. As he toured city and countryside, he was particularly enthusiastic about the parks of London. While
the architecture of the West End resembled that of fashionable neighborhoods in other European capitals, what he found so distinctive was
the vast amount of open space, a cityscape that seemed to be "holding
the country in its lap." London's West End parks conveyed to visitors "a
broad and noble feeling of natural beauty." The landscape of St. James's
Park, he wrote, "seems to you more like a glimpse into one of the love-
liest pleasure-grounds of the Hudson, than the belongings of the great
Metropolis." The sheer scale of Hyde Park and Kensington Gardens left
Downing in a state of "bewildered astonishment" as he marveled at the
"wealth of a city which can afford such an illimitable space for the pleasure of air and exercise for its inhabitants." The West End of London
demonstrated to Downing, as it had to other visitors, the need for public parks in American cities.[22]

Upon his return from England, Downing made the creation of urban parks a personal crusade. His efforts took two directions. First, he
accepted a commission to design the public grounds in Washington,
DC. The site was an L-shaped tract, extending from the Capitol west to
the site of the Washington Monument and then north to the President's
House. In the 1791 plan for the new capital, Pierre Charles L'Enfant
had intended that this space become a "grand avenue," the aesthetic
centerpiece of the city, but in the first half of the nineteenth century the
space was largely ignored. One journalist described the site of the public grounds as a "bleak, unhospitable common" traversed by muddy roads
and devoid of trees "except one or two scraggy and dying sycamores."
Downing welcomed the opportunity both to beautify the nation's capital and to create what he believed would be the first "*real* park in the
United States." In his February 1851 report accompanying the plan for
the public grounds, Downing expressed hope that when completed the
public grounds would demonstrate to other cities the importance of
open spaces within the urban environment.[23]

Downing's design provided grand ceremonial spaces and embellishments suitable for the national capital, such as a triumphal arch as the
grand entrance to the grounds and a dignified setting for the still-
incomplete obelisk of the Washington Monument in the area Downing
designated Monument Park. Yet the design also included more intimate
spaces and quiet walks amid open lawn or stands of evergreen and de-
ciduous trees. A small lake, fountains, and five miles of carriage drives
and pedestrian paths that led visitors through a handsome landscape

were the hallmarks of the plan. Downing expected that when completed, the public grounds would provide an alternative to the "straight lines and broad Avenues of the Streets of Washington" and would make it possible for residents to enjoy "all pleasant and healthful intercourse with gardens and green fields."[24]

President Millard Fillmore adopted Downing's plan in the spring of 1851, and shortly thereafter construction commenced on the initial stages of site clearing and preparation. While work on the public grounds was going forward, Downing adopted a second strategy for promoting public parks: he took up the pen and made the *Horticulturist* a powerful publicist for the cause, focusing national attention on the need for a large park in New York City. In May 1851, Mayor Ambrose C. Kingsland had proposed the establishment of a park at the Jones Wood, a 160-acre site overlooking the East River that extended from Sixty-fourth to Seventy-fifth Streets. While Downing was pleased that New York was considering construction of a park, he had specific ideas about the qualities of landscape that would be necessary to relieve the tedium of a city he described as "this arid desert of business and dissipation." A park had to be more than city squares, which Downing characterized as children's playgrounds, and needed to embrace "broad reaches of park and pleasure-grounds, with a real feeling of the breadth and beauty of green fields, the perfume and freshness of nature." He then advocated the establishment of a park of at least 500 acres in the central area of Manhattan Island north of Thirty-ninth Street.[25]

"The New-York Park," the essay Downing published in the August 1851 *Horticulturist*, outlined both a rationale for park development and a comprehensive reformist agenda he termed "popular refinement." During his visit to England, he had praised the "elevating influences of a wide popular enjoyment of galleries of art, public libraries, parks and gardens, which have raised the people in *social* civilization and social culture to a far higher degree than we have yet attained in republican America." Downing conceded that the common school was merely a beginning, that in order to fulfill its republican destiny the United States needed to promote the kinds of institutions that would provide "the refining influence of intellectual and moral culture" to the working class. His prescription, breathtaking in scope, simultaneously condemned the limitations of a supposedly classless society and held out the possibility of a more enlightened future: "Open wide, therefore, the doors of your libraries and picture galleries, all ye true republicans! Build halls where knowledge shall be freely diffused among men, and not shut up within the narrow walls of narrower institutions. Plant spacious parks in your cities, and unloose their gates as wide as the gates of morning to the whole people." The comprehensive program of popular refinement that Downing advocated included "common enjoyments for all classes, in the higher realms of art, letters, science, social recreations and enjoyments." If successfully implemented, he predicted, such a cultural system would "banish the plague-spots of democracy" and raise the level of civilization in the United States.[26]

Downing died tragically in 1852, at age thirty-six, when the steamboat *Henry Clay* burned in one of the worst disasters on the Hudson. While he did not have the opportunity to translate his ideas into the design of a park, his writings contributed significantly to the establishment of public parks in many of the nation's cities. In 1857, Downing's former partner, Calvert Vaux, persuaded the Board of Commissioners of the Central Park to reject a preliminary plan for development prepared by engineer Egbert L. Viele and hold a competition to determine the park's design. Together with Frederick Law Olmsted, Vaux entered a plan in the competition, "Greensward," that captured first premium. A Connecticut farmer who was a correspondent to Downing's *Horticulturist* in the 1840s and whose writings on parks Downing first published in his monthly, Olmsted found in Downing the example for his own career in refining and civilizing American society. After winning the competition for designs, Olmsted and Vaux were entrusted with the responsibility for developing Central Park, and based on that success, Olmsted became the preeminent park builder and landscape architect of his generation.[27]

Olmsted and Vaux attributed much of their personal and professional success, as well as the popular embrace of public parks, to Downing's influence. In the spring of 1860, when construction had advanced to the point that the lower portion of Central Park was open to visitors, they attempted to place there "some appropriate acknowledgment of the public indebtedness to the labors of the late A. J. Downing, of which we feel the Park itself is one of the direct results." The printed circular accompanying their letters soliciting donations for the memorial included the passage from "The New-York Park" in which Downing outlined the social and cultural benefits of public parks. Although nothing came of this effort, Olmsted again attempted to honor Downing's memory in 1882, by urging "special and reverent attention" to the surviving parts of Downing's plan for the public grounds in Washington, DC. This was "the last and only important public work of Downing," Olmsted wrote, "who was not only a master of the art, but distinctly a man of genius, of whom his country should always be proud." Once again in 1887, Olmsted and Vaux paid homage to Downing when, at the urging of Downing's widow, Caroline Downing Monell, they offered to donate their professional services to Newburgh for the design of a public park "if the city should name the reservation 'Downing Park.' " The two men and their sons prepared a plan for the park in 1889, and Downing Vaux, the son Calvert Vaux had named after his former partner, superintended construction. Appropriately, the highest points in the park overlooked the community of Downing's birth and the scenery of the Hudson River Valley he had cherished.[28]

During his short life, Andrew Jackson Downing profoundly influenced the contours of middle-class culture in the United States. His prescriptions on domestic architecture and landscape design as well as his advice on the treatment of interiors and furnishings had an enormous impact on the homes Americans created and reinforced the culture of domesticity by teaching readers how to create optimal environments for familial life. Through his writings in the *Horticulturist*, Downing advocated a range of initiatives that would improve the quality of rural homes and villages. But it was in cities and adjacent suburbs that this champion of the middle landscape had perhaps his greatest influence. The first issue of *Park International* honored Downing as the "Father of American Parks," while historian Kenneth T. Jackson has described him as "the most influential single individual in translating the rural ideal into a suburban ideal." Downing's crusade for urban parks and suburban communities contributed to the emergence of a new form for metropolitan America—compactly built center cities, spacious parks that provided recreational opportunities for an expanding urban population, and suburbs that enabled families to have a house and a garden while maintaining links to city jobs and social and cultural life. To a remarkable extent, the modern American city still bears the imprint of the ideational structure Downing articulated a century and a half ago.[29]

Notes

1. David Schuyler, *Apostle of Taste: Andrew Jackson Downing, 1815–1852* (Baltimore: Johns Hopkins University Press, 1996), 72, passim. Sedgwick is quoted in

Fredrika Bremer, *The Homes of the New World: Impressions of America*, trans. Mary Howitt, 2 vols. (New York: George P. Putnam, 1853), 1:46; Wilhelm Miller, "Downing, Andrew Jackson," in Liberty Hyde Bailey, comp., *Cyclopedia of American Horticulture*, 4 vols. (New York: Macmillan, 1900), 1:501.

2. Schuyler, *Apostle of Taste*, 10–11, 17.

3. Mark C. Carnes, "The Rise and Fall of a Mercantile Town: Family, Land, and Capital in Newburgh, New York, 1790–1844," *Hudson Valley Regional Review* 2 (September 1985): 17–40; Joel E. Spingarn, "Henry Winthrop Sargent and the Early History of Landscape Gardening and Ornamental Horticulture in Dutchess County, New York," *Year Book of the Dutchess County Historical Society* 22 (1937): 36–70.

4. Schuyler, *Apostle of Taste*, 28–55; Andrew J. Downing, *A Treatise on the Theory and Practice of Landscape Gardening, Adapted to North America* (New York: Wiley and Putnam, 1841), 53–54; *Treatise*, 1844 ed., 10, 73.

5. Andrew J. Downing, *Cottage Residences; Or, A Series of Designs for Rural Cottages and Cottage Villas, and Their Gardens and Grounds. Adapted to North America . . .* (New York: Wiley and Putnam, 1842), i, 19–24.

6. Schuyler, *Apostle of Taste*, 72–84; Andrew J. Downing, *Fruits and Fruit Trees of America* (New York: Wiley and Putnam, 1845).

7. Andrew J. Downing, "Introductory," *Horticulturist* 1 (July 1846): 10. See also Schuyler, *Apostle of Taste*, 90–94, 119–26.

8. Schuyler, *Apostle of Taste*, 132–53; Andrew J. Downing, *The Architecture of Country Houses* (New York: D. Appleton and Co., 1850), xix–xx, 1–48, 135–42, 257–70, 364–460.

9. Andrew J. Downing, "The Influence of Horticulture," *Horticulturist* 2 (July 1847): 9–10; idem, *Treatise*, ii–iii, passim; idem, *The Architecture of Country Houses*, xix–xx, passim.

10. Downing quoted Pope in "Our Country Villages," *Horticulturist* 4 (June 1850): 537. See also Andrew J. Downing, "Domestic Notices. Suburban Embellishments," *Horticulturist* 6 (February 1851): 98; idem, "Citizens Retiring to the Country," *Horticulturist* 7 (February 1852): 61.

11. Andrew J. Downing, "Hints to Rural Improvers," 9–10; idem, "On the Mistakes of Citizens in Country Life," *Horticulturist* 3 (January 1949): 309.

12. Andrew J. Downing, "Our Country Villages," *Horticulturist* 4 (June 1850): 539–40. See also Kenneth T. Jackson, *Crabgrass Frontier: The Suburbanization of the United States* (New York: Oxford University Press, 1985).

13. See the "Map of Village Lots and Cottage Sites at Dearman, Westchester Co. . . . ," Archives of the Hudson River Museum, Yonkers, New York.

14. Downing, "Our Country Villages," 539–40.

15. Ibid., 540.

16. Ibid., 540–41.

17. Ibid.

18. N. P. Willis, "Sale of Mr. Downing's Residence," *Home Journal*, reprinted in *Horticulturist* 7 (November 1852): 527. On residential patterns for urban workers see Sam Bass Warner Jr., "If All the World Were Philadelphia: A Scaffolding for Urban History," *American Historical Review* 74 (October 1968): 26–43.

19. Stuart Blumin, *The Urban Threshold: Growth and Change in a Nineteenth-Century Urban Community* (Chicago: University of Chicago Press, 1976), 1; Mark C.

Carnes, "From Merchant to Manufacturer: The Economics of Localism in Newburgh, New York, 1845–1900," *Hudson Valley Regional Review* 3 (March 1986): 46–56.

20. Schuyler, *Apostle of Taste*, 218–19.

21. Andrew J. Downing, "A Talk about Public Parks and Gardens," *Horticulturist* 3 (October 1848): 154–56.

22. Andrew J. Downing, "Mr. Downing's Letters from England," *Horticulturist* 6 (June 1851): 281–86.

23. David Schuyler, "The Washington Park and Downing's Legacy to Public Landscape Design," in *Prophet with Honor: The Career of Andrew Jackson Downing, 1815–1852*, ed. George B. Tatum and Elisabeth B. MacDougall (Washington, DC: Dumbarton Oaks, 1989), 291–311.

24. Andrew J. Downing, "Explanatory Notes to Accompany the Plan for Improving the Public Grounds at Washington," Records of the Commissioners of Public Buildings, Letters Received, vol. 32, letter 3158 1/2, National Archives and Records Administration, Washington, DC.

25. Andrew J. Downing, "The New-York Park," *Horticulturist* 6 (August 1851): 345–49; Frederick Law Olmsted, "Passages in the Life of an Unpractical Man," in *The Papers of Frederick Law Olmsted*, 5 vols., ed. Charles E. Beveridge and David Schuyler (Baltimore: Johns Hopkins University Press, 1983), 3:84–94.

26. Downing, "The New-York Park," 345–49.

27. See Francis R. Kowsky, *Country, Park, and City: The Architecture and Life of Calvert Vaux* (New York: Oxford University Press, 1998), and Charles E. Beveridge, *Frederick Law Olmsted: Designing the American Landscape* (New York: Rizzoli, 1995).

28. David Schuyler, "Belated Honor to a Prophet: Newburgh's Downing Park," *Landscape* 31 (Spring 1991): 10–17.

29. "Andrew Jackson Downing: Father of American Parks," *Park International* 1 (July 1920): 42–48; Jackson, *Crabgrass Frontier*, 63.

Suggested Readings

Recent books about Downing's life and career include my *Apostle of Taste: Andrew Jackson Downing, 1815–1852* (Baltimore: Johns Hopkins University Press, 1996), which also contains a list of Downing's writings and a bibliographical essay; Adam W. Sweeting, *Reading Houses and Building Books: Andrew Jackson Downing and the Architecture of Popular Literature, 1835–1855* (Hanover, NH: University Press of New England, 1996); and Judith K. Major, *To Live in the New World: A. J. Downing and American Landscape Gardening* (Cambridge, MA: MIT Press, 1997). Also important are the essays published in *Prophet with Honor: The Career of Andrew Jackson Downing, 1815–1852*, ed. George B. Tatum and Elisabeth B. MacDougall (Washington, DC: Dumbarton Oaks, 1989). Several editions of Downing's books are available, including the fourth (1849) edition of *A Treatise on the Theory and Practice of Landscape Gardening* (Washington, DC: Dumbarton Oaks, 1991), which contains an introduction by Therese O'Malley; a reprint of the 1873 edition of

Cottage Residences, prepared by architect George E. Harney and published as *Victorian Cottage Residences* (New York: Dover Publications, 1981); and a reprint of *The Architecture of Country Houses* (New York: Dover Publications, 1969).

3

Francis L. Cardozo
An Early African American Urban Educator

Bernard E. Powers Jr.

Although the South remained a predominantly rural region before the Civil War and the southern economy still rested firmly on the base of plantation agriculture, southern cities performed an increasingly important function and grew at impressive rates of speed. Slavery as gang labor flourished in the countryside as part of the Old South's extractive economy, but nearly 150,000 slaves toiled in urban settings as well by 1860. Bonded African Americans labored in iron works, tobacco factories, cotton gins and presses, chemical plants, tanneries, blacksmith shops, and wharves; they served as domestic workers, waiters, butlers, laundresses, draymen, and porters. Also, approximately one-third of the region's free black population resided in urban areas in the antebellum years. Free blacks worked as barbers, caterers, builders, and teamsters; many owned their own businesses and enjoyed a considerable measure of financial security. African American communities, complete with churches, clubs, and voluntary associations, developed within southern cities, and class distinctions crystallized to separate slaves from free blacks. In some cities—particularly in New Orleans and Charleston—skin color intensified stratification, with light-skinned African Americans assuming leadership positions.

After the Civil War large numbers of African Americans in the South fled their plantation homes for the promise of a new life in nearby urban areas. Hoping to escape the violence of the countryside and recognizing the potential for greater freedom and economic advancement in the cities, the freedmen often took up residence in existing African American enclaves and sometimes created altogether new communities. By 1890 fully 15 percent of the rural black population had resettled in urban areas, and southern cities had become home for 70 percent of the nation's black urban population. The sudden and dramatic influx of African Americans proved unsettling for the cities' white residents, and racial segregation intensified. During and after Reconstruction, heightened economic competition in southern cities left blacks at a disadvantage, and many found themselves shunted into low-skill, low-paying occupations. In the chilling environment of the New South, both freedmen and free African Americans who had long enjoyed higher status found the economic competition fierce. For economic as well as cultural and social reasons, education took on great importance in southern African American communities; the path to freedom and economic advancement led directly through the schoolhouse. The story of Francis Cardozo illuminates the vitally important role played by schools in Reconstruction-era cities like Charleston.

Bernard Powers Jr. received a Ph.D. degree from Northwestern University, Evanston, Illinois, and is currently professor of history at the College of Charleston. He is the author of *Black Charlestonians: A Social History, 1822–1885* (1994) as well as several articles on African Americans in Reconstruction-era Charleston.

Access to literacy was a security matter in the slaveholding South and especially so in antebellum South Carolina, a state that had outlawed slave literacy. The urban environment blunted the effect of such laws because, unlike the countryside, the city provided extraordinary opportunities for slaves to learn. The streets of Charleston, the state's largest and most cosmopolitan city, contained a myriad of signs; newspapers and books were widely available; city slaves sometimes held jobs requiring literacy, and they had frequent contact with literate free blacks. Some free blacks even maintained schools where they clandestinely taught slaves. As 86 percent of white Charleston families owned slaves in 1830, that secret activity often evoked concern.[1]

Charleston's free black population was sizable, and by 1860 one-third of all free black Carolinians resided in Charleston. Southern free blacks were among the region's most highly urbanized groups. In 1860 one-third lived in cities, compared to only 15 percent of whites and 5 percent of slaves. The city's great occupational diversity afforded slaves opportunities to hire themselves out, accumulate money, and purchase their freedom. Free blacks frequently sought the anonymity of the city, and many former slaves migrated there. Freedom meant living within a web of legal restrictions that prevented blacks from enjoying the protections of white citizens. For example, free blacks could not vote or sit on juries. In South Carolina they were normally called free persons of color because of their mixed racial background. In 1860, 75 percent of free blacks in Charleston County were mulattoes, as the mulatto offspring of slave masters had a greater chance of becoming free. Most of the men were skilled workers, as were some of the women. Some accumulated property and even became wealthy. Members of this "free brown elite" intermarried and enjoyed a sophisticated community life, attended white churches, and educated their children in private schools.[2]

Until the late antebellum years, Charleston offered few public schools for its white citizens; the curriculum was rudimentary, and citizens of means had their children privately educated.[3] By the 1850s prescient Charlestonians were calling for improved public education. One reason for their concern was that Charleston, like other major southern cities, had attracted a sizable foreign-born population. At that time, immigrants comprised the majority of the white working class, and civic-minded Charlestonians viewed public education as a means of social control. If the children of affluent families attended the schools, their interactions with working-class children could help reduce potential class conflict. Finally, in the city, blacks and whites often performed the same jobs, which could threaten white supremacy. Recognizing this possibility, William H. Trescot urged educational reforms to elevate whites and maintain "an impassable gulf, between the lowest and humblest form of white labour and the highest development of black." [4] In the late 1850s expenditures for Charleston public schools increased dramatically, curricula were upgraded, and a building campaign was undertaken. One policy was immutable; Charleston's public schools remained available solely to white students.

Public schools for black Charlestonians developed after the Civil War, along with a new class of professionally trained black educators. Many were former free blacks who entered into teaching after benefiting from the educational advantages that antebellum urban life afforded. In Charleston, Francis L. Cardozo personified these developments.

Francis Cardozo was born free in 1837 to Isaac N. Cardozo, scion of a prominent Jewish family in Charleston, and Lydia Williams, a free mulatto woman. He was educated in private schools and employed as a carpenter. Desiring to follow intellectual pursuits, at age twenty-one Francis traveled to Glasgow, Scotland, and enrolled in college to prepare for the ministry. His carpentry skills allowed him to finance his education, and he graduated with honors from the University of Glasgow, winning prizes for classical scholarship. He also studied for three years in Presbyterian seminaries in London and Edinburgh before relocating to New Haven, Connecticut, as pastor of Temple Street Congregational Church in mid-1864.[5]

In the North, Francis Cardozo joined the struggle for racial uplift; in October 1864 he attended the Syracuse, New York National Convention of Colored Men as a delegate from Hartford. Renowned abolitionists such as William Wells Brown and Frederick Douglass were among the delegates. Cardozo was elected a vice president of the National Equal Rights League, which promoted moral reform, education, and African American citizenship rights.

When Cardozo reflected on the likely outcome of the Civil War, he decided he could best serve his race as a normal school or high school principal in the South. In June 1865 he volunteered his services to the American Missionary Association (AMA). The AMA was an organization of evangelical abolitionists that dispatched agents south to provide relief and education for fugitive slaves during the Civil War. Afterward, it promoted freedmen's education and civil rights. The AMA leaders found Cardozo's interests consistent with their plan to establish advanced schools in major southern cities, and they dispatched him to Charleston.[6]

Charleston was occupied by federal troops in mid-February 1865 and immediately attracted a substantial in-migration of rural freedmen. The city's population grew from 40,522 in 1860 to 48,956 by 1870, with freedmen comprising almost all of the growth; correspondingly, blacks increased from 42 to 53 percent of Charleston's population. Former slaves moved to the city to pursue new occupations, to locate family members from whom they had been separated by sale or war, or to seek refuge from hostile former Confederates. The services of churches, schools, and the Freedmen's Bureau were more typically available in cities, further stimulating the in-migration.

In March 1865, James Redpath, an abolitionist journalist, was appointed Superintendent of Education for the military post of Charleston, and school buildings were opened for freedmen's instruction. Charleston became one of the earliest locations for freedmen's education in the state. By April the city freedmen's schools received support from a number of benevolent associations, including the Freedmen's Aid Society of Boston, the National Freedmen's Relief Association, and the American Missionary Association. Thomas Cardozo, the brother of Francis Cardozo, spearheaded the initial AMA efforts. Thomas was born and educated in Charleston and left the city in the 1850s, eventually relocating in Flushing, New York, where he taught school. He returned to Charleston in April 1865 to supervise an AMA school. Thomas Cardozo's school initially had an enrollment of about one hundred students, and he hired six teachers, all of whom had been his classmates in Charleston's free black schools.[7]

At first things went well, and Thomas won the approbation of his superiors and black Charleston. However, when rumors that he had had an affair with a student in New York were verified, he was dismissed. Francis was chosen as his replacement, and the school was named Saxton after General Rufus Saxton, the first assistant commissioner of the Freedmen's Bureau for South Carolina. Francis Cardozo used his array of friends in black Charleston to build support for AMA educational plans, and they eagerly sent their children to his school. Saxton enjoyed immediate success, and its growing popularity was reflected in an enrollment that exceeded 1,000 students by December.[8]

Success did not come easily in the year following the end of the Civil War. One of the difficulties Francis Cardozo faced was working in an atmosphere of racial tension and hostility. A revolution in race relations occurred, and white Carolinians were completely unprepared to interact with free African Americans. The state legislature passed Black Codes that, among other things, severely limited the freedmen's geographical mobility and employment opportunities, while criminalizing certain activities only for blacks (such as possession of firearms). The antebellum racial order changed most rapidly and extensively in cities. Here black and white populations interacted frequently and competed for employment, and black Charlestonians sometimes boldly intruded themselves into public spaces, such as parks and streetcars, that they had been either excluded from or admitted to only with restrictions. As the old racial etiquette eroded in 1865–66, racial confrontations occurred in Charleston.

Hostility toward freedmen's education was palpable in the months immediately following the war. Once Francis Cardozo observed, "One thing especially provokes them, [white Charlestonians] that is our Schools." He also noted that while many visitors came to Saxton School by mid-December 1865, "not a *single Rebel* has ever been to visit us, they pass by on the opposite side and mutter curses as they hear the children sing." Another time, a well-dressed white woman peered through the door of the school "while the children were singing, and said 'Oh, I wish I could put a torch to that building! *The niggers.*' "[9]

Sometimes it was the idea of northern teachers instructing the freedmen that raised the ire of white Charlestonians. Many northern teachers were abolitionists and viewed white southerners as morally bankrupt because they either owned slaves or tolerated the practice. Special concerns were raised when these teachers interacted with African Americans on the basis of equality and encouraged them to assert their rights. Students singing "patriotic" songs with lyrics such as "rally round the flag" or "John Brown's body lies a-mouldering in the grave" or uttering prayers, asking "God [to] bless—Abraham Lincoln—our President—and Liberator," also kindled white enmity.[10]

At times it was not the idea of black education but the locations of the freedmen's schools that white Charlestonians found so troublesome.

The editor of the Democratic *Charleston Daily News* caustically charged that buildings erected for the education of whites and paid for by them "have been used, not so much to educate the freedmen, as to instill into them principles and ideas totally at variance with the opinions of the community in which they are obliged to live." According to the editor, white children were growing up in ignorance at the same time.[11] The motives of white Charlestonians were transparent to Francis Cardozo when he reported, "The Secession School Committee here went to Gen. Saxton asking him to restore the school buildings to them. They admitted that they had no funds to carry on the schools, but still wished them restored, I suppose to shut them up rather than see the colored people educated." Cardozo would not tolerate such a result and told black Charlestonians that they had paid taxes and were entitled to one-half the school buildings. He also urged them "to take the case to the U.S. Supreme Court" if they were not allowed to retain a fair share of the schools.[12] Saxton School was located in different buildings before 1867, depending on which properties the Union Army or the Freedmen's Bureau had available. For the 1865–66 school year, it was located in Charleston's Normal School, one of the city's premiere antebellum schools.

Postwar opposition to black education in Charleston was never as strident or pervasive as in the rural counties because of the city's antebellum tradition of at least limited private education for free blacks. Physical attacks on black schools occurred routinely in the countryside and, at the end of 1865, Freedmen's Bureau officials claimed the rural black schools could not survive without a federal military presence. In Charleston by mid-1866, there was some evidence of whites becoming more tolerant of freedmen's education. In March 1866 a delegation of prominent Episcopal ministers and other men of influence, such as George A. Trenholm, former Confederate secretary of the treasury, visited Saxton School. Francis Cardozo was encouraged and proclaimed the occasion to be "the first movings of the waters in the formation of a public opinion in favor of educating the colored people and giving them their rights."[13]

Cardozo's genial manner, combined with his insider's knowledge of Charleston and its inhabitants, contributed significantly to the success of his school and to his stature as a community leader. When in late 1866 he campaigned for a normal school curriculum and a new building, he won the endorsement of several prominent white Charlestonians, many of whom expressed their approval of him personally. His supporters included George Trenholm, Democratic governor James Orr, and Cardozo's former pastor, Dr. Thomas Smyth. Cardozo was warned not to expect Mayor Palmer Gaillard's approval, but he wanted the endorsement badly and formed a plan to obtain it. Realizing that some leading white Charlestonians looked down on the mayor's family, Cardozo secured endorsements from especially prominent men before going to the mayor. When the mayor was approached with the list of supporters, Cardozo observed him examine the names and smile, "As if [he] had no objections to join in the company of so many 'First Families,' " and Gaillard eagerly signed. The poignancy of this moment did not escape Cardozo, who reported, "I thought it a most singular thing that I should hold the document for a one-armed Confederate officer to sign to educate and elevate the men for whose perpetual enslavement he had lost an arm."[14]

Regardless of public opinion, Francis Cardozo knew that the success of the school depended upon the quality of the faculty. For the beginning of the fall 1865 school term, he retained several of the black teachers his brother had hired. They were all former Charleston free persons of color, and some were experienced teachers or had other qualifications. William O. Weston was a bookkeeper for his family tailoring business who had attended the city's free black schools, where he studied logic, rhetoric, astronomy, algebra, Latin, and Greek. Frances Rollin attended free black schools in Charleston and had the benefit of tutors before studying at Philadelphia's famous Institute for Colored Youth, an advanced school attended by elite African Americans.

During his tenure at Saxton, Cardozo consistently hired African American teachers from the local community, and the national office of AMA supplied additional teachers who were usually northern white women. At the beginning of the 1865–66 school year, Cardozo employed twenty-one teachers—ten southern blacks and eleven northern teachers, including one black. One of Cardozo's greatest frustrations was his inability to find enough high-quality African American teachers. Freedmen's education was so important that he believed it "far better that no colored persons should engage in this work at all, than to have such as would only disgrace the cause, and retard the progress of their own people." Francis had a marked preference for northern teachers because they frequently had more experience and formal training than their southern counterparts. Accordingly, he placed them in the highest and most responsible positions. He often assigned black teachers to less responsible positions but "where they may improve by the superiority of their *white* fellow laborers, and whose positions after-wards they may be able to occupy."[15]

Cardozo's expressed preference for northern teachers led on one occasion to a serious misunderstanding with the home office of the AMA. He was chagrined to learn that personnel there believed he did not want African American teachers sent to his school. Cardozo immediately wrote to Superintendent of Education Reverend Samuel Hunt, stating forth-rightly, "I am sure you are mistaken in saying I requested such a thing. My request was that I should have all *Northern* Teachers. It was and still is perfectly indifferent to me whether they are *white* or *colored*, all I ask is that they be competent for their work, and when I made the request I did so because *Northern* Teachers are more competent than Southern ones." So concerned was he about the potentially damning charges that he requested a written admission of the misunderstanding because, he explained, "If such a report were to be circulated in the city it would hurt my influence very much."[16] Cardozo was not always satisfied with the white northern teachers the AMA assigned, either. Once, he bluntly informed the home office, "I am *disappointed* with the set [of teachers] you have sent me" and charged that they were "inferior" to the faculty from the previous year.[17]

The AMA's stated policy was to create a pool of competent south-ern black teachers, but it sometimes seemed reluctant to recognize their talents. Male teachers were paid more than their female counterparts, and northern teachers were paid more than southerners. Cardozo tried to raise his teachers' salaries, but he sometimes encountered opposition from the New York office when requesting increases for black teachers. This adversely affected morale and made it difficult to retain faculty members. Mary Weston and Frances Rollin were cases in point. Cardozo described Miss Weston as "a most excellent and experienced Teacher" and had her salary increased from fifteen to twenty-five dollars a month shortly after he took over as principal. At that rate, she was still paid less than her northern white counterparts. Cardozo complained to the New York office that "you said those that did work equal to Northern Teach-ers would be paid at the same rate" and requested her salary be increased to thirty-five dollars per month. Miss Weston refused to continue with the AMA without the increase, and Cardozo informed his superiors that she could easily obtain employment with another association in the city at the higher rate, leaving her position to be filled with a teacher costing forty dollars a month. He described the case of Frances Rollin as "pre-cisely similar." Miffed when his request was denied, Cardozo vowed to pay Mary Weston an additional five dollars a month from his own salary. Eventually, the home office relented and agreed to the increase for Miss Weston; even so, she resigned her position by June 1866, probably because of the salary issue. The previous January, Frances Rollin had left the AMA for a higher-paying position at a different school.[18]

The foregoing is only one example of how financial matters strained relations between Francis Cardozo and the New York office of the AMA. The home office constantly demanded that Cardozo reduce the costs of housing the teachers and running the school. One means of cost savings suggested by the home office was to increase the student–teacher ratio to fifty to one, but Cardozo resisted this. In the spring of 1866 he reported an average ratio of forty to one and insisted that his rooms could not accommodate fifty students. He also believed freedmen's classes had to be smaller than those in northern schools, as southern students were "undisciplined" because they had never attended school before. Finally, as the school introduced more advanced subjects and the students became more proficient, they required more individualized instruction in order to maintain quality. Cardozo was sensitive to criticisms over his fiscal management of the school and found dealing with the home office over such matters difficult and sometimes irritating.[19]

Cardozo claimed that Saxton was unique among Charleston's freedmen's schools and vowed to protect its mission. Many of its black teachers were drawn from the city's antebellum free black community, and those with surnames such as Weston, Shrewsbury, Holloway, Rollin, and McKinlay represented some of the most elite families in black Charleston. The school also attracted an extraordinarily high percentage of children who were free before the war. From 1865 to 1867, 25 percent to one-half of Saxton's student body was comprised of free black children, compared with only 10 to 12 percent of the students at Morris Street School, to which Saxton was often compared.[20] Given the comparatively privileged background of many of his students, Cardozo confidently asserted, "We have 750 of the best scholars in Charleston, and I think anywhere in the South." Based on the abilities of the students, the school was divided into primary, intermediate, and grammar departments, but from its inception, Saxton offered no basic curriculum. In the fall of 1865 there were no students at Saxton learning the alphabet, and all could read and spell. To start the new school year in 1867, Cardozo reviewed 600 applicants but selected only 225 of the "more advanced" students. Students with less-developed skills had to attend other schools, at least at first.[21]

One of the other schools was Morris Street School. Constructed for whites in 1860 but housing a freedmen's school after the war, it became the first public school for black Charlestonians in 1867. Many black students were educated in the private schools that proliferated during the postwar years. Shaw School was originally funded by the New England Freedmen's Aid Society and became Charleston's second black public school in 1874. The ease of access to schools in the city contrasted sharply with their relative dearth in the remote rural areas.

At Saxton, Francis Cardozo realized how much he loved teaching, and his interaction with the students reaffirmed his decision to leave "the *exclusive* duties of the ministry for this work." Certain that there was no more noble work than inspiring young people to "love and serve Christ," he hoped to accomplish this goal through the classroom. Cardozo recognized the unique opportunities that now existed, and he understood the crucial role educated men and women were required to play in shaping the destiny of his race. He had witnessed slavery's "corrupting and degrading influences," but now he rejoiced that Christian teachers "with their admirable system, their order and punctuality of exercises and habit must and will entirely alter the . . . very character of this people."[22] Cardozo taught the most advanced class of boys, and when he noticed unusually talented and enthusiastic students, he gave them special attention. Such was the case with three formerly free teenage boys who benefited from several years of schooling before entering Saxton. Now they advanced so rapidly that Cardozo placed them in a special class where he taught them advanced Latin and Greek. All three aspired to the ministry, and Cardozo obtained AMA support for their future enrollment in a northern college.[23]

Cardozo understood the urgent need for educated ministers because across the South, African Americans now declared independence from the white churches they had formerly attended to establish new congregations under their own control. Population density and antebellum traditions of church attendance and leadership, along with higher levels of literacy and wealth, ensured that the growth of new churches would occur most rapidly in cities. Most black Charlestonians gravitated to the new Baptist, African Methodist, and Northern Methodist Churches. As a highly trained cleric, Cardozo found that his talents were in demand. During his first year in Charleston, he preached in churches of different denominations each Sunday and participated in church fund-raising efforts. During his years in Charleston, he acted as the liaison between Presbyterian and Congregational churches in the city and the

AMA. Cardozo was especially suited for this role, as he had antebellum friends in these congregations. The AMA valued Cardozo's efforts and encouraged him to take on greater ministerial responsibilities; but he declined, arguing that the responsibilities at Saxton School were too great.

When Cardozo returned to Charleston, his fondest dream was to establish a normal or teacher training school, but he found most students unprepared for advanced work. After a year of careful training and limited normal offerings, Saxton School produced about 200 pupils who were prepared for a full course of normal training, and Cardozo passionately stated the case to the home office. "It is the object for which I left all the superior advantages and privileges of the North and came South," he declared. "It is the object for which I have labored during the past year, and for which I am willing to *remain* here and make this place my home."[24] Cardozo also informed the office that soon the state would establish its first public school system, making the need for African American teachers more imperative. In the fall of 1866 the AMA agreed with his plans, and Saxton became a full-fledged normal school.

Parents of Saxton students often had professional aspirations for them. The school attracted a disproportionate number of children of antebellum free blacks and, not surprisingly, they dominated the most advanced classes. Many of these students planned teaching careers, and the school soon became an important source of black teachers for South Carolina. Although most Saxton students were freedmen, the school developed an air of exclusivity as a private school with an advanced curriculum. Its unique qualities attracted prominent visitors, including General Oliver O. Howard, Superintendent of the Freedmen's Bureau, who compared it favorably to the best New England grammar schools. No wonder then that after one of its public examinations, a local newspaper reported "our best colored society" was attracted to Saxton because it was considered "the recherché seminary, to which all the aristocracy send their children."[25]

The perception of the school as elite was responsible for conflicts between Cardozo and northern white teachers, who accused him of giving preferential treatment to the children of the free brown elite. For example, Sarah Stansbury, principal for the primary grades, objected when Cardozo's supervisory responsibilities with his students required her to fill in for him, adversely affecting her own pupils and teachers. In exasperation she wrote to New York, "I cannot see why the interests of the Primary [Department] which is already so far behind the Higher

Department . . . should be taxed for the advancement of teachers of the Higher Department." When she showed him the letter, Cardozo directed her not to send it, and Stansbury accused him of acting like a dictator. Cardozo denounced her to the home office as having a disrespectful manner and because, he said, "*She* wanted to govern [the school] and *me* too." This dispute was not merely over administrative style; its subtext was Miss Stansbury's opposition to sacrificing the instructional needs of the freedmen to advance those of the free brown elite. Her feelings became clear when she described her elation after reassignment to teach at a nearby farm. "The children are all ex-slaves which is more than can be said of Mr. Cardozo's school; his own class and Mrs. Chippenfield's are composed I should judge, entirely of freemen's children, many of whom owned slaves before the war." [26]

Cardozo never relished conflict and initially shunned what he described as "the turbulent political arena." Given his vision for racial uplift and the inherently political character of African American education at the time, he could not remain aloof for long. In November 1865, Cardozo attended the Colored People's Convention of South Carolina in Charleston, the city's foremost black political meeting, where delegates denounced racial discrimination and demanded immediate citizenship rights. The resolution that passed, stating that "knowledge is power," asserting that educated people could not be enslaved, and demanding good schools, found particular resonance with Cardozo.[27] In March 1867 he worked with a racially integrated "Committee of Thirteen" to found the Republican Party and write its platform, endorsing the Thirteenth and Fourteenth Amendments to the Constitution and publicly financed common schools. South Carolina was required to revise its constitution in accordance with the Reconstruction Act of 1867 before being readmitted to the Union. Cardozo's friends appealed to his sense of duty as an educated African American to stand for election to the constitutional convention of 1868. He was elected and subsequently chaired the education committee.

Cardozo and other black delegates played a crucial role in writing the constitutional provisions for South Carolina's first statewide system of publicly financed education. Specifically, Cardozo led the successful fight in favor of making school attendance compulsory. He aggressively supported the controversial provisions that provided public schools for all students regardless of race. When opponents argued that this would cripple the system because whites feared integrated schools, Cardozo rejoined that this plan did not require racially integrated schools but did make it possible for black children to attend any school they wished. Based on his experience at Saxton, he confidently predicted that few black Carolinians would want to attend white schools if quality instruction were available in their own schools. Finally, when a literacy requirement was proposed for the franchise, Cardozo doggedly opposed it as hypocritical, "ridiculous," and injurious to the Republican Party. In the end, the literacy requirement was dropped.[28]

The completion of the newly drafted constitution led to a new phase of Cardozo's political involvement. Later in 1868 he accepted nomination to the office of secretary of state on the Republican ticket. Victory made him the first African American statewide officeholder in South Carolina. (He would be elected state treasurer in 1872.)

Cardozo's new responsibilities led him to resign from the AMA, but before leaving, he achieved another goal. To alleviate his school's cramped conditions, in 1867 he persuaded the AMA to purchase a lot on which the Freedmen's Bureau agreed to construct a building. The new brick school was completed in mid-1868 and renamed Avery Institute, after Reverend Charles Avery, a northern philanthropist and supporter of the AMA who provided $10,000 for the project. As Avery's principal of approximately three years departed, the school was physically and pedagogically on the firmest foundation yet.

Following the Civil War, the efforts of the Freedmen's Bureau and various freedmen's aid societies were concentrated on cities because they were centers of transportation and communication and also because the population was more accessible. In cities like Charleston with substantial antebellum free black communities, these organizations were able to capitalize on their previous educational achievements. The leadership provided by Francis Cardozo and the heritage of freedom enjoyed by many of the African American teachers and students at Avery illustrate this point. In 1870 the demand for black teachers increased as South Carolina's first public school system was implemented. By 1880 over 65 percent of Avery's students studied the normal curriculum, and the school's teachers were in great demand.[29]

The rate and extent of social differentiation among African Americans was also most pronounced in cities because the breadth of urban occupational structures provided a wider range of remunerative work and because the educational opportunities were greater there than in the rural areas. Charleston's black community, like most across the South, witnessed its first formally trained teachers, ministers, attorneys, physicians, and other professionals emerge after the Civil War. Of course, many received their preparatory training at schools similar to Avery Institute. Avery's record for producing college-bound students is noteworthy, and its early graduates attended Howard, Atlanta, and Fisk Universities. South Carolina was the only southern state to have a racially integrated university during the 1870s, and several Avery graduates attended the University of South Carolina during this brief period. After Cardozo left Avery, he became a member of the university board of trustees and helped several Avery graduates to enroll there and also at Howard University.[30]

One of the most famous Avery graduates and an example of the accomplishment of its students was William D. Crum. A mulatto free person of color from Orangeburg, South Carolina, Crum graduated from Avery in 1875. He attended the University of South Carolina, completed a medical degree at Howard University, and started his practice in Charleston in 1880. Crum became a local leader and received national attention when President Theodore Roosevelt appointed him collector of customs for the port of Charleston in 1903.[31] William Crum's experience reveals another important legacy of Francis Cardozo's educational work. The advanced schools that emerged after the Civil War tended to reinforce antebellum class divisions within black communities. Most of the students attending Avery were freedmen, but a substantial number were, like William Crum, free persons of color or their descendants. This group's educational and often economic advantages were enhanced by an Avery education. By 1880 at least 40 percent of black Charleston's upper class had been free before the war, and there was often a close association between attendance at Avery and elite status in the city's black community.

Notes

1. Janet D. Cornelius, *When I Can Read My Title Clear: Literacy, Slavery, and Religion in the Antebellum South* (Columbia: University of South Carolina Press, 1991), 18; Richard Wade, *Slavery in the Cities: The South, 1820–1860* (Oxford: Oxford University Press, 1964), 21–22.

2. Ira Berlin, *Slaves without Masters: The Free Negro in the Antebellum South* (New York: Pantheon, 1974), 155, 173, 175.

3. Laylon W. Jordan, "Education for Community: C. G. Memminger and the Origination of Common Schools in Antebellum Charleston," *South Carolina Historical Magazine* 83 (January 1982): 105–6.

4. Walter Fraser, *Charleston! Charleston!: The History of a Southern City* (Columbia: University of South Carolina Press, 1989), 236–37; Jordan, "Education for Com-

munity," 107–8, 112; "Free School System of South Carolina," *The Southern Quarterly Review* (October 1856): 156.

5. Joe M. Richardson, "Francis L. Cardozo: Black Educator during Reconstruction," *Journal of Negro Education* 48 (Winter 1979): 73.

6. F. L. Cardozo to Rev. M. E. Strieby, August 13 1866, American Missionary Association Papers (hereafter cited as AMAP); Joe M. Richardson, *Christian Reconstruction: The American Missionary Association and Southern Blacks, 1861–1890* (Athens: University of Georgia Press, 1986), vii–viii, 113.

7. T. W. Cardozo to Rev. M. E. Strieby, April 29, June 16, 1865, AMAP.

8. F. L. Cardozo to Rev. Messrs. Whipple and Strieby, August 18, 1865, AMAP.

9. F. L. Cardozo to Rev. S. Hunt, December 13, 1865, AMAP.

10. *American Missionary Magazine* 9 (May 1865): 104.

11. *Charleston Daily News*, August 30, 1866.

12. F. L. Cardozo to Rev. Geo. Whipple, October 21, 1865, AMAP.

13. John R. Dennett, *The South As It Is, 1865–1866* (New York: Viking Press, 1965), 218; F. L. Cardozo to Rev. S. Hunt, March 10, 1866, AMAP.

14. F. L. Cardozo to Rev. E. P. Smith, October 25, 1866, AMAP.

15. F. L. Cardozo to Rev. S. Hunt, January 13, 1866, AMAP.

16. F. L. Cardozo to Rev. S. Hunt, December 2, 1865, AMAP.

17. F. L. Cardozo to Rev. S. Hunt, October 16, 1866, AMAP.

18. Richardson, *Christian Reconstruction*, vii; F. L. Cardozo to Rev. W. E. Whiting, December 14, 1865, AMAP.

19. F. L. Cardozo to Rev. S. Hunt, March 27, 1866, F. L. Cardozo to Rev. S. Hunt, March 2, July 4, 1866, AMAP.

20. F. L. Cardozo to Rev. M. E. Strieby, June 13, 1866, AMAP; *American Missionary Magazine* 9 (September 1876): 207–9.

21. F. L. Cardozo to Rev. S. Hunt, November 5, 1866, F. L. Cardozo to Rev. E. P. Smith, October 1, 1867, AMAP.

22. Rev. F. L. Cardozo to Rev. Geo. Whipple, October 21, 1865, F. L. Cardozo to Rev. S. Hunt, March 2, 1866, AMAP.

23. F. L. Cardozo to Rev. Geo. Whipple, May 18, 1866, F. L. Cardozo to Rev. M. E. Strieby, June 13, 1866, AMAP.

24. F. L. Cardozo to Rev. M. E. Strieby, August 13, 1866, AMAP.

25. Rachel Mather to Mr. E. P. Smith, November 15, 1867, AMAP; *Charleston Daily News*, June 4, 1866.

26. Sarah M. Stansbury to Revs. Messrs Hunt and Smith, November 17, 1866, Sarah M. Stansbury to Rev. Mr. Smith, January 10, 30, 1867, F. L. Cardozo to Rev. E. P. Smith, May 28, 1867, AMAP.

27. *Proceedings of the Colored People's Convention of the State of South Carolina Held in Zion Church, Charleston* (Charleston, SC: Leader Office, 1865), 7, 9–10, 23–27.

28. *Proceedings of the Constitutional Convention of South Carolina* (Charleston, SC: Denny and Perry, 1868; reprint, New York: Arno Press, 1968), 689–91, 825–34, 901.

29. Jas. T. Ford to Rev. E. M. Cravath, June 30, 1874, AMAP.

30. *Charleston Daily Courier*, September 3, 1869.

31. *Charleston News and Courier*, March 16, 1880.

Suggested Readings

Anderson, James A. *The Education of Blacks in the South, 1860–1935.* Chapel Hill: University of North Carolina Press, 1988.

Drago, Edmund L. *Initiative, Paternalism, and Race Relations: Charleston's Avery Normal Institute.* Athens: University of Georgia Press, 1990.

Forten, Charlotte A. *The Journal of Charlotte Forten: A Free Negro in the Slave Era.* Edited by Ray A. Billington. New York: Collier, 1961.

Gatewood, Willard B. *Aristocrats of Color: The Black Elite, 1880–1920.* Bloomington: Indiana University Press, 1990.

Jenkins, Wilbert L. *Seizing the New Day: African Americans in Post–Civil War Charleston.* Bloomington: Indiana University Press, 1998.

Lowe, Richard. "The Freedmen's Bureau and Local Black Leadership." *Journal of American History* 80 (December 1993): 989–98.

Powers, Bernard E. *Black Charlestonians: A Social History, 1822–1885.* Fayetteville: University of Arkansas Press, 1994.

Rose, Willie Lee. *Rehearsal for Reconstruction: The Port Royal Experiment.* New York: Vintage, 1964.

Vaughn, William P. *Schools for All: The Blacks and Public Education in the South, 1865–1877.* Lexington: University Press of Kentucky, 1974.

Williamson, Joel. *After Slavery: The Negro in South Carolina during Reconstruction, 1865–1877.* Chapel Hill: University of North Carolina Press, 1965.

4

Alexander R. Shepherd
The Haussmannization of Washington, DC

Alan Lessoff*

As industrial cities grew dramatically in the late nineteenth century, local governments struggled to maintain the provision of everyday services and preserve the health of the citizenry. Rapid physical expansion and mushrooming populations strained existing urban infrastructures, resulting in an apparently limitless demand for more and better-built streets, bridges, sidewalks, streetlights, parks, and, in many instances, docks and beaches. In addition to the provision and maintenance of public works, the occupants of city halls had to be concerned about public health and sanitation. According to one expert, the typical American resident around 1900 annually generated up to 1,200 pounds of ashes from stoves and furnaces, 100 to 180 pounds of garbage, and 50 to 100 pounds of rubbish; the increased demand for refuse collection and disposal led to the widespread establishment of municipal street-cleaning services. At the turn of the century, an estimated 3.5 million horses still traversed the streets of American cities. With the normal, healthy horse producing twenty pounds of manure and a gallon of urine daily, street cleaners faced a Herculean task—just as they did with the prospect of removing the thousands of horse carcasses that accumulated on city streets each year. As well, the use of cesspools and privy vaults proved an inadequate means of removing human waste and safeguarding the quality of the city's drinking water. While some called on private enterprise to solve such health and sanitation problems, most urban residents looked to municipal authorities for results.

In the industrial age, a new group of professionals provided technological solutions to these nettlesome urban problems. Civil engineers and planners—who increasingly received training in colleges and universities and became members of professional organizations, subscribed to esoteric journals, and attended regular conferences—applied their technical know-how in new and innovative ways that earned the United States an international reputation as the trendsetter in municipal problem solving. In New York City alone, the completion of such engineering feats as Central Park, the Brooklyn Bridge, and the new Croton Aqueduct constituted a remarkable record of achievement. The Chicago Board of Sewerage Commissioners imported

*The author thanks Jon Peterson of Queens College and the History Department seminar at Illinois State University for comments on early drafts.

53

Boston city engineer Ellis Cheesbrough to improve its hopelessly inadequate drainage system. Cheesbrough raised the Windy City's street level, installed fifty-four miles of sewers, and conceived a proposal that reversed the flow of the Chicago River to carry sewage away from the public's drinking water supply in Lake Michigan. Thanks in great measure to the widespread installation of sewers and the construction of water filtration facilities, mortality rates in the nation's twenty-eight largest cities fell 19 percent between 1890 and 1900. Increasingly sanguine about the capacity for science and technology to improve the quality of urban life, city dwellers likewise celebrated the ability of municipal engineers and other experts to provide solutions in a disinterested fashion, elevated above the petty concerns of partisan politics. But as the story of "Boss" Alexander Shepherd reveals, the triumph of technology could not guarantee solutions for all of society's ills—nor would bureaucrats and technicians necessarily always be immune from politics.

An associate professor of history at Illinois State University, Normal, Illinois, Alan Lessoff received a Ph.D. degree from Johns Hopkins University, Baltimore, Maryland, in 1990. He is the author of *The Nation and Its City: Politics, "Corruption," and Progress in Washington, DC, 1861–1902* (1994).

O n June 23, 1874, the U.S. Senate put off adjourning for the summer to quarrel over the recent report of a House-Senate investigating committee. The 3,000 pages of documents and testimony concerned not familiar issues such as Reconstruction or railroads, but the profusion of paved, lighted, and tree-lined streets, parks and squares, and water and sewer lines constructed throughout Washington, DC, since 1871. These projects formed the heart of a massive effort to end Washington's reputation as a "struggling, shabby, dirty little third-rate southern town" and to create a capital city "worthy of the nation," as the slogan of the time went.[1]

The bipartisan committee appreciated these accomplishments but could "not but condemn the methods by which this sudden and rapid transformation was secured."[2] The agency responsible, the Board of Public Works, had operated in a haphazard, unaccountable fashion. Influence peddling and conflict of interest pervaded the program. The Board had colluded with federal officials to shift costs for unauthorized projects to the United States. To hide spending of $18.9 million in a plan approved for $6.6 million, city officials had issued millions in vouchers and securities of dubious legality.

Days earlier, Congress had implemented the report's recommendation to abolish Washington's government at the time—the Territory of the District of Columbia—and replace it with an interim commission. In the session's final hours, the Senate now debated one of President

U. S. Grant's nominees to this caretaker commission, Alexander Robey Shepherd. As vice president and de facto head of the Board of Public Works from 1871 to 1873 and then as territorial governor, Shepherd had devised and implemented the "Comprehensive Plan of Improvements" at the heart of the quarrel.

A handsome, charismatic man in his late thirties, six feet tall and 200 pounds, Shepherd inspired admiration in those who embraced the forceful, enterprising spirit of post–Civil War business and politics. Imperious, impetuous, and garish, he appalled those who condemned the willfulness and vulgarity of the era. While the hearings had uncovered no personal corruption on Shepherd's part, they had revealed much tolerance of others' impropriety in the cause of public works. Staunch supporters insisted that a program "to lift the city out of the mud and make it what it should be as the capital of the nation" faced so many obstacles that Shepherd's unorthodox, even unscrupulous methods were in order. Critics such as *The Nation* magazine countered that the turmoil and corruption surrounding the Shepherd program revealed the folly of entrusting complex tasks such as public works to boosterish amateurs: "What we must expect to find in every department of Government so long as a show of activity and energy is preferred to technical knowledge and administrative experience."[3]

Grant's insistence on his protégé Shepherd placed Senate Republicans in a bind. Party members who saw Washington's renovator as a hero would resent Senate rejection. Still, even long-standing allies were annoyed at Shepherd's ruses to force Congress to pay for projects it had never approved. Moreover, Democrats were gleeful to have a Republican city government embroiled in scandal, for this offset the recent exposure of New York's Democratic Tweed Ring. After a "stormy" debate, the Senate voted 36 to 6 against the nomination.[4] The 1874 rejection of Shepherd as District commissioner put a premature end to his political career. In 1880 the former governor, still youthful but now bankrupt, would move with his wife and seven children to Mexico's Sierra Madre mountains, where he would embark on a second remarkable career as a developer of silver mines. In his absence he came to be remembered not as the scoundrel or despot he was labeled at the time, but as "a household synonym for public benefaction,"[5] the leader who had sparked Washington's rise as an attractive capital indeed worth comparison to Paris or Berlin.

Shepherd's Comprehensive Plan was perhaps the most ambitious urban public works program in nineteenth-century America. Still, Washington was hardly alone in its scramble to upgrade its appearance and services. Cities throughout the Americas and Europe took on huge debts to improve streets, water supply, parks, and other services to keep up with unprecedented growth in population and social complexity. In the decade after the Civil War alone, the bonded debt of New York, Boston, and Chicago tripled, Cincinnati's debt rose five times, and Cleveland's increased 1,000 percent.

In an age of rapid governmental as well as industrial and commercial expansion, capital cities attracted special attention. Proponents of embellishing such disparate capitals as Washington and Buenos Aires often cited Paris's Georges Haussmann as inspiration. As prefect of the Seine in the 1850s and 1860s, Haussmann had driven magnificent boulevards through ancient, gnarled central Paris while also upgrading the French capital's parks, markets, water supply, sanitation, and transit. To describe this unprecedented program of urban renewal, contemporaries coined the term "haussmannization." Americans and other foreign admirers, moved by the grandeur and ingenuity of Haussmann's Paris, rarely tried to understand the tumultuous controversy that surrounded the prefect and his program. This controversy underscored the fact that public works are not arcane matters best left to engineers, but vitally concern all urban dwellers because changes to infrastructure can reshape a city's economy and way of life. By driving boulevards through old quarters, lining these boulevards with fashionable apartments, and connecting the new thoroughfares to a ring of railroad stations, Haussmann secured Paris's position as France's political, business, and cultural center, but at the cost of displacing long-established neighborhoods of artisans, shopkeepers, and laborers. The political contentiousness of public works multiplies in capital cities, where urban politics intertwine with national affairs. Like Shepherd an imperious man intolerant of criticism, Haussmann adopted high-handed, irresponsible methods that finally prompted his removal in 1870. Within France, Haussmann came to symbolize the arrogance and venality of his patron, Emperor Napoleon III, whose regime survived Haussmann's ouster by less than a year.

Likewise, the Shepherd controversy concerned the direction of the American nation, as well as official mismanagement and arrogance. The federal city's "ill-kept, noisome, and stinking" appearance seemed to Civil War-era patriots to symbolize the shortcomings of the antebellum Union.[6] A splendid Washington could provide symbolic reinforcement for American national loyalty. A modern Washington could serve as administrative center for the vigorous government that many Unionists hoped would result from a northern victory in the Civil War. In the course of remaking Washington physically, Shepherd and his allies intended to undermine the city's traditional, southern-oriented elite in favor of progressive, northern-minded leadership. Meanwhile, Shepherd's pro-development Republicans also struggled to distance themselves from local radical Republicans. The radicals believed that civil rights for Washington's black population should have equal priority with Shepherd's physical and economic improvements. In theory, the economic and civil rights agendas of Reconstruction-era Republicans were not in conflict: an enterprising, innovative society would be a more open, tolerant one and vice versa. Yet as occurred across the Reconstruction South, implacable white hostility toward black progress forced pro-enterprise Republicans to downplay civil rights to preserve their developmental goals. Shepherd worked to secure Washington as a dynamic, impressive capital even as the radical vision of Washington as avatar of democracy faltered.

Still another source of controversy stirred by Shepherd, Haussmann, and their counterparts stemmed from the sheer novelty of what they attempted. City officials knew how to build adequate, individual streets, water supplies, and sewers. No city, however, had yet devised effective methods for planning transportation, water, and drainage as systems coordinated with trends in business, population, and housing. The municipal engineers, planners, and health experts on whom city dwellers now rely for such tasks did not yet exist as distinct professions, even in France, which emphasized the training of engineers and civil servants. In the United States, with its cult of the self-made man, self-taught contractors such as Shepherd seemed as good as anyone else. The huge sums Shepherd wasted and the technical failure of his pavements and sewers helped to convince urban Americans that professionals should have direct control over infrastructure improvements, even if politicians retained the ultimate say. Even so, streets, water, sewers, and parks remain prolific sources of controversy, as in the days of Haussmann and Shepherd.

Born in 1835, Shepherd was the son of a lumber dealer in southwest Washington. This area had acquired the nickname "the Island" because it was isolated from the rest of the city by the Washington Canal, which stretched along the north side of the Mall where Constitution Avenue now runs. A putrid reminder of the failure of George Washington's dream of making his city a prosperous river port, the canal had degenerated by

Shepherd's youth into a receptacle for garbage, street runoff, and sewage from federal buildings. One of the most applauded of Shepherd's extralegal acts while head of the Board of Public Works would be his diversion of an appropriation for dredging the canal to covering it and making it a main sewer.

Shepherd's father died when the boy was ten. After leaving school as a teenager, the young Shepherd was apprenticed to John W. Thompson, the District's largest plumbing and gas contractor. At a time when urban buildings were acquiring running water and gas lighting, plumbing was a new, booming business suitable for a youth interested in how cities were built. By his early thirties, Shepherd had bought Thompson out and was branching into other city-building enterprises. He invested in construction materials, a street railway, the Washington Market Company, and the *Evening Star* newspaper. His property investments by the early 1870s exceeded $250,000. Estimated to have developed as many as 1,500 houses within ten years, he played a noteworthy role in creating the fashionable neighborhoods of northwest Washington between present-day Farragut Square and Dupont Circle.

Shepherd relished displaying to his hometown that he had arrived. In the suburbs north of the current Florida Avenue, Shepherd and his wife, Mary, acquired a country house. Their townhouse overlooking Farragut Square became the site of lavish receptions. Although a native Washingtonian from a Maryland family that had once owned slaves, Shepherd stood outside the southern-leaning elite, of whom he expressed resentment and who treated him as an upstart. His associates tended to be transplanted northerners or native Washingtonians with northern leanings who were engaged, as he was, in real estate, contracting, utilities, and other city-building enterprises.

With the old elite tainted by southern ties during the Civil War, Shepherd had a chance to rise as rapidly in politics as in business. After a brief Union enlistment in the spring of 1861, Shepherd won a seat on Washington's common council, becoming its president in 1862. Prominent in political offices and civic organizations throughout the 1860s, Shepherd gained a reputation as a dauntless champion of making "our city one of the most beautiful on the face of the globe," as he put the goal in an 1870 speech.[7]

While Washington had developed at a respectable rate, the capital had fallen far short of the expectations of the Founding Fathers. Galling evidence of this pervaded the city. Population leapt from 75,080 to 131,700 during the dramatic 1860s, but people still scattered thinly over the grandiose plan made in the 1790s by French engineer Pierre Charles L'Enfant for a city with several times that number. L'Enfant's famous street system—his radiating 160-foot avenues imposed on a grid of 100-foot streets—had proved far too costly for Washington's taxpayers to maintain. In dry periods, dust from the broad, unpaved avenues covered everything and everyone. After rains, journalist Noah Brooks reported, the streets became "seas or canals of mud," whose "geographical features" were "conglomerations of garbage, refuse, and trash."

The Mall epitomized the city's disappointing condition. Fragmented into eight grounds under the control of separate federal agencies, landscaped piecemeal, encroached upon by railroads, and crowned by the half-finished Washington Monument (abandoned in its scaffolding for want of funds in 1855), the Mall offered, in the words of park designer Frederick Law Olmsted, "a standing reproach against the system of government."[8] Commercial and residential buildings matched the streets and Mall in decrepitude. Nearly all accounts concur with Mark Twain's characterization of the hotels, saloons, offices, and shops along Pennsylvania Avenue as "mean and cheap and dingy." "None of us are proud of this place," remarked Nevada Republican William Stewart in 1869, during a Senate debate over whether Washington should host the centennial exposition eventually held in Philadelphia in 1876.[9] Congress's dissatisfaction with Washington even reached the stage of discussing moving the capital to a midwestern city such as St. Louis.

Those most drawn to the goal of a "worthy" Washington were, like Shepherd, nationalistic, pro-development Republicans. This faction of the party coexisted uneasily with the Republicans' radical faction, whose agenda was to make Washington a model of post-emancipation race relations. During the 1860s, African Americans, mostly former slaves from the Chesapeake region, comprised the most rapidly increasing segment of the capital's population. By 1870 blacks were one-third of the population, long the largest black presence in a major American city. Between 1862 and 1869, Congress responded by passing measures to emancipate the city's remaining slaves, provide schools for black children, desegregrate streetcars, and extend the vote, jury service, and office holding to blacks.

As much as possible, Shepherd and his allies kept their distance from the radicals. Though not a vehement racist, he shared the condescending views of blacks that prevailed in this former slave city. Shepherd's hesitancy to work with the radicals, however, largely resulted from nervousness that the capital's physical and economic development could be paralyzed by the visceral opposition to black rights displayed by the majority of white Washingtonians. An 1866 referendum in which Washington City voted 6,591 to 35 against black suffrage and Georgetown 712 to 1 dramatized the depth of this hostility. When Congress imposed black suffrage on Washington despite such expressions of opposition, the Shepherd group made a strategic alliance with the radicals. In this way, Shepherd's group hoped to persuade the powerful radical Republican faction in Congress to support federal appropriations for Washington's public works. In 1868, in a narrow election marred by violence, this alliance of newly enfranchised black voters, white radicals, and pro-business Republicans elected a white radical, Sayles J. Bowen, as Washington City mayor. Bowen pledged to expand both black rights and public works, but his administration became so mired in squabbling that, far from working to increase spending, the radicals in Congress distanced themselves. Securing federal appropriations would be impossible so long as Bowen remained mayor.

Shepherd switched tactics again. He became head of a Reform Republican movement that cooperated with old-line, mainly Democratic Washingtonians to oust Bowen in favor of a moderate Republican in the 1870 municipal elections. Meanwhile, the Shepherd Republicans lobbied Congress for a territorial government that would consolidate the ineffectual municipalities of Washington City and Georgetown with the outlying portions of the District known as Washington County. With a governor and legislative council appointed by the president and an elected house of delegates and delegate to Congress, this territorial format seemed to meet Congress's demand for more federal control over Washington as a price for federal underwriting of public works.

Congress passed the territorial bill on February 21, 1871, the day the city held a carnival—organized by the omnipresent Shepherd—to celebrate Pennsylvania Avenue's new wooden pavement. Along with the pending State, War, and Navy Building (now the Old Executive Office Building), the rebuilt Avenue signaled Congress's decision to rededicate itself to Washington and to ignore calls to move to the Midwest. President Grant bypassed Shepherd to appoint Henry D. Cooke, brother of financier Jay Cooke, as the first territorial governor. Grant instead placed Shepherd and several allies on the Board of Public Works. As governor, Cooke was ex-officio head of the Board, but he left its operation to Vice President Shepherd, who ran the Board of Public Works as a vehicle for his visions and ambitions, "as though no one else were associated with him," investigators later remarked.[10]

Grant filled the Territory's other appointive offices with reliable Republicans. These appointments in effect handed Shepherd control of all contracts and patronage related to public works. The Shepherd Republicans used their patronage and the enthusiasm surrounding the new government to dominate elections for the house of delegates and congressional delegates. Superficial similarity to Tammany Hall's use of public works contracts and jobs to control New York elections led to the Washington leader acquiring the nickname "Boss Shepherd." While this epithet was useful to opponents who wished to tar Shepherd as a Republican William M. Tweed, Shepherd's movement differed from the machine politics then emerging in many American cities. Typical ward bosses were politicians by trade who delved into contracting or real estate as a way to make money through inside influence. Shepherd and his allies did not disdain such influence peddling, but they remained businessmen first and politicians second. Political machines, moreover, prided themselves on their ability to build loyal support in working-class and ethnic neighborhoods and to deliver votes reliably. Shepherd and his colleagues made little attempt to build constituencies at the precinct or ward level.

Indeed, the Shepherd group devised the Territory to insulate themselves from local voters. In racially tense Washington, nonradical Republicans such as Shepherd realized that they could not build a majority based upon white voters alone, but it would be politically fatal to rely too visibly on the black minority. The answer to Washington's public works quandary, it seemed, was to remove the issue from popular control. Black leaders responded with ambivalence to a government that, while not abandoning civil rights altogether, did treat their goals as problematic distractions. Shepherd's efforts to make Washington "an honor rather than a disgrace to the nation" deserved "earnest, active support," asserted the city's black newspaper, the *New National Era*, which nevertheless expressed "fear" that Shepherd meant "to relieve" Washington's Republican Party "of the influence of its radical element."[11]

Within three weeks after taking office in June 1871, the Board of Public Works submitted its Comprehensive Plan of Improvements. This program would not qualify as a "city plan" in the present-day sense of an integrated set of proposals based on estimates of housing, transportation, recreation, and other needs. Even so, the Shepherd plan embodied a more coherent sense of the intertwined character of streets, water, sewerage, parks, and public buildings than any American urban public works project to that time. In a departure from tradition, Shepherd and his associates proposed to finance two-thirds of the estimated $6.6 million cost of the plan through bond sales and only one-third through assessments on property adjacent to improvements. Until this time, American cities had usually assessed the entire cost of improvements to abutting property. Washington thus became one of the first American cities to accept that pavements or sewers were not simply of concern to the street or neighborhood through which they passed. Cities needed to treat public works as systems, because the condition of sections of a city affected the entire urban environment.

The scale and cost of the Comprehensive Plan prompted a rancorous split between Shepherd's pro-improvement Republicans and the Democratic elite with whom they had cooperated during the campaign for the Territory. Conservative Washingtonians objected that Shepherd's "ill-digested, incoherent, and blundering scheme" contained inadequate controls over the Board of Public Works and that contracts would go to "rings" of political cronies.[12] Supporters retorted that old-line critics were "rich people content with existing circumstances" who fought "progress and manifest destiny."[13] The quarrel over the Comprehensive Plan reflected the division within Washington's business and civic elite over whether the city should weave itself into the northern commercial and cultural orbit or retain its customary orientation toward the Chesapeake and the South.

As soon as Shepherd had pushed the Comprehensive Plan through a compliant territorial legislature, the Board of Public Works contracted for projects throughout the city, but especially downtown and in fashionable areas of northwest Washington. In these areas, public works had the greatest potential for promoting growth by stimulating private investment. Not coincidentally, these were also areas where Shepherd's allies concentrated their own real estate operations. Given the period's penchant for romanticizing entrepreneurship, politically active businessmen such as the Shepherd group easily confused their public responsibilities with their private interests. Territorial leaders made only cursory efforts to avoid conflicts of interest and defended themselves forcefully when questioned, on the grounds that their public and private activities combined to advance the worthy cause of Washington's physical and economic progress. The costly scandals that ensued help to explain why laws and customs regarding conflict of interest have grown more stringent since the 1870s.

The obstructiveness and disdain of elite conservatives reinforced Shepherd's brusque manner of dealing with even well-meaning criticism. Shepherd alienated otherwise well-disposed Washingtonians with his grudging responses to pedestrians inconvenienced by torn-up streets, to neighborhoods bypassed by improvements, and to homeowners who sought compensation for rebuilt plumbing, stairs, and foundations necessitated by changes in street grades. The Board of Public Works did cancel improvement taxes imposed on two prominent senators who returned from a recess in late 1872 to find their houses on ledges ten feet above a regraded Massachusetts Avenue.

Two incidents in 1872 illustrate Shepherd's blunt approach. One Wednesday in early September, when stall keepers at the Northern Liberty Market—dilapidated and slated for replacement—threatened legal action rather than relocate to temporary sheds, Shepherd invited the relevant judge to dinner at his country house. As stallholders cleaned up for the evening, workmen arrived to tear the hall down. In the confusion, two people died: a butcher and a young boy hunting rats with his dog. Shepherd never expressed remorse; the market was "necessarily sacrificed to the public good," he later wrote.[14] In November, when a railroad refused to remove tracks that ran right below the Capitol, Shepherd sent 200 workmen one night to tear them out. "I did that without authority of law," he recalled, "but it was the right thing to do, and the nuisance would not otherwise have been removed."[15]

Supporters from around the country cheered that Washington had found its "Baron Haussmann."[16] Especially given the city's backward reputation, Shepherd's accomplishments were indeed astonishing. By 1874 the Territory had overseen construction of 150 miles of paved roads, 120 miles of sewers, thirty miles of water mains, thirty-nine miles of gas lines, 208 miles of sidewalks, two new markets, and six new schools.

As enemies had predicted, the speed with which Shepherd pushed his program greatly inflated its cost. As an alternative to the time-consuming practice of putting contracts out for bids, the Board of Public Works hastily drew up a list of standard rates that enticed contractors with guaranteed profits. Rather than take pains to design, measure, and estimate work beforehand, Shepherd encouraged contractors to begin streets and sewers quickly. Shepherd then retroactively changed materials, specifications, and work sites. The huge profits ensured by such practices attracted contractors—reputable and otherwise—from around the country. Guaranteed profits also nurtured an unsavory level of brokering and lobbying in city contracts. The revelation that House Appropriations chairman James Garfield had accepted $5,000 to lobby

Shepherd on behalf of a Chicago wooden paving firm damaged the reputation of the future president. As Garfield understood, in the absence of the checks provided by open bidding and careful planning, Shepherd could with little scrutiny channel lucrative work to contractors and building suppliers with political connections to the Republican Party.

By the spring of 1873 the Board of Public Works had already spent over twice its original $6.6 million estimate. Nearly out of cash, the District began to issue floating securities to cover payrolls and keep projects going. Shepherd's allies even manipulated their control of the finances of the Freedman's Savings Bank to divert the hard-earned savings of former slaves to favored contractors. This callous chicanery contributed greatly to the bank's 1874 collapse.

Shepherd and his supporters defended themselves by insisting that much of the debt they incurred properly belonged to a negligent federal government. The Board of Public Works republished decades of statements by presidents, congressmen, and cabinet officers in favor of national underwriting of Washington's infrastructure on the grounds, as an 1835 Senate study had put it, that the L'Enfant Plan had been "calculated for the capital of the great nation" and was "from its very dimensions and arrangements" beyond local resources.[17] Between 1802 and 1871, Shepherd claimed, the United States spent as little as one-tenth what local taxpayers spent on improvements. In 1873 the federal government did spend $3.45 million to subsidize Shepherd's program. Investigators would conclude that this was too little, too late, and too random. Indeed, observers at the time and since suggested that Congress's dawdling prompted Shepherd's uncontrolled spending, because Congress would have to pay rather than let its capital default on its bonds. "I have been kicking my heels at the doors of Congress for five years to obtain appropriations," Shepherd told a House hearing in 1872, "and have invariably been met with the response: Why not do something for yourselves?" If residents "make the start," he insisted, Congress "cannot rid itself of responsibility."[18] One way that Shepherd acted on this threat was by colluding with Major Orville Babcock, the army engineer in charge of federal property in Washington and a close associate of President Grant, to bill the United States for work that Congress had never appropriated.

In 1872, Shepherd's opponents persuaded the House District of Columbia Committee to investigate the Territory. Chaired by one of Shepherd's political allies, the House committee meekly admonished that city officials had become "intoxicated with the spirit of improvement."[19] By the spring of 1873, Shepherd's political position was no longer so secure. A resurgent Democratic Party was making congressional Republicans anxious over scandals brewing around Grant associates such as Shepherd and Babcock. National newspapers disenchanted with Grant, such as the Republican *New York Daily Tribune*, began investigating the capital's finances and contracts. In April and May 1873 the *Tribune* published lengthy exposures of the "bankrupt and irresponsible" Board of Public Works.[20] The city's ability to survive on debt ended in September 1873 when the collapse of Jay Cooke and Company sparked the worst financial panic in decades and, incidently, forced Henry Cooke to resign as territorial governor. Shepherd won confirmation as Cooke's replacement, despite the *Tribune's* sneer that this was an "appointment not fit to be made."[21]

In early 1874, with worried Republican state officials pressuring national leaders to conduct a vigorous investigation, congressional Republicans agreed to a bipartisan House-Senate investigating committee. By late spring, copious evidence of loose administration, dubious financing, and influence peddling had the Territory reeling. Shepherd's fate was sealed when a disenchanted friend, Adolph Cluss, an architect who held the post of engineer to the Board of Public Works, provided details of Shepherd's autocratic governance and of ruses used to saddle the federal government with unauthorized costs. Meanwhile, the story hit the papers of a bizarre scheme to discredit one of Shepherd's upperclass enemies by framing him for the theft of evidence from the safe of a city attorney. This scheme, carried out by professional safecrackers commissioned by the U.S. Secret Service, was never solved. In such a charged atmosphere, only Shepherd's firmest supporters welcomed his nomination to the caretaker commission, though many Republicans continued to express admiration in private.

As passions cooled, the major players in the Washington improvement controversy gradually worked out accommodations on the issues they saw as fueling their quarrel. After gaining a majority in the House of Representatives in the 1874 elections, congressional Democrats reluctantly came to agree with Republicans on the need to complete the Shepherd improvements and to consolidate his debts into federally guaranteed bonds. Leaders from both parties also came to accept Shepherd's major point: that making large, regular federal appropriations was the only way to ensure Washington's steady development. In the government act passed in June 1878 to replace the caretaker commission, Congress promised to contribute 50 percent of the District's expenses in exchange for assuming direct control of the city's budget. This half-and-half plan would survive until eroded by new political and social circumstances early in the twentieth century. Satisfied in their chief demand, Republican business and civic leaders in turn accepted the controversial idea of abolishing local elections altogether and making the appointed commission format permanent. The republic's capital was destined to remain under the rule of appointed officials until the 1970s. Abolition of local self-government satisfied members of the southern-leaning elite, who had persuaded themselves that black suffrage was a root cause of the Shepherd mess. Over the next decades, federal and District officials and the northern-oriented faction within Washington's business community stood by as civil rights eroded in the voteless city and as Jim Crow laws took hold. Washington thus acquired the split personality that characterized it through much of the twentieth century: majestic capital of a great world power, but at the same time, a provincial city oppressive to minorities.

Within two years, Shepherd's impatient, improvisational approach showed in rotting wood pavements, crumbling asphalt, and ill-sealed sewers that ran uphill in places and that entered the Potomac below high tide. The cost in millions of dollars in additional expenditures to replace Shepherd's mistakes became a persuasive argument against placing self-taught contractors in charge of public works. Even Shepherd's close friends in the Army Corps of Engineers, which inherited oversight of the city's infrastructure, were scathing in their criticism of his commencing projects without "data or formulae" and of the "bad workmanship" and "worthless" materials that he had tolerated.[22]

Shepherd's mistakes were proportionate to his ambitions. In this early phase of the development of modern municipal engineering, all American and European cities experienced similar fiascos, though usually on a lesser scale. As cities recovered from their financial devastation following the 1873 Panic, they regained a taste for capital improvements. Yet even in cities where machine-style politics dominated, politicians came to accept the need for cautious financing and expert planning. Post-Shepherd Washington epitomized this trend toward expertise. By century's end, the capital would become a leader in the professionalization of public works, for example by hiring famous experts on asphalt paving and sewer design and by publishing the 1902 McMillan Plan, the country's first modern, comprehensive plan. As was the case with Haussmann's tumultuous transformation of Paris, Shepherd's impetuous drive for a worthy Washington acquired an ambiguous reputation: a signal episode in the movement to create more inspiring capitals and more pleasant, healthful cities, but also an example of the dangers of reckless finance and imperious management.

Given the feeling that Shepherd's misdeeds had been motivated by excessive zeal for a worthy cause, politicians assumed that the youthful, charismatic former governor would remain a force in Washington for decades to come. In November 1876, news of his bankruptcy stunned the city. Associates insisted that Shepherd could easily revive his enterprises. Restless as ever, however, he became intrigued by promising silver mines in the Batopilas River Valley in Chihuahua, Mexico. Given the paucity of roads and rails in northern Mexico, these mines were nearly a month's travel—mostly by pack mule through the Sierra Madres—from Chihuahua city. After a scouting trip in 1879, Shepherd persuaded an investment group to underwrite a $3 million mining company. Five years of hard work, Shepherd assured his wife, "would ensure a fortune."[23]

In the twenty-two years that he spent running the Batopilas mines, Shepherd displayed his normal talent for overcoming obstacles that he had underestimated. He had power machinery carted into the mountains and added tunnels, dams, and reducing plants. Shepherd's imperious streak, energy, and paternalistic stance toward his Mexican workers won him friends among the pro-American technocrats known as *científicos* who surrounded the dictator Porfirio Díaz. While journalists portrayed the large Shepherd family living as Gilded Age aristocrats in a mountain duchy, their life was modest compared to their previous standards. Though nostalgic for Washington's bustle and for public attention, Shepherd returned to his hometown only a couple of times, the first in 1887, while recuperating from an infection contracted when his scalp was torn open against a rock in a tunnel. Old friends and former foes combined to organize an enormous parade along Pennsylvania Avenue, with fireworks, speeches, and a proclamation granting Shepherd, once driven from office amid rancorous conflict, the freedom of the city.

To the first generation to live in a dynamic, attractive Washington, Shepherd came to seem, as one former opponent put it, "a man of great energy, liberal views, and full of enthusiasm" whose plans "startle[d] the whole community," but who precipitated a necessary crisis that pushed the capital up the road of progress.[24] When he died in Mexico in 1902—of appendicitis that could not be treated quickly because of Batopilas's isolation—five teams of workmen carried his casket out of the mountains so that he could be buried in Washington's Rock Creek Cemetery. In 1909 civic leaders erected a statue in front of the new District Building on Pennsylvania Avenue. The statue stood there until 1979, when the District government, in a fit of historical negligence, removed it to an obscure location during a redevelopment project. From its pedestal on the country's main street, Shepherd's likeness could watch over the magnificent, torn city he had indeed helped to shape. With his grand achievements and glaring faults, Shepherd remains a fitting symbol of his hometown.

Notes

1. *The Nation*, March 30, 1871.

2. *Affairs in the District of Columbia*, 43d Cong., 1st sess., S. Rept. 453, Report, vii.

3. *Washington Evening Star*, April 6, 1871; *The Nation*, June 25, 1874.

4. *Baltimore Sun*, June 24, 1874.

5. *Washington Critic*, September 28, 1881.

6. P. J. Staudenraus, *Mr. Lincoln's Washington: Selections from the Writings of Noah Brooks, Civil War Correspondent* (South Brunswick, NJ: Thomas Yoseloff, 1967), 344–5.

7. *Evening Star*, May 25, 1870.

8. Staudenraus, *Mr. Lincoln's Washington*, 116–17; Frederick Law Olmsted to Justin Morrill, draft letter, January 22, 1874, Olmsted Papers, Library of Congress, reel 14.

9. Mark Twain and Charles Dudley Warner, *The Gilded Age: A Tale of Today* (1873; reprint, New York: Penguin, 1994), 177; *Congressional Globe*, 41st Cong., 2d sess., December 22, 1869, 303–4.

10. *Affairs in the District of Columbia*, 43d Cong., 1st sess., S. Rept. 453, Report, xi.

11. *New National Era*, October 26, 1871 (second quote); December 12, 1872 (first quote).

12. *Washington Daily Patriot*, September 25, 1871.

13. *Evening Star*, June 30, 1871.

14. *Payment for Destruction of the Northern Liberty Market*, 54th Cong., 1st sess., May 12, 1896, S. Rept. 926.

15. *Washington Daily Chronicle*, February 26, 1876.

16. *Lippincott's Magazine*, March 1873.

17. Quoted in Howard Gillette Jr., *Between Beauty and Justice: Race, Planning, and the Failure of Urban Policy in Washington, DC* (Baltimore: Johns Hopkins University Press, 1995), 21.

18. *Affairs in the District of Columbia*, 42nd Cong., 2d sess., H. Rept. 52, 586–7.

19. Ibid., iv–v.

20. *New York Daily Tribune*, April 8, 1873.

21. Ibid., September 15, 1873.

22. District of Columbia Commissioners, *Annual Reports*, 1874, 162–5; 1875, 239–45.

23. Quoted in David M. Pletcher, *Rails, Mines, and Progress: Seven American Promoters in Mexico, 1867–1911* (Ithaca, NY: Cornell University Press, 1958), 191.

24. "Address of Ex-Mayor Berret," *Records of the Columbia Historical Society*, 52 vols. (Washington, DC: Columbia Historical Society, 1899), 2:15.

Suggested Readings

Three recent books analyze Shepherd's Washington within the context of the city's overall history and of nineteenth-century American urbanization: Carl Abbott, *Political Terrain: Washington, DC, from Tidewater Town to Global Metropolis* (Chapel Hill: University of North Carolina Press, 1999); Howard Gillette Jr., *Between Beauty and Justice: Race, Planning, and the Failure of Urban Policy in Washington, DC* (Baltimore: Johns Hopkins University Press, 1995); and Alan Lessoff, *The Nation and Its City: Politics, "Corruption," and Progress in Washington, DC, 1861–1902* (Baltimore: Johns Hopkins University Press, 1994). See also William M. Maury, *Alexander "Boss" Shepherd and the Board of Public Works* (Washington, DC: George Washington University Washington Studies, 1975); and James H. Whyte, *The Uncivil War: Washington during the Reconstruction* (New York: Twayne, 1958). On Shepherd's Mexican career, see David M. Pletcher, *Rails, Mines, and Progress: Seven American Promoters in Mexico, 1867–1911* (Ithaca, NY: Cornell University Press, 1958).

Works that place Shepherd's Comprehensive Plan within the development of urban public works include Jon C. Teaford, *The Unheralded Triumph: City Government in America, 1870–1900* (Baltimore: Johns Hopkins University Press, 1984); and Martin V. Melosi, *The Sanitary City: Urban Infrastructure in America from Colonial Times to the Present* (Baltimore: Johns Hopkins University Press, 2000). For a comparison of Washington to Paris, see David P. Jordan, *Transforming Paris: The Life and Labors of Baron Haussmann* (New York: Free Press, 1995).

5

Frank Julian Sprague
The Father of Electric Urban Mass Transit in the United States

Martha J. Bianco

Until well into the twentieth century, most Americans navigated their way around cities on foot. As a consequence, historians have called the city of the preindustrial era the "walking city." Typically confined to no more than two miles in radius—roughly the distance the average pedestrian could walk in an hour or less—the walking city exhibited considerable congestion due to high population densities, small lot sizes, and narrow streets. Before rapid industrialization dispersed economic functions to discrete districts, the production of goods occurred in small shops intermingled within the same blocks. Workers lived near their jobs, often toiling and residing in the same buildings. With the most prestigious residential areas situated near the city center, less desirable land uses and residents of lower status gravitated toward the urban periphery. The reconfiguration of American cities occurred when transportation innovations allowed residences to decentralize.

The first form of urban mass transit in the United States, the 12-passenger omnibus, initially appeared in New York City in 1831 after several years of use in London and Paris. Similar in many respects to a horse-drawn stagecoach, the omnibus operated along a fixed route at regular intervals. Traversing rough cobblestone streets, traveling at speeds of only five to six miles per hour, and charging prohibitively expensive fares of ten to fifteen cents, the omnibus left many potential commuters dissatisfied. At approximately the same time, horse-drawn streetcars commenced operation in Baltimore and New York City. Providing a more comfortable ride on fixed rails, the horse-drawn streetcars carried thirty to forty passengers at speeds of six to eight miles per hour for a flat one-way fare of a nickel. By midcentury, the omnibus and horse-drawn streetcar helped expand the radius of older American cities to three to four miles.

By the late 1830s other forms of urban transportation operated as well. In Boston, Philadelphia, and other eastern cities, steam railroads carried passengers to and from downtowns. Although affluent suburbanites enjoyed the pleasant commute, city residents along the railroad lines objected to the noise, smoke, sparks, and boiler explosions brought by locomotives to their neighborhoods. Cable cars operated quietly and generated no smoke or sparks, but suffered from a series of equally debilitating drawbacks. Ten times as expensive to install as horsecar rails, cables suffered repeated mechanical breakdowns, often with high-speed derailments leading to injuries and fatalities. Financially feasible only in densely settled areas, cable cars thrived in only a handful of cities. In most communities, horse-drawn streetcars continued to predominate.

Yet for all of their advantages, horse-drawn streetcars remained problematical modes of public transit. Reliance upon the 100,000 horses pulling the nation's streetcars led to a host of difficulties. Passengers and onlookers frequently objected to seeing overworked draft animals being beaten by drivers. Played-out horses perished where they fell; carcasses left in the streets attracted flies and emitted a foul odor as they decomposed. Newspaper accounts and municipal records indicated that the typical horse in the city produced an estimated twenty pounds of manure per day. The historian Joel Tarr calculated that by 1900, the 15,000 horses toiling on the streets of Rochester, New York, produced enough manure to fill one acre to a height of 175 feet—enough to breed sixteen billion flies. Thus, by the late nineteenth century, Frank Sprague and others interested in providing safe, convenient forms of urban mass transit had sound reasons for inventing a viable alternative to animal power.

Martha J. Bianco received a Ph.D. degree from Portland State University, Portland, Oregon. She is the author of "Technological Innovation and the Rise and Fall of Urban Mass Transit," *Journal of Urban History* 25 (March 1999), and an entry on Franklin Julian Sprague for the *Encyclopedia of Urban America: The Cities and Suburbs*, edited by Neil Larry Shumsky (1998).

F rom time to time the 25-year-old U.S. Navy ensign would ride the Metropolitan District Underground Railway—the world's only passenger-carrying subway train—to and from the exhibition halls of the Crystal Palace Electrical Exhibition in London. He traveled the subway not as an exhibitor or visitor to one of the first of many grand world's fairs showcasing technological innovations, but as a jury judge and secretary evaluating tests and experiments on dynamos, electric lights, and gas engines. His observations made their way into his *Report on the Exhibits at the Crystal Palace Electrical Exhibition in 1882*, published in 1883. But this 169-page report, commissioned by the U.S. Navy, was not the only outcome of his subway treks to and from the London exhibition.

Powered by coal-burning steam locomotives, the London underground train, however impressive, was dangerous, noisy, and dirty. Although it carried tens of millions of people per year, greatly alleviating surface-street congestion and improving commuter convenience, the

Metropolitan District Underground was poorly lit, with ventilation that was inadequate to handle the smoke, gas, and steam from the locomotives. These conditions impressed the young ensign on his rides. Writing for the professional journal *Electrical World* three years later, Navy officer Frank Julian Sprague commented, "We see, then, that steam locomotion does not present many opportunities to better the condition of the road. Hence we are obliged to turn to some other method of locomotion, and that which promises the most satisfactory solution is an electrical system. I have for a long time been elaborating such a one, and am now convinced that this is the future method of propulsion for the trains."[1]

Within two more years, in early 1888, Frank Sprague watched proudly as what would soon be the world's largest-scale electric streetcar system—with forty cars operating over twelve miles—opened for regular service in Richmond, Virginia. An exceedingly risky venture, Sprague's electrification of the Richmond line was a resounding success despite obstacles at every turn. His tenacity, drive, penchant for risk, and technical expertise in the Richmond enterprise earned Sprague the well-deserved moniker of the "father of electric urban mass transit."

The Age of Energy

Frank Julian Sprague was born on July 25, 1857, in Milford, Connecticut, during an era when inventors and entrepreneurs were rapidly ushering in a revolution in the use of electrical energy. Twenty years before Sprague was born, Samuel F. B. Morse had perfected the use of electric current in the operation of the telegraph. Within a decade—in November of 1847—brokers in England sent stock quotes from London to Manchester, forever changing the nature of the world's financial markets. In 1855 the military used telegraphic communications for the first time during the Crimean War, when operators were finally able to print out Morse code in words.

Sprague's father was a superintendent of a hat-manufacturing plant, a respectable position at the time. When Sprague's mother died in 1866, his father sent Frank and his brother to live with their aunt, a schoolteacher in North Adams, Massachusetts. The Sprague family appears to have placed a high value on formal education and, indeed, it was while in high school in Massachusetts that Frank first demonstrated an aptitude for mathematics, chemistry, and physics. Encouraged by his high school principal to pursue an education in engineering, Sprague determined to take advantage of the free education offered at West Point. He traveled to Springfield to take what he thought were competitive exams for the Army training academy, but found instead that the exams being held were for the naval academy at Annapolis. It was thus by pure chance that Frank Sprague began a career in the U.S. Navy, the best training ground in the United States at the time for electrical engineering.

Sprague developed a keen interest in dynamos and in inventing electrical devices. After his first two years at Annapolis, he visited the Philadelphia Centennial Exhibition of 1876, where he began to follow closely the activities of Thomas Edison and other inventors in the Age of Energy. Edison was the perfect example of de Tocqueville's practical scientist. By the time of his death in 1934, Edison had earned the title of "America's Most Useful Citizen," having been credited with inventions including the electric typewriter, phonograph, synthetic rubber, guided torpedo, and, of course, the incandescent lightbulb.[2]

The Gilded Age: Movers and Shakers Mold the New Economic Order

The riches of the Gilded Age did not belong to everyone. In this era those with entrepreneurial acumen and unfettered self-interest took risks with their investment capital and relied heavily on the innovative genius of brilliant inventors such as Frank Sprague and on the labor of vast hordes of unskilled workers. While some may claim that the public sector had little if anything to do with the engine that propelled the Gilded Age, in fact an important triumvirate of power was responsible for creating the mature industrial economy of this period. That triumvirate—real estate speculators, financiers, and public officials—seized upon the inventions of the scientific innovators and translated them into the shortest road to wealth.

In Sprague's case, he had a few dues to pay before proving his mettle as a worthy investment to members of the triumvirate. In 1880, while still in the Navy, he passed his ensign's examinations and then took a short leave to continue studies on the development of dynamos and motors at the Brooklyn Naval Yard and the Newport Naval Station. Within a year, Sprague caught wind of yet another electrical exhibition, this one in Paris. He promptly requested duty with the Mediterranean Squadron, hoping to make it to Paris in time for the exhibition. Unfortunately, his ship was delayed and he did not reach Paris until the fair had ended.

The Paris Electrical Exhibition of 1882 would have been Sprague's second world-class exhibition showcasing the technological advances of the Industrial Revolution. His first was the Philadelphia Centennial Exhibition of 1876, where he had become familiar with Thomas Edison's work. Fortunately, however, the Crystal Palace Electrical Exhibition had just opened in London, and Sprague received an assignment as a secretary and member of an award jury.

In *Exhibiting Electricity*, K. G. Beauchamp has written of the role of the electrical exhibition for displaying technology. The exhibition of electricity has its origins in trade fairs during the medieval period and in showcase fairs of polytechnic institutes. The Great Exhibition of 1851 came at a time when some of the key electrical devices had been invented—the telegraph and the dynamo, for instance. By the time Sprague attended the Philadelphia Centennial Exhibition in 1876, there had been at least ten other major electrical exhibitions in London, New York, and France.

The Philadelphia Centennial Exhibition of 1876 was the United States' first real foray into the "business" of world's fairs. Philadelphia, of course, seemed the logical location for a fair meant to coincide with the one-hundredth anniversary of the birth of the republic. The purpose of such fairs was only nominally to celebrate and showcase technological innovation. A primary, if not overtly stated, purpose was to advertise the city in which the fair was taking place. Only world-class cities—London, New York, Paris—were home to such grand pronouncements of a city's having arrived on the world scene. City boosters, all members of the power triumvirate of real estate, finance, and politics, raised large sums of money to bring such extravagant displays to their cities. City tourism, capital investment, and population growth usually increased after a successful fair.

Technological advances and the capitalizing and marketing thereof thus offered more than just the shortest road to riches; they were also powerful tools that city boosters deployed in the competition to attract capital and put their city "on the map." Sprague would soon become involved as a pivotal actor in this competition among places to attract investment capital and become world-class cities—not so much in the display of any particular invention at an exhibition, but as the inventor of one of a city's most powerful competitive weapons: a fast, safe, convenient mass transportation system.

From Navy to Private Employee to Company Owner
to Capitalist-Financed Contractor

While at the London exhibition, Sprague met E. H. Johnson, an Edison representative overseeing the latter's incandescent lighting exhibition. It was Johnson who recommended that Sprague seek employment with Edison. In 1883, Sprague resigned from the Navy and went to work for Thomas Edison in New York, where he was assigned to the central station-planning department.

At that time the work for determining the size and location of conductors was entirely manual and very tedious. A large map represented the district in miniature. Spools of wire were actually mounted at the locations of residences and other buildings on the map. The resistance of each spool was then made proportional to the number of incandescent lights used at each site. By trial and error, technicians determined the voltage drop along each of the wires and then calculated the appropriate size for the conductors. Sprague quickly realized that a mathematical model could easily, efficiently, and correctly calculate the conductor sizes without reliance on a large map and miniature version of the electrical system. His training in electrical engineering and his mathematical prowess clearly served him in the capacity of a professional engineer in a company where others worked with much less sophisticated methods.

Sprague's true love, however, remained dynamos and motors, with which he had become familiar while at Annapolis. While continuing to work for Edison, Sprague spent his spare time engaged in his favorite activity: invention. He became increasingly disenchanted with Edison's focus on electric lighting to the seeming exclusion of all other uses of electricity, particularly given his own persistent interest in electric railway transit. "I have not given much thought to the substitution of electricity for horses on surface street cars," Thomas Edison said in an interview for *The Mail and Express* in 1884.[3] Disenchanted with Edison's shortsightedness and having made progress on his own in the development of a railway motor, Sprague resigned from Edison's employ that same year.

Toward the end of 1884, Sprague and E. H. Johnson formed the Sprague Electric Railway and Motor Company, with an authorized capital stock of $100,000, with Sprague owning the majority of the shares. The company immediately proceeded with selling motors, which were manufactured by none other than the Edison Machine Works. The Sprague Electric Railway and Motor Company itself did little; Edison

Machine Works manufactured the motors and independent agents sold them. Sprague was thus able to focus all of his energy on and funnel all profits into research and development. His small scale of operations did not yet require massive injections of capital. In 1886 his enterprise was prospering enough that Sprague broke with Edison and established his own manufacturing plant in New York. The authorized capital stock of the company was increased to $1,000,000—a 900-percent increase in just two years.

Although the Sprague motors were sold predominantly for industrial uses, Sprague's primary interest remained the problem of electrical traction, which he had identified in 1882 during his steam-propelled subway rides on London's Metropolitan District Underground. Certain financiers in New York—Jay Gould, for one—were skeptical of electric traction, possibly because they doubted its safety. As of 1880 city boosters were becoming aware of the benefits of using electricity for lighting, particularly street lighting—a real advantage for extending hours of business. In 1882 electric power became available for commercial distribution in the United States, and more and more homes were wired for electricity as inventors churned out one electric appliance after the other. But by 1886, when Sprague was advocating publicly for electric traction, there had been only a handful of electric railways in operation anywhere, and none of these was sufficiently impressive to attract investment capital. Sprague remained confident, however, that electricity could successfully power street railways on a large scale from a central power plant. He finally had an opportunity to demonstrate his conviction in 1887, when he received a contract to electrify a street railway in Richmond, Virginia, financed by a group of investors from New York.

The New York financiers had visited Richmond to scout out a site for a manufacturing plant. When the group, which included one Maurice B. Flynn, realized that Richmond had only one streetcar company, they saw an opportunity to underwrite a second. The route that interested Flynn and the others featured steep grades, sharp curves, and unpaved streets. Given these conditions, horsedrawn streetcars were clearly out of the question. Although cable traction was the standard in many cities with steep grades, it had not proved the most viable investment. Flynn knew of Sprague's experiments and demonstrations with electric traction in New York and contacted him to enter into what might seem in hindsight an exceedingly risky—if not outright exploitative—contract.

Sprague's self-confidence and unshakable commitment to the idea of electric traction are nowhere as evident as in his acceptance of the

Richmond contract. Rather than a desire for profit, Sprague's primary motive appears to have been his faith in his own scientific reasoning and in the practical applicability of his ideas. Yet this commitment generally did not lead him to act blindly and impulsively. He was a married man with children and an interest in preserving his career, financial solvency, and, indeed, the very idea of electric traction.

Thus, it must have been with nothing short of unwavering certainty that Sprague entered into the Richmond contract in early May 1887. The risks abounded. Not only had no track been laid, but the route itself remained uncertain; the operating conditions of the line were also therefore untested. Despite these unknowns, Sprague signed a contract, agreeing to bear all risk of failure and to supply forty cars, with two motors and accessories for each; all overhead wiring and related equipment; twelve miles of track; and an electric generating plant of 375 horsepower. Most astonishingly, he agreed to a 90-day completion date for the entire operation. He would receive no payment until the railway had operated successfully for sixty days, at which time he would be paid $110,000 in cash.

The Electric Era

Sprague's electrification of the Richmond line was a success and marks the effective beginning of the electric streetcar era. The line began regular operation on February 8, 1888, with a handful of cars. Thirty additional cars were added on May 4, which the American Electric Railway Association proclaimed as National Railway Day. The success of the Richmond operation did not come easily. Sprague understood the problems of his predecessors, but unlike them, he had far more professional expertise and training. Unfortunately, he also had serious time and money constraints. Although the line opened for regular operation on February 8, 1888, Sprague encountered blow after blow. Serious problems arose with overhead switches, insulation, lightning, and motor brushes. The rail tracks spread apart and sank into the mud. Derailments were common along the many curves, where there were no guardrails. Keeping the trolley attached to the overhead wires was as challenging as ever.

By the fall of 1888, Sprague had addressed each of the difficulties, including the trolley problem: he tried over fifty different trolley poles before finding a universal swiveling pole that exerted upward pressure. More important, though, he had overcome all the weaknesses of his predecessors' systems. His system featured technical characteristics that allowed for large-scale operation, including two motors on each car, mounted underneath by what was known as a "wheelbarrow suspension."

The most significant impact of the Richmond installation was its rapid duplication in other cities. Henry M. Whitney, president of Boston's West End Street Railway, came to Richmond to observe Sprague's operation in the summer of 1888. Whitney and his general manager, Daniel F. Longstreet, were concerned about what would happen if a number of cars became concentrated on a short section of track, creating a bottleneck situation. They doubted that the overhead wiring could furnish enough electrical current to handle such an occurrence. Sprague demonstrated that a jam of up to twenty-two cars could be moved, convincing the Bostonians to finance the second major urban electric transit line.

By 1890 hundreds of electric cars plied the streets of urban America —from Minneapolis, Cleveland, St. Louis, and Pittsburgh, out west to Tacoma. Of these installations, Sprague supplied the equipment for about half. The Sprague Company's capitalization increased by an additional $200,000 in common stock and $400,000 in preferred stock—the latter purchased by the Edison Electric Light Company, forming the new Edison General Electric Company. Once again, Sprague found himself an employee of an Edison organization, having taken the post of consulting engineer to Edison General Electric. And once again he found himself in disagreement over technical matters and he resigned, this time turning his attention to yet another area of invention—electric elevators.

At the 1853 Crystal Palace Exposition in New York, four years before Sprague's birth, Elisha Otis had demonstrated an elevator. Otis's major contribution was the invention of a safety device to prevent the elevator car from falling should one of the supporting cables break. The first elevator—powered by steam, not electricity—was installed in a New York department store in 1857, the year of Sprague's birth. Hydraulic elevators were in place by 1870, and the city that came to have the greatest number of elevator-dependent skyscrapers during the Gilded Age was Chicago.

Skyscraper technology was a product of the Industrial Revolution, relying on knowledge pertaining to metal engineering; the adoption of steel as a lightweight alternative to iron; new organizational methods of construction whereby a single general contractor became responsible for the construction of the entire building, from start to finish; heaters and incandescent lighting that allowed work to proceed in cold weather and at night; and, significantly, new market forces that created a whole new class of workers: managerial and clerical workers employed in the growing FIRE (finance, insurance, and real estate) sector. Skyscrapers also were a function of central city density, which precluded horizontal expansion in the central business district. Firms wanting to be downtown had to build up, not out.

Having rebuilt itself out of the ashes of the Great Fire of 1871, Chicago appeared to the U.S. Congress to epitomize the American spirit when it came time to choose the site for the 400th anniversary of Christopher Columbus's expedition to America. The World's Columbian Exposition, held in Chicago in 1893, featured displays of all the latest inventions. The city itself was home to most of the great skyscrapers of the time, including the tallest building in the world, the 21-story Masonic Temple, with sixteen Otis elevators. These elevators all operated independently, however. They could not be controlled by a master switch, and hence their operation could not be coordinated to accommodate variations in use among the cars.

Sprague had been dabbling in elevator technology for years; in 1884 he pioneered the use of electric instead of hydraulic power to propel elevator cars. In 1891 he formed the Sprague Electric Elevator Company and in 1892 undertook the largest installation of elevators in the world—600—in the Central London Railway. Shortly thereafter, Sprague sold his elevator company to the Otis Elevator Company and turned his attention to the development of a multiple-unit (MU) control system, whereby a single master switch in the basement of a building could control the movement of any individual elevator or all of them together. He was also interested in experimenting with the MU control system in the operation of electric traction so that an entire train could be controlled from either end of *any* car. His goal was for individual cars to operate completely independently of one another. He finally had the chance to demonstrate his idea in 1897, when the South Side Elevated Railway of Chicago was reorganized and its management decided to electrify in the process.

Sprague was less eager to take advantage of the Chicago opportunity than he had been for the Richmond opportunity a decade earlier. Although he did envision application of the MU system to traction, his immediate interest remained with elevators, and he was hoping to secure a large elevator contract in London. Also, the 40-year-old innovator, now a navy lieutenant, had recently fallen while installing elevators in New York's Waldorf Astoria Hotel, and he was still on crutches when A. D. Lundy, representing Chicago's South Side Company, approached him. Nevertheless, Sprague agreed to bear all risks of the project and even furnished a $100,000 bond in case he failed to fulfill his contract. He also agreed to have one mile of track with six cars completely equipped and ready for testing with the MU system within two and a half months, again at his own expense. Upon satisfactorily supplying and installing equipment for an additional 114 cars and demonstrating successful operation, Sprague would receive $300,000.

Sprague not only agreed to these remarkable terms at a time when his plans for the MU system for electric traction existed only on paper but, while still on crutches, he also decided to go ahead with his London trip anyway. To compound matters, a strike in his shops brought production of necessary equipment to a standstill. One month before the demonstration due date, Sprague still had nothing to show. Incredibly, but true to his nature, he was able to get two of the six promised demonstration cars up and running one day beyond the due date, with the remaining cars up within another week and a half. To prove how easy the MU system was to operate, Sprague put his 10-year-old son at the controls. Within one year, 120 cars were in operation and the South Side Elevated's net earnings increased 400 percent, with the value of its stock rising more than 300 percent, from $32 per share to $105 per share. In 1902, General Electric, which had earlier absorbed Edison General Electric, bought out the Sprague Electric Company for $1 million, stating that there was "no other way . . . to get possession of . . . [the multiple-unit control system] patent which was absolutely necessary to our business."[4]

Sprague's Legacy

In 1904 the 47-year-old Sprague looked back over his decades of accomplishments and concluded, not unjustifiably, that "the electric railway has become the most potent factor in our modern life."[5] Indeed, the 1890 census counted 5,700 miles of horse-car track and 1,260 miles of electric track. Within three more years—six years after Sprague's Richmond demonstration—there were 12,000 miles of streetcar track, 60 percent of which had been electrified. By the end of 1903, 98 percent of the country's 30,000 miles of track were carrying electric streetcars.[6]

After electrifying the Chicago line, Sprague went on to serve as a consultant for other streetcar system electrifications. He also continued to engage in the activity at which he had always excelled: invention. He formed the Sprague Safety Control and Signal Corporation in 1906, having become interested in automatic railroad signaling. During World War I he served on the Naval Consulting Board and assisted in the development of depth charges and delayed-action fuses. In 1927 he invented an automatic control system to allow two elevators, one local and one express, to operate in the same shaft. Not long thereafter, he contributed to the construction of the automatic train control.

Frank Sprague was an entrepreneur and inventor, but first and foremost a scientist. His commitment to and belief in the scientific method of inquiry are clear from his published articles on his work but also from the honorary degrees he received from a number of universities. On May 16, 1911, the American Institute of Electrical Engineers awarded him its highest award, the Edison Medal—only the second time the award had been given. On October 25, 1934, at the age of seventy-seven, Sprague died of pneumonia, still in the process of working to bring new inventions to light. His contributions to urban transportation and, indeed, urban form were many. His invention of large-scale electrified transit systems allowed cities to expand beyond the 10-mile limit of the streetcar city: the electric streetcar suburbs extended twelve, fifteen, and even twenty miles out. Although many social scientists decry suburbanization—particularly automobile suburbanization during the post–World War II era—for contributing to the death of the central city, some of Sprague's inventions contributed to the strength and special identity of the central business district.

Electric streetcar suburbanization increased the segregation of land uses and, in doing so, left to the central business district those functions and characteristics associated with the modern downtown: office buildings and department stores, civic buildings, cultural venues, parks and plazas, even universities and hospitals. The skyscraper, facilitated by Sprague's contributions to elevator technology, still stands as the symbol of a vibrant downtown, whose skyline draws the focus toward the center rather than outward.

Despite Sprague's contributions to the definition of the downtown, in many metropolitan areas decentralization has eroded the economic strength of the central city. It is not uncommon for those cities that retain a vibrant urban core to boast a viable radial and circumferential rail system, whether heavy (rapid) or light rail. It is Sprague's multiple-unit control system that makes possible urban transit as we know it today, and it is that system that has justly earned him the title of the "father of electric urban mass transit."

Notes

1. Frank J. Sprague, "Application of Electricity to Propulsion of Elevated Railroads," *Electrical World* 7 (1886): 27–44. Excerpted in Gerrylynn K. Roberts and Philip Steadman, *American Cities and Technology: Wilderness to Wired City* (London: Open University, 1999), 50.

2. Craig Wollner, *Electrifying Eden: Portland General Electric, 1889–1965* (Portland: Oregon Historical Society, 1990), 7.

3. Quoted in Harriet Chapman Jones Sprague, *Frank J. Sprague and the Edison Myth* (New York: William-Frederick Press, 1947), 9.

4. Letter from A. G. Davis of the General Electric Patent Department to F. P. Fish, General Counsel of General Electric, February 1, 1910; historical files of the General Electric Company, Schenectady, New York. Quoted in Harold C. Passer, "Frank Julian Sprague: Father of Electric Traction, 1857–1934." In William Miller, ed., *Men in Business: Essays in the History of Entrepreneurship* (Cambridge: Harvard University Press, 1952), 234.

5. Quoted in Kenneth T. Jackson, *Crabgrass Frontier: The Suburbanization of the United States* (New York: Oxford University Press, 1985), 115.

6. Jackson, *Crabgrass Frontier*, 111.

Suggested Readings

Beauchamp, K. G. *Exhibiting Electricity*. London: Institute of Electrical Engineers, 1997.

Bouman, Mark J. "Luxury and Control: The Urbanity of Street Lighting in Nineteenth-Century American Cities." *Journal of Urban History* 14 (1987): 7–37.

Bruegmann, Robert. *The Architects and the City: Holabird and Roche of Chicago, 1880–1918*. Chicago: University of Chicago Press, 1997.

Condit, Carl W. *American Building Materials and Techniques from the First Colonial Settlements to the Present*. Chicago: University of Chicago Press, 1982.

Cowan, Ruth S. *A Social History of American Technology*. New York: Oxford University Press, 1997.

Dyer, Frank Lewis, and Thomas Commerford Martin. *Edison: His Life and Inventions*. New York: Harper Brothers, 1929. At *http://www.jhalpin.com/metuchen/tae/ehlai0.htm* (last updated by Jim Halpin, September 17, 1999).

Ford, Larry R. *Cities and Buildings: Skyscrapers, Skid Rows, and Suburbs*. Baltimore: Johns Hopkins University Press, 1994.

Granovetter, Mark, and Patrick McGuire. "Shifting Boundaries and Social Construction in the Early Electricity Industry, 1878–1915." At *http://*

sasweb.utoledo.edu/sasw/PORACVEN.htm (last updated, December 7, 1998).

Hamond, John Winthrop. *Men and Volts*. New York: J. B. Lippincott Company, 1941.

"History of Electricity." At *http://historia.et.tudelft.nl/wggesch/Werkgroep Geschiedenis der Elektrotechniek* (last updated, March 15, 1999).

"History of Electricity Use." At *http://www.bydesign.com/fossilfuels/links/html/electricity/electric_history.html* (last updated, January 7, 2000); Link Center fossilfuels.org, "One Thousand Links for Learning How North America Uses Fossil Fuels." At *http://www.bydesign.com/fossilfuels/links/index.html* (last updated, March 19, 2000).

Jackson, Kenneth T. *Crabgrass Frontier: The Suburbanization of the United States*. New York: Oxford University Press, 1985.

McShane, Clay, and Joel A. Tarr. "The Centrality of the Horse in the Nineteenth-Century American City." In *The Making of Urban America*, edited by Raymond A. Mohl, 105–30. Wilmington, DE: Scholarly Resources, 1997.

Miller, John Anderson. *Fares, Please! A Popular History of Trolleys, Horsecars, Streetcars, Buses, Elevateds, and Subways*. New York: Dover, 1941, 1960.

Misa, T. A. *A Nation of Steel: The Making of Modern America, 1865–1925*. Baltimore: Johns Hopkins University Press, 1995.

Passer, Harold C. "Frank Julian Sprague: Father of Electric Traction, 1857–1934." In *Men in Business: Essays in the History of Entrepreneurship*, edited by William Miller, 212–37. Cambridge: Harvard University Press, 1952.

Roberts, Gerrylynn K., and Philip Steadman. *American Cities and Technology: Wilderness to Wired City*. London: Open University, 1999.

Sprague, Frank J. "Report on the Exhibits at the Crystal Palace Electrical Exhibition, 1882." Washington, DC: Government Printing Office, 1883.

_____. "Application of Electricity to Propulsion of Elevated Railroads." *Electrical World* 7 (1886): 27, 36, 118.

_____. "The Multiple Unit System for Electric Railways." *Cassier's Magazine* 16, no. 4 (August 1889): 460.

_____. "Lessons of the Richmond Electric Railway." *Engineering Magazine* 7, no. 6 (September 1894): 789.

_____. "Some Personal Notes on Electric Railways." *Electrical Review* 40, no. 7 (February 15, 1902): 227.

_____. "The Electric Railway." *Century Magazine* 70, no. 4 (August 1905): 522.

_____. "Digging in the Mines of the Motors." *Journal of the American Institute of Electrical Engineers* 53, no. 5 (May 1934): 703.

Sprague, Harriet Chapman Jones. *Frank J. Sprague and the Edison Myth*. New York: William-Frederick Press, 1947.

Tarr, Joel A. "Urban Pollution: Many Long Years Ago." *American Heritage* 22 (October 1971): 65–69, 106.

Tarr, Joel A., and G. DuPuy, eds. *Technology and the Rise of the Networked City in Europe and America*. Philadelphia: Temple University Press, 1988.

Tocqueville, Alexis de. *Democracy in America*. New York: Random House, 1981.

Twain, Mark, and Charles Dudley Warner. *The Gilded Age: A Novel*. Hartford: American Publishing Company, 1873.

Willis, C. "Light, Height, and Site: The Skyscraper in Chicago." In *Chicago Architecture and Design, 1923–1993: Reconfiguration of a Metropolis*, edited by J. Zukowsky, 119–39. Chicago: Art Institute of Chicago, 1993.

Wollner, Craig. *Electrifying Eden: Portland General Electric, 1889–1965*. Portland: Oregon Historical Society, 1990.

6

Charles A. Comiskey
Baseball as American Pastime and Tragedy

Douglas E. Bukowski

The connections between sports and American cities have proved firm and long-lasting. In the colonial period, tavern keepers sponsored competitions in bowling, cockfighting, cricket, and bearbaiting. During the same years, residents of seaboard cities founded private sporting clubs for horse racing, yachting, and other athletic contests. In the nineteenth century, bareknuckle boxing became very popular in cities, even though its illegality in many places meant that prizefights had to be held in secret. Daily newspapers and specialty journals such as the *American Turf Register*, the *Clipper*, and the *National Police Gazette* regularly reported the results of athletic contests and sparked heightened interest in them. Although respectable families initially denounced the drinking, wagering, and hooliganism associated with the predominantly male sporting crowd, by the late 1860s many reformers and clergy defended sport for the lessons it imparted about teamwork and fair play as well as its wholesome influence on youth. Rising population densities, expanding communication and transportation networks, and increases in leisure time and discretionary income contributed to a growing fascination with sports during the age of urban industrial expansion.

A descendant of the English game of rounders, baseball surpassed cricket as the most popular team sport in America by the time of the Civil War. Recent arrivals in the cities from the nation's small towns and farms found escape from the hurly-burly of urban life in bucolic baseball stadiums, small islands of greenery surrounded by acres of concrete. Immigrants rapidly mastered the rules and customs of the national pastime as part of their Americanization. Excluded from professional baseball in 1898, African Americans formed their own teams that played in segregated settings until after World War II. Urban entrepreneurs founded or purchased baseball teams, cultivated political contacts in order to secure expensive municipal services at a discount, and sought to foster the public's support for the local teams. As owner of the Chicago White Sox, Charles Comiskey established an institution of enduring significance for Chicagoans, and his experience demonstrates how sport touched the lives of countless urbanites and helped establish an identity for a city.

A lifelong Chicago White Sox fan, Douglas Bukowski received a Ph.D. degree from the University of Illinois at Chicago in 1989. He is the author of *Baseball Palace of the World: The Last Year of Comiskey Park* (1992); *Navy*

Pier: A Chicago Landmark (1996); and *Big Bill Thompson, Chicago, and the Politics of Image* (1998).

The first sixty years in the life of Charles Albert Comiskey could have been scripted by Horatio Alger: the son of an immigrant literally walks away from a blue-collar job for the game of baseball, which leads him to fame and fortune. But in the sportsman's last twelve years, Alger gave way to Theodore Dreiser, and Comiskey found himself caught up in possibly the first great celebrity scandal of twentieth-century America.

Charles Comiskey was born in 1859, three years after baseball's arrival in Chicago. The boy no less than the city found the game irresistible. By the time he turned seventeen, Comiskey was ready to make a living at baseball. Along the way, he joined in creating a national pastime, not to mention an urban-centered big business.

Comiskey's father may have wanted him to take a different career path. John Comiskey was an Irish immigrant who eventually entered the world of Chicago politics as an alderman. Comiskey was able to arrange jobs for his son as an apprentice plumber and a teamster, but neither occupation satisfied the youngster. (Later, as a team owner, Comiskey also passed on the chance to follow his father into politics. "I'd rather win a pennant than an election," he said in answer to the suggestion he run for mayor of Chicago.)[1]

One day in the summer of 1876 the teenaged Comiskey was driving a wagon filled with bricks destined for the new Chicago city hall. On his way, he passed a ball game in progress. Seeing that one team badly needed pitching, Comiskey left the wagon to volunteer his services as a reliever. Thus was born a baseball career, though Comiskey soon moved from pitcher to first base, where he excelled as a professional for thirteen seasons.

Comiskey might have been spared both fame and notoriety had Americans not fallen so in love with the game of baseball. On the whole, they agreed with the poet Walt Whitman, who said, "I see great things in baseball; it's our game, the American game." Baseball also grew into a great enterprise and, as Calvin Coolidge once noted, the business of America is business. Fans who attended games worked—or worshiped—in a kind of factory, Coolidge might have added.[2]

Baseball is descended from the English game of rounders, which features a bat, a ball, and bases. The game itself evolved over time, the legend as well as the rules. That Abner Doubleday did not in fact invent baseball in 1839 while living in Cooperstown, New York, matters little. The story endowed baseball with a bit of engaging myth. So did the game's early history. From its colonial roots, baseball grew in popularity along the East Coast during the 1830s and 1840s. The first organized team to leave behind a record was the Knickerbocker Base Ball Club of New York City. In 1845 the team chose as its playing field a clearing in rural New Jersey, close to Hoboken. The site was known as Elysian Fields, the same name used for paradise in ancient Greece.

The Knickerbockers, for their time, consisted of young, upwardly mobile professionals desirous of some healthful exercise. Fans soon divined a connection between the game and good morals. As baseball swept into Brooklyn, not yet a part of Gotham, one New Yorker observed, "God speed the churches and ball clubs of our sister city!" Baseball in its early days also carried an element of class conflict. Teams of workers and capitalists squared off on the diamond in a way they could not at work.[3]

Surprisingly, the Civil War worked to baseball's advantage, though not for reasons long held—that it provided something for prisoners of war to do. Prison camp conditions were too debilitating for the playing of games. However, soldiers between battles found exercising the bat and ball a pleasant way to pass the time.

Admission to games was charged as early as 1858. During the war, the first-ever permanent baseball facility debuted in Brooklyn, along with a regular 10-cent admission fee. Soon after 1865, the amateur ideal began yielding to the realities of professionalism. Americans found that they enjoyed rooting for a winner and, if paying salaries to players translated into more victories, so be it.

William Marcy Tweed helped the process along. "Boss" Tweed, as the powerful if unofficial head of New York government was more commonly called, liked his baseball, to the point that players for his Mutuals team tended to find themselves with city jobs. Similar to a later New York owner, Tweed boasted a team payroll virtually impossible to match. Luckily, the cartoons of Thomas Nast never savaged baseball as they did Tweed. While Tweed's methods may have been extreme, they were part of a growing trend. In Chicago, for instance, the teenaged Albert Goodwill Spalding landed a good-paying job with a wholesale grocer. Spalding was valued more for the talent he brought to the company baseball team than for his skills as a stock boy.

In 1869 the Red Stockings of Cincinnati became the first team to declare openly that it operated as a professional, not an amateur, undertaking. Seven years later, the National League was founded along the same lines. If baseball came with more than a few paradoxes, Americans did not seem to notice or care. Fans were about to take to their hearts a game that was in equal measures rural and urban, simple and complex, amateur and professional.

There is no denying baseball's past in colonial and small-town America, or its growth in cities of the Gilded Age. The game thrived in a place like Chicago, which grew from a settlement of fifty residents in 1830 to a city of 112,000 by the time of Charles Comiskey's first birthday in 1860. The Chicago National League entry began play sixteen years later, when the city's population surpassed 300,000. In 1900, Comsikey located his new American League team on the south side of a city with a population of 1.7 million people. The story repeated itself with other professional teams—they chose cities remarkable for sudden population growth. At the same time, people who crowded into cities were often uncomfortable with their new surroundings. They had been raised in a culture that viewed cities the way Thomas Jefferson did, "as pestilential to the morals, the health and the liberties of man." Urbanites who dared break with their rural past needed a security blanket nonetheless, in green if possible.[4]

While teams often built parks at the edge of town where real estate prices were low, the urban landscape always caught up. This growth of the cityscape made the insides of a ballpark that much more important as the playing field became an island of green in a sea of concrete. And when a player from Pocahontas, Iowa, or Nanticoke, Pennsylvania, stepped onto the field, he allowed fans to look beyond the city's rooftops to see their own rural past, real and imagined.

Giving fans a team and players to cheer and identify with may have been baseball's greatest contribution to city life. A team's fan base crossed class and ethnic, if not often racial, lines. The lawyer and mechanic mixed in the bleachers while immigrants cheered their countrymen on the field (even as the National League in the late nineteenth century preferred to hire only WASPs for its umpires). As a second-generation Irishman, Charles Comiskey came with his own cheering section.

Baseball did not lack for critics, especially when played on Sunday or at a ballpark that tolerated alcohol, cursing, and gambling on or off the field. Still, religious and civic leaders also realized that the game could be made into an object of civic virtue. The cities of post–Civil War America created something that had never much existed in society—leisure time along with the disposable income to enjoy it. The ballpark at least promised an activity on which time and money were well spent, as opposed to the dance hall, amusement park, or saloon, or so critics believed. For their part, owners periodically tried to foster wholesome conduct on the field and in the stands, if with varying degrees of success. The game emerged as the one city seduction that civic leaders could tolerate. They saw only a simple child's game that adults were fortunate enough to play or to watch other adults play. But there was more: baseball was a perfect metaphor for the complexities of city life in the Industrial Age.

Baseball emphasized interdependence, as did cities and corporations. Fans took their cue from the dugout. Managers provided leadership as politicians and bosses did in everyday life; a double-play combination exhibited the same kind of teamwork expected of workers on the factory floor or in the office. Moreover, following the game was not unlike making one's way up the corporate ladder. There were always figures to comprehend (Batting Average and Earned Run Average or sales and GNP), together with levels of organization (players, coaches, and owner versus workers, foremen, and owner). It may have been more than a coincidence that the American League was formed in 1900 and US Steel a year later.

The inventions that made the modern corporation and city possible also exerted a profound influence on baseball, starting with transportation. The railroads took teams from city to city while streetcars brought fans to the ballpark. The results of a game were then subject to the same process as might befall an important business meeting—they were typed up, transmitted by telegraph or telephone, and delivered to the intended party. Andrew Carnegie no doubt received such news privately; for nearly everyone else, there was the daily newspaper. Just like baseball, journalism came of age in post–Civil War America. Joseph Pulitzer and William Randolph Hearst learned that reporting on sports, baseball in particular, was good business.

The success of the National League showed baseball to be more than just a game, notwithstanding the ruling by Supreme Court Justice Oliver Wendell Holmes in 1922 that baseball failed to qualify as "trade or commerce in the commonly accepted use of those words." It qualified to the many brewers and streetcar magnates who invested in teams. These men had a product or service to sell, and baseball promised to increase their bottom line.[5]

If fans insisted on treating baseball as a game rather than a business, owners were happy to oblige; doing so allowed them to hide how poorly they paid most of their players. Albert Spalding, who went from player to owner to sporting goods tycoon, explained management's view of the sport. Spalding spoke with none of the sentimentality typically associated with baseball: "Like every other business enterprise, baseball depends for results on two interdependent divisions, the one to have absolute control and direction of the system, and the other to engage— always under the executive branch—the actual work of production." John D. Rockefeller could not have put it better.[6]

The young Comiskey began producing for teams in such midwestern cities as Dubuque, Elgin, and Milwaukee. Two years after splitting his time between the Dubuque Rabbits and a job selling candy and magazines to passengers on the Illinois Central Railroad, he broke in with the St. Louis Browns. The team belonged to the American Association, then seeking parity with the National League. The 23-year-old Comiskey immediately established himself at first base and within three years became player-manager of the Browns.

An average hitter with a lifetime .264 mark, Comiskey stood out for his defense and innovations. He liked to play off the bag at first, a little-used strategy at the time. By cutting down on the number of ground balls making it through the right side of the infield for hits, Comiskey modernized defensive play. He also showed the advantages of having the pitcher cover first base and the infield play in or back depending upon the situation. Comiskey's style of play and managing led the Browns to four straight pennants between 1885 and 1888, but not all of his ideas proved popular. Players apparently shied away from their manager's concoction of chilled oatmeal water to maintain energy.

Comiskey played for a team owned by Chris Von der Ahe, a German-born boardinghouse operator and saloon keeper. Von der Ahe was said to be so ignorant of baseball that he once bragged of having the biggest baseball diamond in the world; advised by Comiskey that diamonds had uniform dimensions, the owner then boasted he was in possession of the biggest infield. The mercurial Von der Ahe probably taught Comiskey that it was better to own a ball club than to work for someone who did.

Though he was paid a generous $8,000 by 1889, Comiskey left the Browns the following year to take part in a players' revolt against organized baseball, the National League included. Players had long complained about salaries. Though better paid than many fans in their jobs, players made just a fraction of the money taken in by owners. The average player salary in 1880 did not exceed $1,500. Another complaint centered on the reserve clause. In 1879 the National League declared that teams could reserve exclusive bargaining rights with a set number of their players; both the National League and the American Association agreed to an expanded version of the reserve clause in 1883. For nearly 100 years, this legal maneuver would serve to indenture players to the teams that held their contracts. Ballplayers generally had no choice but to accept the salary offered or go to another club when traded.

The 1880s were an unsettled decade for organized baseball, to the benefit of players. The American Association was one of several upstarts challenging the National League. More teams meant an increased demand for services, along with higher player salaries. Then in 1885 the Brotherhood of Professional Base Ball Players organized for better pay and an end to the reserve clause. Leadership of the group felt confident enough to launch its own league in 1890. The Players' League, which attracted Charles Comiskey as one of over 100 players to its eight teams, hoped to bring the more established leagues to their knees, but shaky finances led to its demise after just one season.

Had Comiskey worked at a Chicago steel mill or meatpacking plant, he would have faced the likelihood of being blacklisted for union activity. But baseball was more forgiving, if only because the offender in question was so highly talented; the willingness to bend rules for its moneymakers would become a hallmark of the entertainment business. After one more season in St. Louis, Comiskey joined Cincinnati of the National League as a player-manager. He would never again exhibit the same interest in player issues.

It was in Cincinnati that Comiskey met sportswriter Byron Bancroft "Ban" Johnson. While the two quickly struck up a friendship, the Cincinnati owner, John T. Brush, so disliked Johnson's critical reporting that he maneuvered to have the journalist take over the rival Western League. The hope was for him to fail, but Johnson succeeded to the point that in 1900 he was able to transform his collection of teams into the American League. Heading up a new franchise in Chicago was Johnson's friend, Charles Comiskey, who had been owner of a Western League team in St. Paul, Minnesota, since 1895.

Comiskey proved as innovative an owner as he had been a player. In St. Paul he improved his offense just by bringing in the fences in right field to make his seven left-handed hitters greater home-run threats. That same kind of imagination was needed in Chicago if Comiskey hoped to challenge the more established National League club. He started by borrowing that team's old nickname, the White Stockings, and making it his own. By 1906, Comiskey's White Sox had their first World Series win, against the crosstown rival Cubs.

When Comiskey had played in St. Louis, the Browns sought to draw fans by charging twenty-five cents for admission, half of the National League ticket price. Comiskey employed his own version of this strategy in Chicago by designating 25 percent of the seats as bleachers, the most affordable. He reasoned that lower per-ticket revenue was worth the risk because it "gives a greater number of fans a chance to see my team, and that is the big thing with me."[7]

Comiskey also moved to increase his fan base with a new ballpark. Baseball facilities had always tended toward slapdash, wooden creations vulnerable to collapse or fire. The first modern stadium of steel and concrete, Shibe Park, opened in Philadelphia in 1909. Comiskey wanted the same kind of home for his team on the South Side of Chicago. Construction began on St. Patrick's Day in 1910 and finished four months later. Comiskey allowed his star pitcher, Ed Walsh, to assist in the design. It was no surprise that Walsh called for generous dimensions that would make home runs difficult for the opposition; the resulting pitcher's park stood for eighty years. "The most modern and best equipped Ballpark in the world," reads a postcard of the time. Comiskey is shown surveying his park on its grand opening. The man seen leaning over the railing in the upper deck is just fifty years old, in the prime of his baseball life.[8]

The ballpark may have been Comiskey's most enduring legacy. It was the work of architect Zachary Taylor Davis, who four years later designed the home of the Chicago Whales of the Federal League. (After that league's collapse in 1916, the Cubs moved into what came to be known in the 1920s as Wrigley Field.) Davis understood the cityscape of the South Side. The brick facade of Comiskey Park not only reflected the surrounding neighborhood but it also helped the stadium to resonate with fans as a place of play and even of faith. The park's most distinctive feature was a series of arches that circled the field. Looking from the inside out, it was as if Davis had executed a series of church windows, with scenes of urban life in place of stained glass. The effect may have been more than coincidence, for Davis also designed churches. Much later, when baseball enjoyed a renaissance fueled by nostalgia for a perceived simpler time, Comiskey Park was identified as one of the "green cathedrals" of the game.[9]

The ballpark opened on July 1 with a loss to the St. Louis Browns. Thus began the run of one of Chicago's unique social institutions. By putting his team on the South Side, Comiskey gave it a working-class sensibility; this section of the city was the location of the Union Stock Yards and steel mills as well as countless small factories. The South Side was also home to many of Chicago's immigrants.

With baseball recognized as the national pastime, Comiskey Park initially served as an outpost for Americanization. Newcomers, whether from Europe or the South, cheered the White Sox, thereby showing they were true fans and, by extension, good Americans. A black man could not play major league baseball in 1917, but in Chicago at least he could watch from the stands at Comiskey Park: "I wish you could have been here . . . to those games," wrote one participant of the Great Migration to a friend back home. "T. S. and I went out to see Sunday game witch [*sic*] was 7 to 2 White Sox and I saw Saturday game 2 to 1 White Sox."[10]

Comiskey's ballpark stood on the border of white and black Chicago. In the summer of 1918 a teenaged Langston Hughes visited the South Side from his home in Kansas. On his first Sunday in Chicago, Hughes "set out walking alone to see what the city looked like. I wandered too far outside the Negro district, over beyond Wentworth, and was set upon by a group of white boys, who said they didn't allow niggers in that neighborhood. I came home with both eyes blackened and a swollened jaw."[11] The incident, like the race riot the following summer, took place just blocks from the ballpark, and yet the racial strife that marked so much of twentieth-century Chicago never really touched Comiskey Park. However much he failed in other areas, Charles Comiskey—along with those family members who controlled the team until 1959—did right on the issue of race. In time, his ballpark welcomed the Chicago American Giants, a Negro League team, and the annual Negro League All-Star game. And it was at Comiskey Park that boxer Joe Lewis became heavyweight champion of the world in 1937.

Not only did the Comiskey family pursue a policy of racial tolerance, but their ballpark witnessed the fall of the color line in American League and Chicago baseball. Larry Doby of the Cleveland Indians followed Jackie Robinson into the majors when he pinch-hit against the White Sox on July 5, 1947. Four years later the White Sox acquired a black outfielder from Cleveland. Minnie Minoso established himself both as the first black on a Chicago major league team and the most popular player in White Sox history.

In Chicago baseball evolved into a defining passion. The Cubs—especially after chewing-gum manufacturer William Wrigley took over in 1921—were the North Side team, WASP and middle class. The White Sox drew the denizens of the South Side, Catholic, Jew, and black Baptist alike. Bill Veeck noticed the difference in fans when he bought the White Sox from the Comiskeys in 1959. "The Cub fan comes from the suburbs and from out of town. He will come to a Sunday game, preferably after an early-morning round of golf, to relax. To the White Sox rooter there is nothing casual or relaxing about baseball."[12] Quite the opposite, Veeck observed. "Wake him up in the middle of the night, ask him who he is and he will say, 'I am a carpenter and a White Sox fan.' He may or may not have inherited his trade from his father, but the chances are very good he inherited his rooting interest in the Sox. This kind of family solidarity can only come out of adversity and trial by fire."[13]

Veeck did not exaggerate. Charles Comiskey's team connected with fans on a profoundly personal level that could not be measured by attendance alone. The relationship is best explored in the works of James T. Farrell, whose grim literary realism was always tempered by a love of baseball and the White Sox. In Chicago at least, the White Sox provided followers an escape from the real world of strikes, depressions, and all the other forms of urban uncertainty.

At Comiskey Park the factory worker did in fact rub shoulders with the artist (the writers Nelson Algren and Simone de Beauvoir dated there) and the politician. Charles Comiskey had so succeeded in stitching his team into the everyday fabric of South Side life that mayor and fan Richard J. Daley allowed the city air-raid system to go off when the team won a pennant in 1959. "The city council passed a resolution decreeing that there be hilarity in the streets and shouting and celebration," Daley explained of the decision that had more than a few residents fearing the Soviets were about to attack.[14]

Daley's enthusiasm for the White Sox—or, for that matter, Mayor Harold Washington's—was the product of decisions Charles Comiskey made nearly a half-century earlier in cementing his standing with fans. Comiskey made his new park available for church functions, barbeques, and picnics, fairs and auto polo, an event that did little for the condition of the playing field. Asked why he allowed so many non-baseball activities, Comiskey replied, "The fans built the park, didn't they?"[15]

The press willingly portrayed Comiskey as a man of the people; he had worked hard to ensure nothing less. The new ballpark included a special area, the Bards' Room, where Comiskey lavished food and drink on reporters. This perk was not the only one enjoyed by those covering the White Sox. Reporters following the team on road trips also had comfortable sleeping berths on Pullman cars, courtesy of Charles Comiskey.

Another of Comiskey's ambitious undertakings was his world tour of 1913–14. Long interested in expanding the popularity of baseball overseas, Comiskey first thought of taking his team on tour after the 1906 World Series; as an experiment the following year, the White Sox spent part of spring training in Mexico City. The opportunity presented itself in full following the 1913 season, when manager John McGraw and his New York Giants agreed to join Comiskey on a 4-month sojourn over four continents.

Not all players from the two teams wanted to spend their off-season away from home, so the venture became something of an all-star affair. (Cleveland second baseman Nap Lajoie agreed to go until he learned that a world tour meant traveling by boat. "Too damp a prospect," he reasoned.) After a barnstorming tour across the United States, the two teams sailed in late November, only to cross the Pacific in a typhoon.[16]

The teams opened in Japan in December, including a game in Tokyo on the seventh and a trip to the city of Nagasaki. Other stops included China, the Philippines, and Australia. During their visit to Ceylon (Sri Lanka), the teams were feted by Sir Thomas Lipton, who gave each guest ten pounds of boxed tea. While sightseeing in Egypt, catcher Ivy Wingo tossed a ball over the Sphinx to outfielder Steve Evans. The tour ended in London with a game before King George V. Everyone returned via the *Lusitania*, arriving back in the States just in time for spring training.

The player who drew the most attention—including an invitation to the palace of the khedive of Egypt—was a spare outfielder for the Giants who hit above .250 just once in his 6-year major league career. The athlete in question was barely a year removed from his gold-medal performance at the Olympics, and he was a Native American. Jim Thorpe generated the kind of international acclaim that Comiskey hoped all ballplayers would in time.

The outbreak of World War I ended Comiskey's plan to tour Africa or South America. Still, the owner of the White Sox was confident that, "If we can carry out our missionary program, in ten or twenty years we may have a real world's series in which all the nations of the world can enter teams. The game has the backbone to make it live and be popular wherever introduced." Indeed, baseball would go international, if not as soon as its prophet predicted.[17]

World travel did not diminish Comiskey's interest in winning. The owner of the White Sox possessed an exceptional competitive drive, as a story suggests. He supposedly ordered a meal of lobster at a restaurant. When the waiter arrived with the food, Comiskey asked why his lobster had only one claw. Told that the other claw had been cut off in battle, Comiskey demanded, "Bring me the winner!"[18]

Comiskey was confident he could fill his team with winners. Among his purchases from other teams were center fielder Oscar "Happy" Felsch for $12,000; left fielder Joseph Jefferson "Shoeless Joe" Jackson for $31,500; and second baseman Eddie Collins for $50,000. In current figures, Comiskey spent just under $1.6 million for three ballplayers. It was Comiskey's great flaw that he found it easier to buy players than to pay them. In St. Louis, Comiskey had joined other players who bolted to the Players' League in 1890 on the grounds that "I couldn't do anything else and still play square with the boys." But as an owner he came to believe that "The man who does not keep track of the payroll has no business in baseball." Comiskey practiced his convictions all too well.[19]

Contrary to popular belief, the White Sox were not the worst-paid team of the time; Comiskey only made it seem that way. The real problem lay in the fact that, while he had assembled first-class talent that would win pennants in 1917 and 1919, Comiskey paid and treated players as though they were second-rate. White Sox players were expected to make do with less meal money on the road than most teams provided, and they had to pay the cost of laundering their uniforms. Dirty wash provided the name for baseball's worst scandal.

During the 1919 season, Comiskey declared, "Crookedness and baseball do not mix. It has become immeasurably more popular as the years have gone by. It will be greater yet. This year, 1919, is the greatest season of them all." What Comiskey failed to know or chose to ignore was that player salaries had seriously eroded in the face of 100 percent inflation during the period from 1914 to 1918. Professional players had increasingly turned to gambling as a way to augment their incomes, with throwing games a part of the deal. Major league baseball overlooked a growing industry problem until it was too late.[20]

White Sox first baseman Charles "Chick" Gandil took the initiative late in the 1919 season. Ultimately, Gandil arranged to have six other players conspire with him to throw the World Series to the underdog Cincinnati Reds; an eighth player, third baseman George "Buck" Weaver, declined an offer to participate. With some $80,000 shared by the conspirators, the White Sox lost the best-out-of-nine series, five games to three.

Watching his team, Comiskey immediately sensed that something was wrong. After the Series, Comiskey covered himself by offering $20,000 to anyone with knowledge of a fix; at least one gambler came forward with details. But rather than go public with the information, he took a gamble of his own, that widespread suspicions about a Series fix would blow over by the next season. That winter, he even gave four of the players involved in the scheme substantial raises.

However, another set of gambling allegations together with a friendship gone bad conspired against Comiskey. Late in the 1920 season, a Cook County grand jury convened to determine whether there had been an attempt to fix a Cubs' game that year. When the investigation stalled, American League president Ban Johnson provided the judge with information that led to indictments against the eight so-called Black Sox. Johnson and Comiskey had long since become enemies, in large part because Comiskey saw himself as Johnson's equal. The indictments were Johnson's revenge against an owner he thought had grown too arrogant.

Although the players were found not guilty of a gambling conspiracy, the trial left Comiskey and his team devastated. In the wake of the scandal, baseball rushed to create the position of commissioner and offered the job to federal judge Kenesaw Mountain Landis. The commissioner immediately ruled against the eight Black Sox remaining on the team, saying: "There is absolutely no chance for any of them to creep back into Organized Baseball. They are and will remain outlaws."[21] The team that Comiskey had so carefully constructed now lay in shambles, as did his reputation. Comiskey had become an unwilling participant in a new phenomenon, the celebrity scandal. The leisure time and mass media that made possible the business of baseball also lent themselves to fans following—and enjoying—the travails of a celebrity caught in wrongdoing. Comiskey had long exploited willing journalists to fashion his image as the caring, principled sportsman. The scandal, regardless of verdict, changed everything. Stories of a less-than-saintly Comiskey sold newspapers.

When Judge Landis banned the eight players, seven of them starters, he deprived Comiskey of the talent he needed to compete. The blow came at the worst possible time, with the emergence of Babe Ruth and the New York Yankees. Baseball was about to experience a golden age of unprecedented popularity, but Charles Comiskey would not be part of it.

In the first nine full seasons at their new ballpark, the White Sox outdrew the Yankees eight times as they led the league in attendance in four of those years. High attendance translated into revenue for Comiskey to buy players. In 1920, with Ruth moving from the Boston Red Sox to New York, the Yankees became the first team in major league history to draw over a million fans, a feat they repeated seven out of the next nine seasons. As White Sox attendance dropped in the wake of the scandal, Comiskey found it ever harder to spend the money to keep up. In 1931, the last season Comiskey ran the team before his death that October, the White Sox finished fifty-one and one-half games out of first place.

Although Comiskey was elected to the Baseball Hall of Fame in 1939, fans have been far more sympathetic to two of the Black Sox players. For decades, Buck Weaver and Shoeless Joe Jackson tried unsuccessfully to clear their names. Weaver in particular had a strong case, given that he did not take any money; Judge Landis banned the third baseman for not informing on his teammates. While Jackson received $5,000, it is also possible that, after the 1919 Series, he tried to give the money to Comiskey, who refused to see him.

Following their deaths in the 1950s, Jackson and Weaver were portrayed both in print and on screen as victims of an unscrupulous owner. Charles Comiskey still contributes to a popular culture he helped create, but now as caricature rather than innovator. He is not accorded the privilege of stepping out from the rows of Iowa corn onto the new Elysian Fields. As for the Chicago teenager who walked away from his wagon for the pitcher's mound, he has all but vanished.

Notes

1. Eliot Asinof, *Eight Men Out: The Black Sox and the 1919 World Series* (New York: Henry Holt and Company, 1987), 51.

2. Charles C. Alexander, *Our Game: An American Baseball History* (New York: Henry Holt and Company, 1991), quote opposite x.

3. Harold Seymour, *Baseball: The Early Years* (New York: Oxford University Press, 1989), 24.

4. Charles N. Glaab, ed., *The American City: A Documentary History* (Homewood, IL: Dorsey Press, 1963), 52.

5. Alexander, *Our Game*, 135.

6. Robert F. Burk, *Never Just a Game: Players, Owners, and American Baseball to 1920* (Chapel Hill: University of North Carolina Press, 1994), 53.

7. G. W. Axelson, *"Commy": The Life Story of Charles A. Comiskey* (Chicago: Reilly and Lee Company, 1919), 67–68.

8. Postcard in author's possession.

9. Philip J. Lowry, *Green Cathedrals: The Ultimate Celebration of All 271 Major League and Negro League Ballparks Past and Present* (Reading, MA: Addison-Wesley Publishing Company, 1992), 1–2.

10. Emmett J. Scott, ed., "More Letters of Negro Migrants of 1916–1918," *Journal of Negro History* 4, no. 4 (October 1919): 458.

11. Langston Hughes, *The Big Sea* (New York: Hill and Wang, 1963), 23.

12. Bill Veeck with Ed Linn, *Veeck as in Wreck* (New York: Fireside, 1989), 336.

13. Ibid.

14. Don Hayner and Tom McNamee, *Chicago Sun-Times Metro Chicago Almanac* (Chicago: Bonus Books, 1991), 153.

15. Axelson, "Commy," 192.

16. Douglas Bukowski, "When Baseball Met the Sphinx." *Chicago Tribune*, March 29, 2000.

17. Ibid.

18. Asinof, *Eight Men Out*, 50.

19. Ibid., 50; Axelson, "Commy," 302.

20. Axelson, "Commy," 318.

21. Alexander, *Our Game*, 126.

Suggested Readings

Alexander, Charles C. *Our Game: An American Baseball History*. New York: Henry Holt and Company, 1991.

Asinof, Eliot. *Eight Men Out: The Black Sox and the 1919 World Series*. New York: Henry Holt and Company, 1987.

Axelson, G. W. *"Commy": The Life Story of Charles A. Comiskey*. Chicago: Reilly and Lee Company, 1919.

Barth, Gunther. "Ball Park." In *American Urban History*, edited by Alexander B. Callow Jr. New York: Oxford University Press, 1982.

Bukowski, Douglas. *Baseball Palace of the World: The Last Year of Comiskey Park*. Chicago: Lyceum Books, 1992.

Burk, Robert F. *Never Just a Game: Players, Owners, and American Baseball to 1920*. Chapel Hill: University of North Carolina Press, 1994.

Chicago Tribune. March 29, 2000.

Glaab, Charles N., ed. *The American City: A Documentary History*. Homewood, IL: Dorsey Press, 1963.

Hayner, Don, and Tom McNamee, eds. *Chicago Sun-Times Metro Chicago Almanac*. Chicago: Bonus Books, 1991.

Hughes, Langston. *The Big Sea*. New York: Hill and Wang, 1963.

Lowry, Philip J. *Green Cathedrals: The Ultimate Celebration of All 271 Major League and Negro League Ballparks Past and Present*. Reading, MA: Addison-Wesley Publishing Company, 1992.

Palmer, Pete, and John Thorn, eds. *Total Baseball: The Ultimate Encyclopedia of Baseball*. New York: HarperCollins, 1993.

Reichler, Joseph L., ed. *The Baseball Encyclopedia*. New York: Macmillan Publishing Company, 1985.

Scott, Emmett J., ed. "More Letters of Negro Migrants of 1916–1918." *Journal of Negro History* 4, no. 4 (October 1919): 412–65.

Seymour, Harold. *Baseball: The Early Years*. New York: Oxford University Press, 1989.

Veeck, Bill, with Ed Linn. *Veeck as in Wreck*. New York: Fireside, 1989.

7

Lillian Wald
Meeting the Needs of
Neighborhoods, 1893–1933

Judith Ann Trolander

In 1883 the Reverend Andrew Mearns published a pamphlet, *The Bitter Cry of Outcast London*, detailing the sordid living conditions of the poor in East London slums. Moved by the Reverend Mearns's exposé and determined to bring aid and comfort to the suffering masses, a group of Oxford University students founded the first settlement house, Toynbee Hall, in London the following year. Refusing simply to provide the poor with relief funds, these first settlement house workers sought to bridge the gulf between rich and poor that had developed in industrial cities by taking up residence in the slums—by "settling" in poor neighborhoods. They hoped to make their settlements oases of culture and refinement in urban jungles, safe havens where the poor had access to social and recreational activities otherwise absent from their lives. Toynbee Hall also emphasized the importance of education to workers by offering university extension courses and sponsoring special lectures.

The idea of the settlement house quickly caught on in the United States. After spending several months in residence at Toynbee Hall, Stanton Coit, a minister of ethical culture, moved to the Lower East Side of New York City in 1886 and founded Neighborhood Guild, the nation's first settlement house. Other reformers quickly followed Coit's lead in cities throughout the industrial northeast and midwest, founding six settlements by 1891 and seventy-four by 1897. By the turn of the century, over 100 settlements operated in American cities; by the outbreak of World War I, the number exceeded 400. Reformers typically located their settlement houses in the city's ethnic enclaves in the hope of contributing to the socialization of the immigrant masses. Although most of the settlement houses abjured religious affiliations and affirmed their secularity, Protestant and Catholic churches operated settlements that evangelized as openly as did their city missions. The story of Lillian Wald is the story of how reformers sought to use settlement houses as a means of dealing with the intractable problems of poverty and social dislocation in the polyglot cities of the industrial age.

An expert on the settlement house movement, Judith Ann Trolander received a Ph.D. degree from Case Western Reserve University, Cleveland, Ohio, in 1972 and is currently professor of history at the University of

Minnesota, Duluth. She is the author of *Settlement Houses and the Great Depression* (1975) and *Professionalism and Social Change: From the Settlement House Movement to Neighborhood Centers, 1896 to the Present* (1987).

Louis Pink, a leading public housing and social welfare activist in the first half of the twentieth century, characterized Lillian Wald and other urban reformers of her generation as "a yeast in the community—trying to make people realize the necessity for a different world, a better community. . . ."[1] Wald was part of a network of reformers centered in the settlement house movement during the Progressive Era. Settlement houses were typically located in disadvantaged urban neighborhoods. The settlement workers' general purpose was to meet the needs of their neighborhoods. They attempted to do so both through daily activities of a mostly educational and recreational nature and also by working to bring about fundamental social reforms. Their method was unique. Consisting of mostly college-educated residents living in the settlement house and bolstered by nonresident volunteers, they sought to gain added insights into urban poverty and tried (not always successfully) to develop a neighborly, as opposed to a client, relationship with the surrounding poor people. Residing in the neighborhood brought added authority to their efforts to advocate for and interpret the poor to the larger community. To finance their efforts and win support for their causes, they reached out to some of the era's wealthiest philanthropists. Next to Jane Addams, who established Hull House in Chicago in 1889, Lillian Wald with her Henry Street Settlement on New York's heavily immigrant Lower East Side was the most prominent settlement house worker in America. As such, she was at the center of much urban social reform.

Progressive reformers such as Wald saw modifying the physical and social environment as the key to solving problems of urban poverty. Wald's neighborhood, the Lower East Side of New York, was popularly regarded as an East European Jewish immigrant neighborhood. However, another famous Progressive Era reformer, Jacob Riis, documented in his famous book, *How the Other Half Lives* (1890), and through his photographs the existence of a wide variety of ethnic groups there, including some small enclaves of African Americans and the adjacent Chinatown. Many newly arrived immigrant families lived in 6-story walk-up tenements. Their apartments were likely to consist of just three rooms, the largest of which was about ten feet square. With the occupants of three other apartments on their floor, they shared a toilet in a closet off the hallway. They were the lucky ones. Others lived in cellar rooms with standing water on the floor or slept on the streets. Open space for recreational activities was virtually nonexistent. Contagious diseases, especially tuberculosis, were rampant. Wages were so low that many individuals had to work ten or more hours a day just to support themselves. Public schools existed but offered classes only in English, which was a real struggle for youngsters used to speaking Yiddish or Italian at home. At times, families were so desperate for additional income that they ignored compulsory school attendance laws and sent their children to labor in the neighborhood's sweatshops. While simply surviving was a challenge, many immigrants energetically and realistically sought to better themselves.

At the same time, other New York neighborhoods glittered. The well-to-do lived in fashionable midtown Manhattan. Broadway offered the best theater in the country, the Metropolitan Museum of Art was the leading museum of its type, and Central Park was the most famous of the large urban parks in the United States. However, these amenities, although only a mile or so away from the Lower East Side, might as well have been in another country, given their relative inaccessibility to the impoverished residents of the Lower East Side. In fact, by the end of the nineteenth century, urban dwellers around the country had largely sorted themselves out into neighborhoods by social class. Settlement houses in New York and elsewhere sought to address problems of social class isolation along with problems of poverty.

Lillian Wald's background ideally suited her to settlement house work on the Lower East Side. She was born into an affluent Polish and German Jewish family in 1867 in Cincinnati, Ohio. Her parents had migrated to the United States eighteen years earlier as children. Her father was a successful merchant who sold optical supplies and moved his family first to Dayton, Ohio, and then to Rochester, New York. The rural-to-urban migration was under way, but most preferred to make their moves in small steps, from farm to small town or from a medium-size city to a large one. Wald chose the largest, New York, when, in 1898 at the age of twenty-one, she entered the School of Nursing of New York Hospital.

Like many other German-Jewish immigrants of the mid-nineteenth century, Wald's family had adopted Reform Judaism. With the increase in persecution of Jews in eastern Europe, however, a second, much larger wave of Jewish immigrants headed for the United States in the late nineteenth and early twentieth centuries. Along with Italians, they constituted the two leading groups of what was the largest wave of migration to the United States. These immigrants were urban-oriented and headed for neighborhoods where people spoke their language, where the synagogues and other institutions important to them existed, and where they could afford housing and find work. These newer Jewish immigrants preferred Orthodox Judaism, but many of the second generation of more prosperous and more assimilated Jewish immigrants reached out to the new arrivals. Lillian Wald quickly became an innovative liaison between the older, philanthropic Jewish community and the desperately needy new Jewish immigrants, although she never learned to speak Yiddish.

In addition to her affluent Jewish background, Wald had a practical asset—her professional nursing skills. After nursing school, she worked in an orphanage as a staff nurse. At this time, some youngsters were in orphanages because they had only a single parent who could barely support herself. Private welfare could be undependable, and no government programs existed to aid mothers in keeping their youngsters at home. Small towns might informally make arrangements to help out destitute children, but the problem grew larger with the greater size and impersonality of cities, generating a growing reliance on orphanages. Wald found the place she worked to be cold, overcrowded, too regimented, with low-quality care, and basically a bad social environment for its homeless youngsters.

Recognizing that she could do little to improve the orphanage, Wald left after a year to take some courses at the Women's Medical College of the New York Infirmary, and she volunteered to teach some classes in health and hygiene for immigrant women on the Lower East Side. Mrs. Betty Loeb, the wife of banker Solomon Loeb and a member of the philanthropic German-Jewish banking clan that included Jacob Schiff and the Warburgs, sponsored the classes. One day a tearful youngster came, begging Wald to visit her sick mother, who was covered with dried blood after hemorrhaging while giving birth two days before. The family of seven lived in a 2-room apartment, subleasing corners with makeshift mattresses to boarders. Wald cleaned the sick mother, her baby, and the squalid tenement, and promised to return. With that experience, she committed herself to living and working on the Lower East Side of New York.

Financed by Jacob Schiff, Wald and a friend and fellow nurse, Mary Brewster, moved into an apartment on the Lower East Side in 1893. Wald was already familiar with two other Lower East Side settlement houses. The first was University Settlement, established in 1886 as the first settlement in the United States and modeled after Toynbee Hall, in London. The other was College Settlement, the second to be established in the United States and where Wald lived for a time before finding her Lower East Side apartment. The better-known Hull House in Chicago, Jane Addams's settlement, opened just weeks after College Settlement, in 1889. Wald was unique in combining the idea of visiting nurses actually living in the neighborhoods of their patients with the settlement concept, and she founded what was originally called Nurses Settlement. Two years later, Jacob Schiff gave Wald a Federal-style row house at 265 Henry Street that became the headquarters of the renamed and rapidly growing Henry Street Settlement.

By 1917 the Visiting Nurse Service at Henry Street employed 134 nurses caring for nearly 33,000 patients.[2] As for the social settlement side in 1917, Henry Street had one of the best programs of clubs and classes plus recreational and cultural activities among settlements in the United States. Its head, Lillian Wald, had become nationally known for her contributions to a variety of reforms, including such urban issues as innovations in public schools, housing, playgrounds, city planning, social welfare, child labor, working conditions, and anti-vice campaigns. (Other causes dear to Wald, such as peace and women's suffrage, were not specifically urban so they are not covered here; but Wald gave them high priority along with urban matters.) Support for Henry Street's programs had broadened from the Schiff-Loeb-Warburg clan to include other philanthropists, and Wald extended her reach through other influential politicians and reformers.

In addition to developing contacts among different groups to support her causes, Wald made excellent use of the demonstration project approach to social reform. Her educational projects at Henry Street illustrate that method. Knowing the overcrowded tenements of her immigrant youngsters, Wald began opening "study-rooms" in 1907. In addition to providing "a quiet, restful place" where youngsters could do their school assignments, she also provided what she termed "coaching," meaning publications on current topics and volunteers who might play the role of parents in more affluent households, helping their children with schoolwork. Wald claimed that this project at Henry Street so impressed the New York Board of Education that it subsequently set up study rooms in a number of New York schools.[3]

Another example of Wald's use of demonstration was the settlement's approach to home economics classes. New York schools had cooking classes, but they were taught in the upper grades, after many Lower East

Side girls had dropped out. Furthermore, the school laboratory hardly resembled the kitchens of the tenements. Wald rented a typical tenement flat, equipped it inexpensively, and used it to teach housekeeping to young women in her neighborhood. Similar centers sprang up in other parts of the city, and Wald praised New York's school superintendent for identifying them with school instruction.[4] Henry Street also offered other innovative school programs, such as kindergartens, adult education, and education for the retarded.[5] In fact, Wald convinced the Board of Education to let a neighborhood teacher of the retarded establish ungraded classes "for the physically handicapped and for those with learning disabilities."[6] She also convinced the School Board to hire the first school nurse by initially offering to pay half the woman's salary while she proved her worth. Elsewhere, settlements pioneered in offering English and citizenship classes, then convinced their local boards of education to take them over and expand them. When Henry Street began its vocational counseling service in 1920, it was one of the first in the United States. These educational activities were one way in which settlements aided the desire of many immigrants to move up in American society.

Progressive reformers such as Wald believed that another major answer to poverty besides education was to improve the physical environment or living conditions of their neighbors. Among New York settlement leaders, Mary Simkhovitch, head of Greenwich House and a colleague of Wald's, took the lead in working for housing reform. New York set the standard for the rest of the country in passing a model housing code. Enforcement was a perennial problem. In 1929 "the secretary of the New York State Board of Housing asked Lillian Wald to submit a summary statement" for use with the state legislature on the subject of housing code enforcement.[7] However, government-subsidized public housing would not come until after Wald's retirement when, several blocks away from Henry Street Settlement, the federal government opened one of the first public housing projects in the United States, Vladeck Houses, in 1939.

During the Progressive Era, the leading housing reformer in the United States was Lawrence Veiller. While he was best known as a national expert on housing codes, which many cities were adopting for the first time, Veiller teamed up with Wald in 1905 to deal with another city planning issue. New York was just starting to build its subways but had an extensive system of elevated railways that were cheaper to build, but noisier, dirtier, and more dangerous. New York was proposing to expand its elevated system in the Lower East Side. Wald and Veiller led the protest campaign, which involved other Lower East Side settlements and organizations and made use of letter writing and petitions to the city council. They won. The Lower East Side did get a subway line and eventually, decades later, New York dismantled the last of its "els."

Wald was also active on behalf of playgrounds. Shortly after acquiring the Henry Street house, she converted its neighboring yard into a playground. In the morning, it served the settlement kindergarten. In the afternoon, it offered supervised play for older children; in the evening, the settlement used it for festivals and dances. Meanwhile, New York had acquired land for a park and playground on the Lower East Side, but that land was still vacant. In 1898, Wald joined with other settlement house leaders and reformers to organize the Outdoor Recreation League. As a result of the League's efforts, four years later, the reform administration of Mayor Seth Low committed to building that park and playground. Wald was so involved in the lobbying that when the measure passed, two city officials immediately phoned her with the good news.[8] She was even more effective in convincing the authorities to establish playgrounds as part of schools. When some people raised concerns about mayhem and vandalism, Wald pointed to her experience with the Henry Street playground and offered to advise the schools about management and even to provide volunteer playground inspectors. Nationally, the playground idea had arrived from Germany, but local communities needed to see the playgrounds of settlements, which functioned as demonstration projects, and also needed the prodding and lobbying of the settlement workers and other playground reformers before committing public funds to playground systems. Most inner-city neighborhoods were like the Lower East Side, where about the only space for a ball game was the street. Reformers such as Wald argued that wholesome, supervised play in the outdoors would build the right character, thus promoting a reform in the physical environment of the neighborhood as a solution to juvenile delinquency.

The Country Life Movement also influenced settlement house workers. This antiurban movement drew on people's love of nature to promote everything from the expansion of city park systems to rural camping experiences for urban youngsters. Advocates believed that it was psychologically beneficial for people to have direct contact with nature. That could be especially difficult for youngsters in inner-city neighborhoods to achieve, so many settlement houses, including Wald's Henry Street, acquired rural camps and ran summer camping programs.

Wald's concern about the urban environment also led her into some peripheral involvement with city planning. During the 1920s, the most innovative city planning group was the Regional Planning Association of America, which implemented the British garden city concept with two developments in the greater New York area—Radburn and Sunnyside. Radburn in particular was an attempt to create a total community outside New York where residents could live, shop, and hold a job, all within Radburn's boundaries. There, housing backed onto interior greenways and varied from single-family dwellings to a 92-unit apartment building. Pedestrian underpasses allowed people to walk throughout the community without ever having to stand at a curb waiting for motor vehicles to drive by. Normal mushrooming growth and urban sprawl were avoided by planning enough dwellings at the start to accommodate the target population and not allowing any more growth after that. The community was also a limited dividend project (investors would get a modest return, not as much as the market would bear), but construction costs were so high that the working poor could not afford to live there. The experiment, begun in 1928, failed as a result of the Great Depression; but even had it succeeded, it would have offered no solution to housing people with incomes like those in Wald's Lower East Side neighborhood. That Wald was a member of the Regional Planning Association of America probably says more about the elite, reform-minded circles in which she moved than it says about her influence on this city planning concept.

Social welfare was more particularly Wald's area of expertise. In her well-known book, *The House on Henry Street*, Wald mentioned the unanimous opinion among social workers gathered at the 1909 White House Conference on Children that orphanages were bad for children and that programs that would substitute foster care or would keep the child with a natural parent were preferable. She underscored that position with human-interest stories drawn from her own experiences. For example, while the staff nurse for a New York orphanage, she was asked to cure a head cold for a boy so that he could be admitted. When she tried to cheer him up by asking what he wished for, he told her that he did not want her to cure his head cold, so he would not have to "go to the orphan asylum."[9]

States began to adopt mothers' pensions in 1911. At Henry Street in 1912, a resident, Alice Gannett, joined forces with another New York settlement house worker to form an organization to promote the adoption of mothers' pensions. It may have been a sensitive issue for Wald, because private relief-giving agencies, including Jewish Relief, opposed government-financed mothers' pensions. Perhaps that was why, having described in her book the need to keep youngsters in their homes if at all possible, Wald then mentioned programs in Australia without ever using the controversial "mothers' pensions" phrase. The settlement organization evolved into a state commission to study the problem and then secure passage of a mothers' pension program in New York.

Wald was more courageous in campaigning openly for the election of New York governor Franklin D. Roosevelt as president in 1932. She had served with Harry Hopkins (Roosevelt's right-hand man for relief as governor of New York and later as president) on New York's Welfare Council. Wald had seen Roosevelt's work relief experiments in New York, and she would live to see Roosevelt take the mothers' pension idea national with the passage of the federal Aid to Dependent Children program in 1935. Wald knew that Roosevelt was well aware of the desperate relief situation in cities, and she may have sensed that he would be willing to break new ground in meeting urban needs. Indeed, he did so when his presidential administration became the first to routinely bypass state governments to meet the needs of cities directly. That direct federal government–city relationship has persisted since 1933.

In 1912 one of the agencies opposing mothers' pensions in New York was the Charity Organization Society, a federation of private relief-giving agencies. Similar groups appeared in large cities around the United States in the late nineteenth century. These organizations were needed because as cities got bigger, private relief-giving agencies proliferated. Before the establishment of the Charity Organization Societies, it was quite easy for a dishonest poor person to go to one agency and get a handout, then go to another agency in another part of the city with the same story of need in order to get a second handout, and so on. Charity Organization Societies maintained central listing services of those receiving aid. They investigated their claims and then referred them to one of their member agencies, which actually give assistance to the poor. The Charity Organization Societies did not even raise funds for their member agencies.

Then, in 1913, Cleveland successfully carried out what became an annual fund-raising drive for over fifty of its local charities, some of them settlement houses. The idea of what today is called United Way spread rapidly to most large cities. However, in the largest cities, New

York and Chicago, joint fund-raising was more difficult and the organizations set up to do it were relatively weak. Wald continued to spend much time throughout her career raising funds directly for Henry Street, and she was quite talented in doing so. In raising her own funds, she maintained maximum autonomy for Henry Street.

That autonomy allowed Wald to engage in promoting labor reforms that the business sector in general opposed. The reforms included attempts to abolish child labor, improve wages and working conditions, and promote labor unions. In working on these issues, Wald had plenty of allies among other settlement house workers and reformers. One of the most important was Florence Kelley, who became a resident of Henry Street. In the 1890s, Kelley had been a Hull House resident in Chicago and was employed by Illinois's liberal governor as the state's chief factory inspector. When the political winds shifted in Illinois and Kelley lost that job, Wald tried to help her gain a similar position from New York's reform-minded governor, Theodore Roosevelt. When no appointment materialized, Kelley took the position of head of the National Consumers League, an organization that she made influential in campaigns against child labor and for better working conditions. In 1904, Kelley also took a local settlement house organization that Wald and others had formed earlier and reconstituted it as the National Child Labor Committee.

One of Wald's biographers commented, "Nothing drove her so incessantly as the sight of children put to work," whether they were hawking items in the streets or working in a sweatshop.[10] Like many Progressive Era reformers, Wald and Kelley were willing to turn to the federal government to help alleviate the problem. Over breakfast in 1905, they happened on a newspaper article describing the federal government's dispatch in investigating the boll weevil's damage to cotton crops. It occurred to Wald that if the federal government could investigate crop damage, it could also investigate damage to children. With the support of Kelley and other social workers, Wald proposed the establishment of a federal agency charged with protecting the welfare of children. In 1906, Wald met with President Theodore Roosevelt and successfully secured his support for the establishment of the Children's Bureau. When Congress refused to go along, Roosevelt staged the first White House Conference on the Care of Dependent Children in 1909. Eventually, under President Taft, the Children's Bureau became a reality in 1912. Its first head was Julia Lathrop, a resident from Hull House.

Meanwhile, Wald and labor reformers were pursuing other strategies. One of these was the formation of unions. Shortly after moving to Henry Street, Wald allowed a group of strikers to meet in the settlement's backyard. She also arranged for one of the striking women to meet with a group of philanthropists. When the women won their strike, they invited Wald to attend the contract signing. In 1894, Wald had met another labor activist, Leonora O'Reilly, when both were members of the Social Reform Club. O'Reilly had worked in factories since she was eleven. Eventually, O'Reilly moved into an apartment next door to Henry Street and put together Local 16 of the United Garment Workers' Union. When the parent body refused O'Reilly's group financial and organizational support, Wald helped out with meeting space and also personally urged the male-dominated union to include the women. She remained a consistent supporter of the labor union movement.

Disillusioned with the American Federation of Labor's halfhearted attempts to organize women workers, both Wald and O'Reilly joined the executive board of a new organization, the Women's Trade Union League. Unique in the way that it gave both working-class and middle-class women policy-making positions, the Women's Trade Union League sought to improve working conditions by organizing consumer boycotts, joining picket lines, and raising bail money for jailed strikers. However, Wald had to walk a careful line in supporting unions in order to remain in the good graces of the wealthy backers of Henry Street. On one occasion when she described the desperate circumstances of some strikers to Jacob Schiff, he gave her money to help them but told her to keep his identity as the donor a secret from their union. Wald also helped strikers in Lawrence, Massachusetts, in 1912 when she personally escorted some of their children away from the violence to live temporarily with families on the Lower East Side. In addition, Wald arranged for one of those strikers to address a meeting at Henry Street. That did cost her the support of one or two donors, but she persisted in her commitment to empowering the working class.

What really brought an advance in state regulation of factories as well as union membership was the 1911 Triangle Shirtwaist tragedy, in which 146 women workers trapped on the eighth, ninth, and tenth floors of a burning building lost their lives. The horrific sight of most of these women choosing to jump to their deaths, some hitting the sidewalk and others being impaled on the iron spikes of the fence that surrounded the building, galvanized New Yorkers to pass laws regulating factory conditions and generated considerable sympathy for the union movement. Wald was one of the trusted professionals who spoke to both sides and who used her influence politically to find solutions.

Another major urban reform during the Progressive Era was cleaning up local politics, or dislodging corrupt political bosses and changing the structure of local government by enhancing the role of the expert through such innovations as the city commission and city manager forms of government. As the country's largest city, Wald's New York was too complex for a city commission or city manager. She also resisted the temptation to wage war on a local ward boss, as Jane Addams had tried with scant success in Chicago. Instead, Wald's approach to politics was to support reform candidates and issues. At times, she could act like a machine politician herself. One biographer explained that during an election, Wald "would mobilize the members of the Henry Street household and clubs to distribute literature, speak at meetings, and act as poll watchers."[11] Her first involvement in municipal politics was supporting the successful campaign of reformer Seth Low for mayor in 1901. With Wald, issues were more important than personalities. If she needed support for a cause, such as nighttime garbage removal in her neighborhood, she did not hesitate to approach a politician she had not supported at campaign time. She cultivated a host of connections, from city bureaucrats to powerful politicians, such as Herbert Lehman, governor of New York in the early 1930s and a volunteer club leader at Henry Street going back to 1899. She counted among her friends Eleanor Roosevelt and President Franklin D. Roosevelt's mother, Sara. If a letter to Franklin Roosevelt failed to produce what she wanted, Wald had Sara apply pressure. One biographer described how Sara Roosevelt contacted her son's secretary to see that Wald got a presidential telegram to be read at a dinner that both Wald and Sara Roosevelt were attending.[12] Wald was charming, capable, well-informed, tactful, and very much a part of a remarkable network of reformers.

A number of these reformers were attracted to some issues with strong moralistic overtones, particularly the movement to do something about prostitution. Wald believed that immigrant women were more susceptible to being lured into prostitution because they were more vulnerable. Also, she thought low family incomes, lack of privacy in overcrowded tenements, and lack of wholesome recreational outlets contributed to the problem. She made a number of speeches on the issue. New York was one of the cities that appointed anti-vice commissions during the Progressive Era. In 1910, when John D. Rockefeller Jr.

accepted the appointment as head of New York's anti-vice commission, Wald spoke out about the need to have women on the commission. She did not want reformers to vent their wrath on the prostitutes, but rather to focus on the underlying causes of prostitution. Nevertheless, the goal of most anti-vice commissions of the era was to stamp out red-light districts in the naive belief that that would end prostitution. It did not. Three years after the Rockefeller commission, in testimony before a legislative committee, Wald objected to the use of plainclothes policemen to trap women prostitutes, recommended the appointment of policewomen to patrol the streets, criticized the courts for their treatment of prostitutes, and opposed New York's law requiring prostitutes to be medically examined for venereal disease as legalizing the double standard. Wald's views were among the more enlightened in this anti-vice crusade. Likewise, she was quicker than most settlement workers to downplay the issue of Prohibition (enacted in 1920 and the cause of much organized crime during that decade) when she endorsed the urban, Catholic, Democratic, and anti-Prohibition New Yorker, Al Smith, for the presidency in 1928.

Another moral issue, but one that most Progressive reformers ignored, was civil rights. The Lower East Side was home to some African Americans, and Wald made sure that they were welcome at Henry Street. She also recognized that a group of blacks living several miles away, near what today is Lincoln Center, needed settlement house services. She opened a branch of Henry Street, Lincoln House, to serve them. Her most significant contribution to civil rights, however, was to join a 1909 group of settlement house workers and reformers in New York headed by Mary White Ovington, which founded the National Association for the Advancement of Colored People (NAACP). When the NAACP held its first national conference in New York, the reception was held at Henry Street because it was one of the few places in New York that would accept an interracial group. But Wald feared reprisals if this group sat down to dinner together, so attendees had to eat while standing. She also withdrew from active membership in the NAACP once that group was firmly launched. Furthermore, while she hired black women as visiting nurses, she refused to allow them to eat in the nurses' dining room. As one biographer summed up Wald's record on civil rights, she "was ahead, yet still part of her time."[13]

With all of these weighty issues, Wald did not forget the finer elements of culture. She had the good fortune to be in the cultural capital of the United States, but if her working-class neighbors had any

opportunity at all to go to the Metropolitan Museum of Art, it would
have to be on Sundays. Therefore, Wald led a successful petition campaign to keep the museum open on Sundays. As for working-class interest, the Metropolitan subsequently conceded that they "were well
represented" on that day.

Wald also got Henry Street caught up in the creativity of cultural
life in New York. Besides social clubs, the settlement offered classes in
photography, carpentry, and other skills. In 1904, Irene and Alice
Lewisohn, along with Rita Wallach Morgenthau, volunteers from socially prominent families, began giving dance and drama lessons at Henry
Street. In 1915 they opened a nationally known experimental theater at
the settlement, called the Neighborhood Playhouse. Henry Street further expanded its performing arts program in 1927 when it began its
Music School. While the quality of Henry Street's arts offerings drew
on the cultural vitality of its New York setting, other settlements elsewhere emphasized the arts in their programming in varying degrees. In
so doing, they underscored the connection of the performing arts with
urban life, even for the so-called culturally disadvantaged.

By 1933, Lillian Wald was in poor health. She recognized the need
to yield the executive leadership of Henry Street Settlement to a new
generation. As president of the settlement house board, Wald helped to
pick her successor, Helen Hall. Hall was a settlement worker from Philadelphia who was active in working for better welfare programs. She was
not a nurse, and Wald recognized that it was time to split the Visiting
Nurse Service that she had created from Henry Street.

In spite of her failing health, Wald's retirement was fairly active.
She may have indulged in anti-urban nostalgia in selecting a house on a
pond in Westport, Connecticut, as her retirement home. She had acquired the place in 1917 as a vacation retreat; now it was her permanent
home. She also had time to publish her second book, *Windows on Henry
Street* (Boston: Little, Brown and Company, 1934), thus paralleling the
publishing pattern of the best-known settlement house worker, Jane
Addams, who had recently published *The Second Twenty Years at Hull
House*. Other settlement workers of Wald's generation were also publishing books about their settlement experiences. The publishing reflects the philosophy of Progressive Era reformers who believed that
people were essentially good and that social problems existed in urban
neighborhoods mainly because the larger population was unaware of
them. Their function as settlement house workers in the Progressive
tradition was to make people in general aware of what life was like in

the impoverished neighborhoods. Hence, they sprinkled their writings with numerous human-interest stories, but with the purpose of describing needs in such a way that the larger society would find and support solutions to the problems. Much of that basic optimism had dissolved by the time Helen Hall's generation took over the settlement house movement.

Wald died on September 1, 1940, of a cerebral hemorrhage. She was remembered in many ways, not least of which was the naming in 1947 of a Lower East Side public housing project the Lillian Wald Houses. Henry Street Settlement still exists, with its headquarters at the same address. Instead of serving a neighborhood of largely East European Jewish immigrants, however, the dominant immigrant group today is Dominican. The neighborhood remains a mixed one, and Henry Street is still attempting to meet the needs of its current neighbors. It is also proud of its past history and the varied reform efforts and accomplishments of Lillian Wald.

Wald was central to furthering many urban improvements. She did not invent the visiting nurse idea, but she did much to develop it. She encouraged public schools to have ungraded special education classes, school nurses, and study rooms with tutors. She helped to bring about better housing for the poor and to expand New York's playgrounds. She did her bit to bring about better social welfare programs, fought child labor, was instrumental in the idea of forming the federal Children's Bureau, and helped to improve working conditions and expand unions. She participated in the establishment of several major reform groups, including the Women's Trade Union League and the National Association for the Advancement of Colored People. Politically, she was a realistic and well-respected advocate of reform; and with all that, she still found the time and resources to help her neighbors cultivate the arts. Lillian Wald was part of much that was the best of urban Progressive reform.

Notes

1. Louis Pink, Oral History Project, Columbia University. Quoted in Allen F. Davis, *Spearheads for Reform: The Social Settlements and the Progressive Movement, 1890–1914* (New York, 1967), 243.

2. Doris Groshen Daniels, *Always a Sister: The Feminism of Lillian D. Wald* (New York, 1989), 39.

3. Lillian D. Wald, *The House on Henry Street* (1915; reprint, New Brunswick, NJ, 1991), 103.

4. Ibid., 107–9.

5. Judith Ann Trolander, "A Historical Glance," in *Voices of Henry Street: Portrait of a Community* (New York, 1993), 10.

6. Beatrice Siegel, *Lillian Wald of Henry Street* (New York, 1983), 56.

7. Judith Ann Trolander, *Settlement Houses and the Great Depression* (Detroit, 1975), 121.

8. Beryl Williams Epstein, *Lillian Wald: Angel of Henry Street* (New York, 1948), 157.

9. Wald, *House on Henry Street*, 125–26.

10. Siegel, *Lillian Wald*, 58.

11. Daniels, *Always a Sister*, 53.

12. Ibid., 30.

13. Ibid., 51.

Suggested Readings

Carson, Mina. *Settlement Folk: Social Thought and the American Settlement Movement, 1885–1930*. Chicago, 1990.

Coss, Clare, ed. *Lillian D. Wald: Progressive Activist*. New York, 1989.

Daniels, Doris Groshen. *Always a Sister: The Feminism of Lillian D. Wald*. New York, 1989.

Davis, Allen F. *Spearheads for Reform: The Social Settlements and the Progressive Movement, 1890–1914*. New York, 1967.

Epstein, Beryl Williams. *Lillian Wald: Angel of Henry Street*. New York, 1948.

Siegel, Beatrice. *Lillian Wald of Henry Street*. New York, 1983.

Sklar, Kathryn Kish. *Florence Kelley and the Nation's Work: The Rise of Women's Political Culture, 1830–1900*. New Haven, 1995.

Trolander, Judith Ann. *Settlement Houses and the Great Depression*. Detroit, 1975.

Wald, Lillian D. *The House on Henry Street*. New Brunswick, NJ, 1991 (originally published New York, 1915).

———. *Windows on Henry Street*. Boston, 1934.

8

Billy Sunday
Urban Prophet of Hope

Lyle W. Dorsett and Nancy Grisham

Religion has served a variety of functions in American cities. The desire to worship led to the planning and founding of new communities. From the Puritans in Boston to the Quakers in Philadelphia to the Mormons in Salt Lake City, religious groups have endeavored to construct what John Winthrop called "a Citty upon a Hill." Even where secular considerations clearly accounted for the location of new communities, religious beliefs determined how residents created neighborhoods, wrote laws, identified values, and regulated behavior. The creation of sacred space helped define public space as churches, synagogues, parishes, cemeteries, and, in some instances, schools gave definition to cityscapes. Before government began providing a significant share of the social services in cities, religious groups did so by default. Church-affiliated organizations offered forms of health care, death and burial benefits, poor relief, and other types of aid to society's unfortunates.

In the industrial cities of the late nineteenth and early twentieth centuries, the sweeping demographic changes occasioned by immigration and the relocation of much of the middle-class population to suburbs had important implications for religious institutions. Whereas some clergy followed their well-to-do congregations out of the cities, others chose to remain and minister to the needs of the working classes. Following the leadership of eminent Protestant theologians such as Washington Gladden and Walter Rauschenbusch, the Social Gospel movement called for the churches to foreswear single-minded obeisance to salvation and tend to the suffering of the masses in the temporal world. Thus, the "institutional church" operated kindergartens, nurseries, and health clinics just as the YMCA and the YWCA sought to improve the physical and moral well-being of young newcomers to the city.

While denominations under the sway of the Social Gospel movement devoted more attention to the suffering of the urban poor, the vicissitudes of urban life offered fertile ground for traditional Christian evangelism. High levels of poverty, crime, and immorality brought nineteenth-century revivalists such as Charles G. Finney and Dwight Moody into the cities. Although these evangelists often spoke of the symbiotic relationship between environment and sin, their principal aim remained the conversion of souls. In the early decades of the twentieth century, evangelists such as Billy Sunday and J. Wilbur Chapman brought Christianity's message to millions of city dwellers; their careers reflected the significance of religion at a key time of urbanization.

Lyle W. Dorsett is professor of educational ministries and evangelism at Wheaton College, Wheaton, Illinois. He is the author of several books, including *Billy Sunday and the Redemption of Urban America* (1991) and *The Pendergast Machine* (1968). Nancy Grisham is a graduate student at Wheaton College.

For nearly a quarter of a century, Billy Sunday was a household name in the United States. Between 1909, when he first found mention in the pages of the *New York Times*, and 1935, when that great daily urban paper covered his death and funeral in detail, people even marginally aware of current events had heard of the former major league baseball player who was preaching about sin and salvation to large crowds throughout urban America. Not everyone who knew of the famous Baseball Evangelist admired him. Plenty of vocal critics lambasted his flamboyant style and criticized his religious message. But Sunday had millions of ardent defenders, and these loyalists were just as outspoken in praise of the preacher as the opposition was in its disdain.

Billy Sunday became a prominent part of the landscape of American culture because he represented hope. He preached a message of hope for urban people who felt spiritually confused. He also gave hope to the millions of poor, rural, and small-town dwellers who migrated to the cities looking for an escape from the poverty and drudgery of unmechanized rural life. Sunday's life manifested the promise of American life. He became a hero, in part at least, because his life was a Horatio Alger–like rags to riches story. Born on a farm and orphaned at an early age, this lad climbed out of rural poverty and an orphanage to become a big league baseball player, a gifted orator and preacher, and a man who found himself in the company of the nation's political and economic elite.

Billy Sunday's life spanned one of the most tumultuous eras in American history. Born during the Civil War, he grew up in the late nineteenth century when the United States shifted from a predominantly small-town and rural nation into a nation of industry and cities. Indeed, in 1860 only nine cities had populations numbering 100,000 or more, but by 1900 there were thirty-eight cities with over 100,000 inhabitants. During the next twenty years that figure increased to sixty-eight cities. Industries demanded thousands of new workers, and the prospect of high wages drew many Americans to the cities from the farms and small towns. In fact, from 1860 to 1900 alone, over 18 million people streamed into the cities from villages and farms; one of them was Billy Sunday.

While the farm-to-city movement supplied people for urban enterprises, the quest for a better life also lured European immigrants to the cities. European immigration to the United States increased after the Civil War, reaching 5,200,000 in the 1880s—the peak for the century. Although immigration declined slightly during the 1890s because of an economic depression, it surged to over 8,200,000 in the first ten years of the twentieth century.

This urban industrial revolution caused problems unprecedented in American history. Housing, transportation, and utility and sewage facilities could not keep pace with the growth. Existing police and fire protection, like schools and medical care systems, could not meet the growing needs. In some industries, wages did not rise to expected highs because of labor gluts or market fluctuations. Urban political bosses took advantage of the problems to build powerful political machines. Consequently, abject corruption was one more ill added to the ugly list of social problems that included child labor, gambling, substance abuse, and prostitution.

These conditions sparked an urban reform movement that was far from unified in its approach to solving the widespread problems. Some reformers urged more government regulation, while others called for nonpartisan political reform. Liberal progressives urged the socialization of natural monopolies, and conservatives advocated unbridled competition among private entrepreneurs. One faction of the progressives called for a return to rural virtues manifested in voluntary associations and neighborhood-led reform. Still others saw conservative biblical Christianity as the panacea for all the social, political, and economic troubles. These religious leaders proclaimed that even if the greedy and exploitative institutions were reshaped and the personnel changed, problems would not disappear until the hearts of people were reformed. Billy Sunday emerged as a leader among this faction of Christian reformers.

William Ashley Sunday was born on November 19, 1862, in Storey County, Iowa. His father, William Ashley Sunday Sr., was a farmer who had recently left home to serve as a Union soldier in the Civil War. W. A. Sunday Sr. died five weeks after Billy's birth, leaving his wife, Mary Jane, so poverty-stricken that she eventually had to break up the family. The oldest child, Albert, left home and set out on his own at the age of fifteen. Mrs. Sunday then placed Billy and his brother Edward in the Union Soldiers' Orphans' Home in Glenwood, Iowa.

Sunday's early years were marked by poverty, disappointment, and personal loss. Even his time at the Soldiers' Home was disrupted when the state closed it and sent the children to a new orphanage 300 miles away in Davenport. Despite the early hardships, these years helped forge the youngster into a man of determination and perseverance. Living in rural Iowa nurtured in him a love for open spaces and the discipline of farm labor. At the Davenport Orphanage he received a basic education, learned personal hygiene and discipline, and discovered that he had a natural athletic ability. The orphanage director and his wife were kind people who taught the boys to pray and to memorize Bible verses. All these influences began shaping the man who would markedly affect urban America.

When Billy was fourteen, he and his brother left the orphanage because Ed was too old to stay there. Billy secured employment on a nearby farm, where he remained until he was almost eighteen. Then he decided he wanted more advantages than rural Iowa could offer, so he became one of the millions who migrated to the cities. Sunday's first move took him to the small city of Marshalltown, Iowa. Although it was an agricultural community, he saw it as a first step away from farm labor. Furthermore, the Marshalltown Fire Brigade baseball team recruited him because of his great running speed. Sunday found employment in a furniture store that gave him enough money to live and the free time to play baseball.

Within two and a half years, Billy Sunday had become famous in Marshalltown for his baseball skills as a base stealer and strong left fielder. He helped the team gain a reputation that captured the interest of a celebrated and undefeated team in Des Moines. The Marshalltown nine was challenged to come and play against Des Moines on a $500 side bet and a share of the gate money. The Marshalltowners took the bet, whipped the big-city men, and established Billy Sunday's prowess against the best players in the state.

One of Sunday's supporters at the game was the aunt of Chicago White Stockings' captain and general manager, Adrian "Cap" Anson. Aunt Em enthusiastically reported Billy's baseball exploits and repeatedly urged Cap to give him a tryout with the White Stockings. Cap agreed and wired Billy an offer to try out for the team. Billy made a bold move—he resigned his job, spent his life savings of $6.00 on a suit, and headed to Chicago on borrowed money.

Sunday had never seen a city the size of Chicago. With a population of over half a million, Chicago boasted factories, tall buildings, countless entertainments, and people constantly on the move. The Iowa farm boy later recalled that he had never imagined anything like this existed in America. The city was teeming with immigrants who spoke languages he had never heard. The emigrant from rural Iowa felt agonizingly out of place. When he met Anson and his team, Sunday felt like a country bumpkin. Sporting an out-of-style, ill-fitting green serge suit, he was introduced to the team. "My hair was long," he remembered, "and I sure looked like the hayseed that I was, compared to those well-groomed men, members of that famous old team."[1]

In the 1860s and 1870s, political machines in urban America helped make baseball a prominent feature of the landscape. They often sponsored teams and encouraged the public to attend games. The prosperity of the 1880s enabled large numbers of people to pay a gate fee of twenty-five or fifty cents. The revenue enabled teams to attract and pay good players. In 1883, Sunday secured a place on the elite 12-man squad of the Chicago White Stockings. He would stay with the team, honing his skills, through the 1887 season.

One Sunday afternoon in 1886, after a few drinks in a Chicago saloon, Billy and some of his teammates were walking through the streets. At the corner of Van Buren and State Streets, they encountered a horse-drawn contraption called the Gospel Wagon, complete with brass band, singers, and a preacher on a mobile evangelistic mission. This spectacle was a far cry from the formal churches of rural America. Billy Sunday and his friends had stumbled on a small group of people who had taken religion out of the pews and into the streets. "We sat on the street curb listening to men and women playing on cornets and trombones and singing gospel hymns that many of the churches have blue-penciled as being too crude for these so-called enlightened days," Sunday recalled years later, "but these hymns stir memories that drive folks back to their mother's God and Christ."[2]

Sunday and his friends had encountered an evangelism team from Pacific Garden Mission, which had been founded in 1877 and was typical of city rescue missions of that era. Sunday and his pals heard singing and preaching out on the street, and they went to investigate the program directed toward the city's drifters and homeless people who were in search of jobs, food, and clothing. Many of the mission's clients were addicted to alcohol or drugs, while some were simply out of work and needing help. The street missions had arisen to reach people on society's fringes.

That afternoon in 1886 one of the preachers, Henry Monroe, walked over to Billy and his pals and invited them to hear a message and stories about some people who "used to be dips (pickpockets), yeggs (safe-blowers), burglars, second-story workers, drunkards, and have done time in the big house, and today are sober, honest, have good homes and are trusted, and respected." He encouraged them to hear stories "of women who used to sell their womanhood to whoever would buy, were slaves to dope and drink, and are now married and have children of their own." He asked them to "come down to the mission and hear stories of re-deemed lives that will stir you, no matter whether you have ever been inside of a church or have wandered away from God and decency."[3]

Sunday maintained that when he heard these words, something deep inside his soul began to stir. Although he made good money, lived in the city, and enjoyed some success as a major league baseball player, this invitation piqued his interest to investigate Monroe's claims. Billy re-called that he stood up on those powerful legs and told his teammates, "Boys, I bid the old life good-bye."[4]

Sunday remembered that some of his teammates laughed, some smiled, and others shrugged their shoulders and looked with mingled expressions of admiration and disgust. Despite their reactions, he went down to the Pacific Garden Mission to hear hymns and stories about people's lives that had changed after they decided to follow Jesus Christ. After the presentation of songs and stories, listeners were encouraged to come to the front of the mission hall, confess their sins, and pledge to obey the teachings of Christ.

Billy Sunday did not respond immediately. Instead, he thought through what he had heard and pondered its meaning for his life. While he was aware that he lacked personal fulfillment in life, he was not cer-tain that Christianity was his answer. It would be several days before he attended another meeting, followed by several successive visits during the next few weeks. Finally, he could no longer resist the pull in his soul. He walked to the altar at the front of the room. A former society woman, Mrs. George R. Clarke, who volunteered her time to the mis-sion, placed her arm around Billy and whispered, "Young man, God loves you. Jesus died for you and he wants you to love him and give your heart to him." It would later be written on a plaque in the Pacific Garden Mission, "the ball player could no longer resist. He swung clum-sily around the chairs, walked to the front and sat down. Henry Mon-roe came to his side and they knelt for prayer." Elijah P. Brown, Billy's biographer, reported that Mrs. Clarke had pointed to a cross on the wall and, "Little by little she brought him to see clearly that eternal life is God's free gift, and being such, it must be received as a gift, through childlike faith in the finished work of Christ."[5]

This event proved to be life-changing for Billy Sunday. He described it as the lifting of a great burden. He also noted that he was no longer interested in drinking and gambling. Furthermore, he developed a keen interest in the Bible and in knowing God's direction for his life. Soon he joined the Chicago Central YMCA Bible Training Class, boldly joining in a study of all sixty-six books of the Bible. He also began attending the Jefferson Park Presbyterian Church on Chicago's fashionable West Side.

As word got out that the National League player was serious about his faith, he began receiving requests to tell his story. An unusually gifted communicator despite his lack of training, Sunday could captivate an audience with his vivid illustrations and fascinating stories. Some people felt he had an almost magical ability to capture his listeners' attention. Those who shared his faith in Jesus Christ maintained that Sunday possessed an empowerment of the Holy Spirit that enabled him to be so effective in his speaking. One observer noted, "There was a charm and freshness about [his speaking] that was a constant surprise."[6]

One of Sunday's new friends at the Presbyterian Church introduced him to Amelia Thompson. Nell, as her friends called her, was from a prosperous family. Through Billy's persistence, they eventually began dating. With Nell's encouragement, Billy began taking classes at the Evanston Academy, a college preparatory school located on the campus of Northwestern University. The university had hired Billy as a coach of its baseball team, so he enrolled in classes at the prep school. Because his grammar and writing skills were weak, he invested time during the winter of 1887–88 in remedial English classes. These efforts became part of the ministerial preparation that this rural Iowan needed to ready himself for America's cities.

Billy Sunday and Nell Thompson were married in 1888, the same year Billy was traded to the Pittsburgh Pirates. From the outset of their marriage, Nell was a powerful source of support and encouragement in Billy's life. Although his baseball career continued to improve, he felt more and more drawn toward his Bible studies and volunteer ministry at the YMCA.

In 1890 the Sundays had their first child, Helen. Billy was just hitting his stride as an athlete and had completed eighty-eight games with Pittsburgh with a batting average of .257. With two-thirds of the season over, he was traded to Philadelphia, where he played thirty-one more games. During the 1890 season, Billy stole eighty-four bases, a substantial feat that made him a national sports celebrity. When the season ended, he was offered the best salary he had ever received in the National League. The proposed $400 a month for seven months was several times higher than the average industrial worker's wages of $380 a year. While he felt the pull of money, Billy also sensed the tug of committing his life to something that would bring hope rather than mere entertainment to the nation's urban dwellers.

Sunday spent the winter of 1890 agonizing over the direction of his career. Instead of signing a lucrative baseball contract, Billy asked for and received a release from his agreement so that he could enter full-time ministry work. But just as life seemed settled, he received an even more attractive baseball offer. The Cincinnati Red Stockings pursued him with a salary of $3,500 for seven months. Although that was an extremely generous salary in 1890, Sunday sensed God calling him to preach the gospel that had changed his life and given him peace and hope.

In a bold move that would set the course for the rest of his life, Billy said good-bye to professional baseball. He astounded many observers by accepting a position with the YMCA for only $83.33 a month. Billy Sunday walked away from fame and money to invest his life in urban social reform. From 1890 until his death in 1935, the Baseball Evangelist spent his energy telling people that the answers to their personal problems and the nation's urban ills were to be found in Jesus Christ rather than in material success. Sunday considered the path he walked to be the path many people had traveled from the rural farmlands into the cities of urban America. He acknowledged that he had also joined them in saloons, thinking the city might hold life's happiness and purpose. But Sunday insisted that it was not until he was introduced to Christianity and decided to obey Christ's teachings that emptiness and dissatisfaction left him.

Clearly, Sunday's personal religious experience brought in its wake a powerful sense of calling. He believed that answers for the root problems that gripped urban women and men had to be found in a personal relationship with Jesus Christ. This belief led him to take the position with the YMCA and to commit his life to preaching what he saw as the hope of urban America.

A keen sense of purpose notwithstanding, the new path was not always easy. In 1892 the Sundays' second child, George, was born. Billy needed to support a wife and two children on a small salary just when the depression of 1893–94 engulfed the nation. Although their income was modest, the Sundays were grateful for what they had. All around, they saw widening misery, especially for the lower economic classes. With the stock market downturn came rising unemployment, and many Americans were engulfed by hardship.

Growing social and economic problems served as the impetus for new programs of social Christianity. The Social Gospel movement, as it was labeled, spread rapidly with its local welfare agencies providing food, fuel, clothing, medicine, and temporary shelters. Local missions such as Chicago's Olive Branch and settlement houses like the one founded by Graham Taylor opened throughout Chicago and other metropolises. Although Billy Sunday offered verbal support for Social Gospel programs, he put all of his efforts into proclaiming the message he had heard at Pacific Garden Mission. Relief work was good, to be sure, but he still believed that all men and women needed to "get right with God" before their deepest problems could be solved.

Whether one agreed with Sunday or not, his message was clearly, boldly, and colorfully proclaimed. Some observers found the new evangelist to be entertaining. Others saw him as an obstreperous buffoon. Ever growing numbers of listeners, on the other hand, responded enthusiastically to his challenge to turn from the sinful, self-centered life to one dedicated to God.

One man who took a liking to Sunday's preaching was a well-known evangelist named J. Wilbur Chapman. Born in Indiana and educated at Oberlin College, Lake Forest College, and Lane Seminary, Chapman was less than four years Sunday's senior but was light-years ahead in education, poise, and experience. A close friend and associate of D. L. Moody, Chapman heard Sunday preach. He liked what he heard, took the Baseball Evangelist on as his associate, and for several years taught the young man with the rough, country edges how to dress, speak, and get along in polite religious circles. Billy Sunday traveled through the nation with Chapman, studying his mentor's sermon preparation methods and preaching style. He worked with Chapman from 1893 to1896, receiving a rich apprenticeship as an itinerant evangelist. When Chapman stepped down from his ministry to take a position as pastor of a Philadelphia church, Billy was suddenly without a mentor or an income. He was now on his own.

In January 1896, Sunday was invited to hold an evangelistic meeting in Garner, Iowa. He accepted the invitation and thus ended his apprenticeship. From this point forward, he would never be without speaking invitations. Although it was not the end of the difficult times for Billy and Nell Sunday, it was the beginning of a new era in his life and career. From 1896 to 1907, Billy preached in seventy different communities. Twenty-eight of the documented revivals were in Iowa, and twenty-four were in Illinois. This resident of Chicago traveled the Midwest by rail and came to call these communities the Kerosene Circuit, because most were agricultural service communities with populations of 1,000 to 7,000 people who had no electric lights, natural gas, or indoor plumbing.

Gradually, Billy attracted larger crowds and spoke in larger urban areas. He began by renting tents to accommodate his listeners, but eventually hired work crews to build wooden tabernacles for his multiweek crusades. His ministry and appeal were increasing, and in these early days he never made pleas for money. Sunday had come from rural America and understood the attitudes of the people. Even in the larger cities many urban dwellers were only a short time off the farm. He understood them, spoke their language, and was sensitive to their needs. His authenticity helped him win the people to his point of view and build an increasingly large following. He told the congregations that he wanted them to find peace and hope. While he stressed that people needed God, his speech was colorful, his illustrations vivid and earthy. Wherever he preached, there was a recurring theme in his messages. Sunday told people, "Going to church don't make anybody a Christian any more than taking a wheelbarrow into a garage makes it an automobile. . . . No hypocrite in the church, or out of it, is going to get into heaven." He was also quick to caution people not to follow him, saying, "If you follow some of the star preachers you will be lost in the woods, but if you follow Christ you will be sure to land in heaven."[7] The basic message he declared was:

> Years ago, Jesus came to take up his abode in my heart and life.
> I am Honored. He is my guest, and will be until the end.
> 1. I believe that the Lord Jesus Christ died for me.
> 2. I have accepted Him as my Savior.
> 3. I have confessed Him before the world.
> 4. I trust Him from day to day.

Billy Sunday believed that many of his listeners were bound by habits that they could not break. He knew they were in broken relationships: many lived in inner pain with a fear of death. Those who moved to urban America might change their circumstances, but this new situation did not change the deeper issues in their hearts. He would ask, "What can be done? Here is a watch. It does not run. Would you say, 'Give it new surroundings'? No, you'd say, 'Give it a new mainspring.'" Then Billy would tell of the new mainspring in his life that had changed him and given him new life:

> I know salvation has done four things for me:
> 1. It has made me a happier man.
> 2. It has made me a better man.
> 3. It has made me more useful.
> 4. It has given me hope.

He would then tell people that if they would "get right with God" through faith in Christ, they could be assured of eternal life in heaven. He encouraged them to "Surrender to Christ and stop drinking up your paycheck. . . . Get right with God and spend more time with your wife and children. . . . Follow Christ and earn money for your family by doing an honest day's work. . . . Become a Christian and stop using tobacco. . . . Be Christ's man and do more with your life than play cards and dance." Many less fundamentalist Christians accused Billy of taking a legalistic view of the faith. He responded by calling attention to the fact that many Christians lived lives that outwardly appeared to be no different from the lives of non-Christians. He was grieved by this and called them to live changed lives through genuine repentance. Sunday argued that modern urban Christianity had moved away from the Bible's teachings. He derisively labeled preachers who doubted the truth of the Bible as "modernist." Sunday often said, "Nowadays we think we are too smart to believe in the Virgin birth of Jesus, and too well educated to believe in the resurrection." He thought that belief was the reason "why people are going to the devil in multitudes."[8]

The outspoken preacher bluntly stated that his main goal was to point to unbelievers in Jesus Christ and to exhort backsliders to renewed commitment to Christian discipleship. After he had finished a message, he would step down in front of the platform and ask people to take his hand and say, "I am a sinner but I want to follow Christ," or "I am an errant believer and I want to renew my commitment to be a disciple of Christ." People responded well to these so-called altar calls. By the late 1890s it was reported that 100 to 200 repentant souls per night came forward.

While Sunday was traveling the Midwest holding meetings, Nell stayed home to care for their four children: Helen (1890), George Marquis (1892), William Ashley Jr. (1901), and Paul Thompson (1907). Increasingly, Billy was on the road, leaving the responsibilities of the home and family to Nell. Being away from the children was difficult for him and the family. Therefore, in 1908 they made the decision to begin working together, with Nell as Billy's administrator. They would travel together, taking the children along as much as possible. Sunday often received invitations to preach multiweek "revivals," as he dubbed them, in large cities. Nell traveled with him much of the time, but frequently they had to leave the children at home with a housekeeper.

Sunday's fame spread rapidly in the early twentieth century. The newly independent evangelist, who had preached his first series of meetings in January 1896 in Garner, Iowa, eventually conducted over 250 crusades in all sizes of towns and cities in the United States. Although he was invited to hold evangelistic meetings in other countries on several continents, he believed that he should restrict his ministry to the United States. He conducted his American preaching engagements nightly over two or three weeks, with morning and afternoon meetings held for special-interest groups such as women's clubs, businessmen's groups, youth gatherings, and Sunday school teachers. From 1896 until his death in 1935 the zealous evangelist maintained a hectic schedule of travel and preaching.

William A. Sunday ultimately preached to over 100 million people. Approximately one million people responded to his altar calls when they were asked to walk his famous "sawdust trails" and commit their lives to Jesus Christ. The "sawdust trails" were his trademark, taking their name from his early campaigns in the Pacific Northwest where the floors of meeting halls and hastily constructed tabernacles were covered with sawdust. This material was free or inexpensive, and the mud, melted snow, and dust could be easily swept away after each meeting.

By the 1920s, Christians and non-Christians alike recognized the noted Baseball Evangelist as an American phenomenon who had preached the gospel to more people in more cities than anyone in world history. When he conducted extensive crusades of several weeks' duration in such places as San Francisco, Chicago, Cleveland, Boston, New York, and Philadelphia, Sunday's meetings were daily front-page news for weeks at a time. Statistics of attendance and altar call respondents were considered newsworthy. In addition, many newspapers reprinted his sermons verbatim, allowing millions more to feel their impact.

A theatrical man, he could make audiences laugh as well as weep. He dined with presidents and socialized with leaders in the sports and entertainment world; he enjoyed renown as one of America's most admired men and befriended the nation's economic power elite. A human dynamo famous for his energy and enthusiasm, Sunday earned over one million dollars, sought the nomination for president of the United States on the Republican ticket, and ran for vice president with the Prohibition Party. He also sold a syndicated column to numerous newspapers and published books of his sermons that sold thousands of copies.

Although Sunday never attended college or seminary, the Presbyterian Church ordained him in 1903. Despite being recognized as an independent evangelist, he remained a Presbyterian all his life. Up until World War I, that mainline denomination enjoyed its name association with America's most famous preacher; by 1917, however, some Presbyterian leaders were embarrassed that the Reverend Sunday carried ordination papers from their church. By that time, he was earning so much money that it brought shame to the Presbyterian Church and nearly caused them to set a limit on their preachers' earnings. Sunday was accountable to no one for his income and expenses. He received no salary but paid his expenses from the offerings collected from his audiences. Usually, he gave away the nightly offerings, after paying rent and workers, to a local charity. He kept only the final night's "love offering" for himself, but that one night might bring over $100,000 in a major city, and Sunday's income became a subject of criticism among many people. Although he remained above any scandal and much of his income went to charities, many observers felt suspicious that this preacher who taught about Jesus Christ, the poor Nazarene, earned such large sums of money.

Most of the criticism directed against Sunday stemmed from his identification with conservative causes. He openly endorsed Republican candidates for political office. Beyond that, he ardently campaigned for the prohibition of the sale of alcoholic beverages during the 1910s. Indeed, many of his contemporaries credited his enthusiasm for the Prohibitionist cause with the passage of the Eighteenth Amendment to the U.S. Constitution. It must be noted, on the other hand, that he was no genuflective right-winger. In the early twentieth century, he took the lead in pushing for the rights of African Americans. He insisted, even in the Deep South, that his services be open to blacks along with whites. This stance won him the admiration of large segments of the black population. Of course, it also brought an onslaught of rancor from hard-core racists in the country.

Sunday's popularity waned after 1930 because he was older, some of his causes were less celebrated, and some of his Republican political friends (such as Herbert Hoover) became unpopular after 1929. Nevertheless, he always had a large following. Crowds thronged to hear him preach. When he died, an estimated 15,000 to 20,000 people streamed past his open casket at Chicago's Moody Church. His followers came from every ethnic group and from all walks of life. He spoke a language people understood and called them back to traditional values during a time of great change. He was the de facto leader of those who wanted to keep biblical, conservative Christianity alive in an increasingly secular society.

Although countless people testified to making first-time commitments to Christ under his preaching and numberless throngs recommitted their lives and took encouragement from the famous preacher, Sunday's life was marred by family difficulties. The Sunday children became a source of much pain for their parents. Only Helen seems to have been a strong Christian. She married Mark Haines, they had a son named Paul, and she died at age forty-two from complications of a disease similar to multiple sclerosis. The three sons, on the other hand, were overly indulged by parents who felt guilty about leaving them alone for weeks on end with their sister or a housekeeper. Unruly and seldom disciplined, all three boys suffered from drinking problems and led promiscuous lifestyles, and they died young and out of fellowship with the Christian community.

During his lifetime, Billy Sunday was faulted by people for failing to raise his boys well, and he was ridiculed by the press and by some church leaders for his excessive income, but these were minor criticisms compared to the attacks leveled against him by some Christian leaders for his altar calls at the end of each service. Sunday believed that people could and must make a decision to repent and follow Christ, so he encouraged people to do precisely that. Many predestinarians found this invitational style of evangelism, which became much more popular as other evangelists and ministers copied Sunday, to be theologically errant. Sunday was denounced as an Arminian by many Calvinists. Some even called him a heretic.

In the final analysis, regardless of his methods, Sunday brought a modicum of reform to urban America. Countless thousands of lives were changed and drinking establishments, gambling dens, and houses of ill repute were closed down forever in some of the communities where he preached. Billy Sunday inspired many Americans and annoyed many others, but millions of people found hope in the midst of their despair as a result of his decades of preaching.

Notes

1. Lyle W. Dorsett, *Billy Sunday and the Redemption of Urban America* (Grand Rapids, MI, 1991), 19.

2. Ibid., 24.

3. Ibid., 25.

4. Ibid., 26.

5. Elijah P. Brown, *The Real Billy Sunday* (New York, 1914), 40.

6. Dorsett, *Billy Sunday*, 31.

7. These quotations and the ones that follow are from undated newspaper accounts in the Sunday Family Papers, microfilm edition, Archives of the Billy Graham Center, Wheaton College, Wheaton, Illinois (hereafter cited as Sunday Papers).

8. Sunday Papers.

Suggested Readings

Brown, Elijah P. *The Real Billy Sunday*. New York, 1914.

Bruns, Roger. *Preacher: Billy Sunday and Big-Time American Evangelism*. New York, 1992.

Dorsett, Lyle W. *Billy Sunday and the Redemption of Urban America*. Grand Rapids, MI, 1991.

McLaughlin, William G. *Billy Sunday Was His Real Name*. Chicago, 1955.

9

Albion Fellows Bacon
Indiana's Frenzied Philanthropist

Robert G. Barrows

During the years that industrialization reshaped American cities, women typically faced exclusion from the men's organizations and political institutions that spearheaded the efforts at civic improvement. Eager to contribute to reform campaigns and to expand their influence outside the confines of the household, women formed clubs that provided avenues for their social activism. (Some women's clubs originated for the purposes of social interaction and cultural refinement and later turned to reform activities, while others remained dedicated solely to literary or artistic endeavors.) In cities of all sizes, women's clubs addressed the dearth of parks, playgrounds, libraries, public health clinics, day care facilities, shelters for the homeless, and other social welfare institutions. Members conducted education campaigns, raised funds for new programs and facilities, and lobbied for local, state, and federal legislation to regulate child labor, conditions in the workplace, and maternal and infant health care. During the Progressive Era, women's clubs constituted a powerful interest group whose reform crusades commanded the attention of elected officials and politicians in the cities.

By the 1890s membership in women's clubs had increased so significantly that an umbrella organization developed to coordinate activities nationwide. The General Federation of Women's Clubs (GFWC) provided a clearinghouse for ideas, held national meetings, and published materials for widespread distribution. African American women and members of other racial and ethnic minorities often faced exclusion from GFWC affiliates and therefore had to form their own clubs. Organizations such as the National Association of Colored Women and the National Council of Jewish Women initiated their own neighborhood and civic improvement projects. Membership in women's clubs peaked in the 1920s—the GFWC reported having two million members at that time—before other opportunities arose for women to influence public policy. Having occupied leadership positions and honed organizational skills in these clubs, women entered the political arena in order to advance the same causes for which they had already been fighting. The story of Albion Fellows Bacon illustrates how a woman could, first as an individual crusader and later as a club member, fight successfully for urban reform.

Robert G. Barrows received a Ph.D. degree from Indiana University, Bloomington, and is associate professor of history at Indiana University-Purdue University at Indianapolis. He is the author of *Albion Fellows Bacon: Indiana's Municipal Housekeeper* (2000) and coeditor of the *Encyclopedia of Indianapolis* (1994).

Historians of American urbanization have often concentrated on a few metropolitan giants to the exclusion of hundreds of second- and third-tier cities. While granting the economic and cultural importance of the largest urban places, it is now apparent that smaller cities were also important in the process of urbanization. In 1900 slightly more of the country's urban residents lived in cities with populations smaller than 100,000 than in places of 100,000 or more. Although often overlooked, Scranton, Dayton, Grand Rapids, and the like were as much a part of the nation's urban experience as were the more frequently examined New York, Chicago, and San Francisco.

Such myopia has also affected the study of urban reformers of the late nineteenth and early twentieth centuries—especially women reformers. Few would dispute the impact, for example, of Chicago's Jane Addams and her Hull House colleagues on turn-of-the-century social welfare efforts. But the emphasis on Addams and a few other high-profile individuals has obscured the hard work and valuable contributions of scores of second-tier reformers whose lives and careers have been too little examined and whose accomplishments are seldom acknowledged. Albion Fellows Bacon was one such person.

Albion Fellows was born in Evansville, Indiana, in 1865, the same year the Civil War ended and Abraham Lincoln was assassinated. She died, also in Evansville, in 1933, the same year Franklin Roosevelt was inaugurated and the New Deal began. Her life thus spanned an epoch congruent with "the shaping of modern America." It was a time when social and cultural transformations occurred at all levels, from the national to the local to the individual. It was also an era that witnessed "the rise of the city." And it was a time of profound change for American women. Albion Bacon's life reflects both new possibilities and lingering limitations.[1]

Although born in Evansville, Bacon spent most of her youth in a nearby rural hamlet—McCutchanville—where her widowed mother had been reared and where relatives still lived. Growing up in this pastoral setting influenced Albion's sensibilities and the pattern of her adult life. In her late forties, she still described her youth in rapturous terms. Moving from the city had been, she wrote, "like waking from a grey dream into a realm of colour and light." She "wandered in a maze of delight" and thought the area "a wonderland, with Heaven among its hills and fairy-land in its hollows." Well after she had moved back to the city and become known as an urban-oriented reformer, she reflected that she had managed to retain a "vision of those wind-swept, sun-crowned hills, and the feeling of those great free spaces." It was this memory, she acknowledged, "that makes our cities choke me."[2]

During her childhood, community activities revolved around the church and the school. McCutchanville's first church was initially considered nondenominational, but by the Civil War era it had become a Methodist congregation. This simple frame structure was still in use when the Fellows family returned to McCutchanville in the early 1870s and it became the church of Albion's youth. Looking back as an adult, she described herself as a devout child who was brought up in a heavily religious atmosphere. The members of her extended family went to church faithfully and attended occasional revivals. She joined the church at age eleven and remained a devoted member of the denomination all her life.

The McCutchanville school was the other major institution in young Albion's life. She later recalled that during her first two or three years, she was "so paralyzed by fear of my teachers . . . that I learned *nothing.*" Later, with gentler instructors, she overcame her fears and learned readily. She remembered that her sense of wonder at the natural world followed her into the schoolhouse. In her first years, "arithmetic was as occult as Hindu numbers, and the parsing of the older grammar classes seemed to me some weird incantation, though the verses they parsed became a part of my very fibre." Her sister Annie (two years older) also provided a glimpse at the curriculum; Annie remembered never being bored since she could listen to the older students' recitations whenever she tired of her own work: "Many an incident in history and many an extract from Webster's speeches or from Shakespeare's plays were learned simply by listening to the higher classes recite."[3]

In retrospect, Albion also acknowledged the influence of her peer group on her development. She recalled "how much more the playground taught than the school room, the playmates than the teacher!" Indeed, she credited "the equal rights of that playground . . . and the exercise to the full of every girl's abilities" with preparing her to function effectively in situations and institutions dominated by men. Writing at the height of the early twentieth-century agitation for women's suffrage, she observed that "years before the wave of feminism had swept over the country, little streams were hastening down to swell the great river, from other springs as obscure as this country school."[4]

In other ways as well, the girls' education continued beyond the walls of the schoolhouse. Their household was one where books were present, prized, and read. Verse attracted both Albion and Annie, and they often recited poems while engaged in household chores. They read an older sister's collection of poetry and also found much of interest in their father's theological library: Foxe's *Book of Martyrs*, Aesop's fables, *Pilgrim's Progress*. ("Lives of Great Men," Albion later observed, "are like hasheesh to an imaginative child.") There were children's magazines over the years, and when these were exhausted, the sisters turned to adult periodicals such as *Harper's Weekly* and *The Christian Advocate.*[5]

With such voracious and precocious reading habits, it is not surprising that the sisters also tried their hands at writing. Albion recalled years later how "amidst our work Annie scribbled stories and I verses with illustrations." In their early teens, both girls submitted verses to a poetry journal. They were thrilled when, with no advance notice, their contributions appeared some time later. "The intoxication of actually seeing our verses in print," Annie recalled, "sent us about with our heads in the stars for days."[6]

In 1881 the family moved back to Evansville. Albion entered the city high school that fall and graduated in two years, after a period of intense and highly focused intellectual effort. Reminiscing in her early sixties, she described her course of study and her teachers as "wonderful" and claimed that her "intellectual awakening" took place during these two years: "I wanted, not just to lead, but to learn. To know—to know! I realized it was only a beginning, a foundation, but I felt I could go on studying all my life." She also recalled, with a sense of embarrassment, that during high school she had "learned nothing but books." She subsequently realized that during her travels to and from school, she had been blind to the reality of urban life. Her focus on her classes to the exclusion of the city around her at least paid academic dividends: she was salutatorian of her class.[7]

Both of Albion's parents, as well as both of her sisters, had completed some collegiate instruction, and she was anxious to do the same. The family's financial resources had been stretched to the limit, however, and her mother could not afford the expense. So Albion taught herself shorthand in six weeks and accepted a position as private secretary to her great-uncle, a local attorney. She continued with this work, as well as serving as a court stenographer, until her marriage. She claimed, in retrospect, that this experience was more valuable than college courses would have been. "It was," she came to believe, "the making of me. It gave me a balance, a discipline, a schooling, I could have had nowhere else." Besides becoming knowledgeable about business correspondence and legal records and phraseology, she learned "to go without fright into public buildings, to keep my own counsel, and to avoid feminine flutterings." Often the only woman in a courtroom, she also learned, as she put it, to " 'see men as trees walking,' with perfect forgetfulness of them and of myself." This ability served her well in later years when her public activities took her to such male preserves as commercial clubs and the state legislature.[8]

In 1888, shortly after she and Annie returned from a 3-month tour of Europe, Albion married Hilary Bacon, a successful merchant who had moved to Evansville from his native Kentucky in 1873. The couple, both of whom had been boarding with relatives, set up housekeeping in the same suburban neighborhood where they already lived. Following the custom of the day for middle-class women, Bacon quit gainful employment when she married. She gave birth to daughters in 1889 and 1892, followed by twins (a girl and a boy) in 1901, and seemed to settle into a comfortable domesticity. It was a sheltered life, but a life with which she seemed outwardly content during the late 1880s and early 1890s.

Beginning shortly after the birth of her second child, Bacon experienced a prolonged bout of ill health that was diagnosed with the catch-all term "nervous prostration." The physical manifestations of the syndrome were extreme fatigue, and Gilded Age physicians routinely blamed it (especially in the case of women patients) on excessive mental stimulation and prescribed extended periods of bed rest. It seems likely that, at least for Bacon, the cause was not overstimulation but rather the absence of appropriate outlets for her intelligence and creativity. She was well-read, high school educated, and bright. She was artistically creative, with serious interests in writing, art, and music. She had worked prior to her marriage, holding responsible positions in a male-dominated profession. And she had made the "Grand Tour" of Europe. What she needed, in short, was activity that forced her (or allowed her) to move beyond the sheltered life of self and family. She eventually found such activity, as did many other women during the early twentieth century, in voluntary associations and social welfare campaigns. Bacon serves as an example of historian Anne Scott's observation that "able, ambitious women gravitated" to such organizations and endeavors because it was in such settings that they could "create impressive careers," albeit "careers from which the income was psychic rather than material."[9]

Reared in a rural environment and a Victorian atmosphere, Bacon was, like many turn-of-the-century Americans, troubled by the pernicious effects of late nineteenth-century industrialization and urbanization. So, again like many of her contemporaries, during the first decades of the twentieth century she sought to improve conditions that she perceived to be physically unhealthy and morally unwholesome. She contrasted her idyllic childhood in McCutchanville with the experiences of impoverished children in congested cities and longed to do something to ameliorate the condition of the latter. She took very seriously Christian, and especially Methodist, mandates for social service, writing in 1915 that her involvement in reform activities had "grown from an act of religious consecration."[10] She became, in time, an influential "municipal housekeeper," a Progressive-Era term for women who applied their (supposedly inherent) domestic skills to social problems plaguing their communities.

Bacon's efforts in this regard began modestly and with a maternal motivation: her first excursion into civic work was to seek an improved playground at her daughters' school. She subsequently learned that some children of poor, working-class parents had come to school while suffering from communicable diseases such as scarlet fever. Stunned by this revelation, Bacon volunteered to serve on the sanitation committee of the city's Civic Improvement Association. She later admitted that she had no idea what the poorer children's homes were like or precisely what needed to be done. But, as she put it, " 'sanitation' had a remedial sound, and something was wrong, and I wanted to take hold somewhere."[11]

Her early work on the sanitation committee gave Bacon "a pleasant sense of light responsibility." But as she began to educate herself, her evolving interest was marked by changes in behavior. Formerly, when passing an alley, she had turned away rather than confront disagreeable sights and smells. Now she stopped, looked, sniffed the air, noted the presence of children playing. Instead of searching first for poetry in magazines and newspapers, she now sought articles on sanitation and began to pay attention to local politics. To the novels on her reading list she added works such as *How the Other Half Lives* (1890), Jacob Riis's vivid description of tenement life in late nineteenth-century New York City. After completing this volume as well as several other works by Riis, she found her mind becoming "a saturated solution of slums."[12]

Evansville, like most American urban areas, had been profoundly affected by the linked phenomena of immigration and industrialization during the late nineteenth century. In 1850 it was a commercial center of some 3,300 residents; thirty years later, it was a manufacturing city of almost 30,000. By 1900 a population of 59,000 made it the second largest city in Indiana. The new arrivals, most of whom came either from the rural tri-state region (southern Indiana, southern Illinois, western Kentucky) or from Europe, were attracted by the opportunities for employment in flour, grist, and lumber mills, furniture manufacturing, and tobacco processing. By 1880 over 3,000 men, women, and sometimes children were employed in Evansville's shops and factories. Twenty years later, some 14,000 residents worked in manufacturing, many of them in low-skill, poorly paid positions, and their economic circumstances were frequently reflected in their dwellings.

Bacon began volunteering as a "friendly visitor" for the Associated Charities of Evansville, visiting the poor in their homes and functioning as a lay social worker. She later organized and directed the Evansville Flower Mission, which delivered flowers cut in middle-class gardens to the city's poor and sick. She also helped organize a Working Girls' Association to assist farm girls and women who had been attracted to Evansville from its hinterlands by the availability of industrial employment. Over a period of several years, as these various activities increased her awareness of and familiarity with Evansville's "other half," she came to the conclusion that alleviating poor housing conditions was essential if other social welfare efforts were to have any chance of success.

Bacon's reputation rests chiefly on her work as a housing reformer. She began her activity in this vein by urging the addition of tenement regulations to a proposed building ordinance for Evansville. When that ordinance stalled, she concluded that a statewide approach would be more fruitful and set about crafting a state tenement law. During the spring of 1908 she sought information from all over the country. Two of her correspondents were Jacob Riis and Lawrence Veiller, the latter the author of the New York tenement law of 1901 and the nation's acknowledged expert on housing reform. Both men provided useful advice, and over the summer Bacon drafted a proposed state law and sought support for it.

One organization offering such support was the Indianapolis Commercial Club (forerunner of the city's Chamber of Commerce), which agreed to support the proposed legislation. But there was one catch. The club's leaders, many quite savvy about legislative affairs, informed

Bacon that the bill would stand a better chance of passage if it were presented by someone considered nonpartisan and apolitical. "We will do all we can to push it," they told her, "and we will stand back of you and do whatever you want done, but you will have to be the leader. . . . You will have to come to the legislature."[13]

Bacon had never anticipated direct involvement in the legislative process and was taken aback by the club's demand. "I saw myself," she remembered a few years later, "with horror, a married woman with a 'career.' I saw my family, whom I had never left except for a few days, suffering for my care; . . . my husband, with a southern man's ideas of such things, his indulgence already strained. I saw my friends, disgusted at such publicity. I saw enemies, frowns, brickbats!" She remonstrated that she had never seen a legislature in action, did not know what to do, and wanted no honor for herself. The club members stood firm, however, and Bacon eventually agreed to their request. She "took the leap," she recalled, "with the desperate deliberation of a suicide who jumps into the icy water."[14]

While she was initially reluctant to take on such a public role and never became entirely comfortable in the spotlight, Bacon rose to the challenge and was remarkably effective as an unpaid lobbyist—an "ambassador of the poor"—on behalf of government regulation of housing conditions. Between 1909 and 1917 she attended every biennial session of the Indiana General Assembly to push that agenda. In three of those sessions (1909, 1913, and 1917) she came away with meaningful legislation.

The 1909 law applied only to multifamily dwellings, was to be enforced by local health boards rather than the State Board of Health, and was amended to affect only the two largest cities in the state (Indianapolis and Evansville). Although disappointed with the result, Bacon viewed it as simply a first step. Responding to subsequent complaints by real estate men and architects in the two cities, she organized several meetings to discuss alterations in the law and brought in Lawrence Veiller, then secretary of the National Housing Association and author of two recent books on housing reform, to serve as an outside expert and assist with the deliberations. New legislation, drafted by Veiller, was shepherded by Bacon through the 1911 legislative session, only to be defeated by opponents' questionable tactics on the last day of the session. While disappointed in the outcome, she judged that the methods employed to scuttle the bill might well give the housing movement "just the touch of sympathy and interest the cause needed."[15]

At first, Bacon had run virtually a one-woman crusade, but she quickly attracted others to the cause and helped to educate them on the issues and coordinate their efforts. The Indiana Federation of Clubs (IFC), the state affiliate of the General Federation of Women's Clubs, was particularly important in extending the lobbying effort throughout the state. Bacon spoke to the IFC twice in the months just following the 1911 legislative session. At a summer event, where she told them "A Tale of the Tenements," the audience "sat hushed for a moment" and then "rose and pledged support to the housing movement." That October, at the IFC's annual convention, Bacon gave an address titled "Women, the Legislature, and the Homes of Indiana" that detailed the story of the previous winter's legislative defeat. She then asked for the federation's support of future housing reform efforts and suggested that the IFC adopt "The Homes of Indiana" as its slogan. The federation members not only agreed to these requests, they created a standing housing committee and made Bacon its chair. Later that fall she helped to form the Indiana Housing Association, the first such state-level group in the country. So during 1912, as she carried the housing reform message throughout Indiana, Bacon was serving not just as a self-appointed spokeswoman but as a representative of the IFC and the housing association.[16]

Her lobbying and networking paid off during the 1913 General Assembly. A bill that was a virtual clone of the 1911 housing legislation attracted support from groups and individuals throughout the state. The measure passed the Senate handily. When it became stuck in a House committee, Bacon published a lengthy letter entitled "The Housing Bill" in the *Indianapolis News*. She began by enumerating objections that had been raised against the measure and then refuted each argument. She noted that the legislation "does not mean that anything must be provided which decency does not demand. . . . Simply light and air, water, drainage, provision for waste and a degree of privacy, without which decency is difficult and home life is impossible." But it was not, she stressed, simply a matter of decency or starry-eyed humanitarianism. "Against the great cost [to] the state in caring for crime and dependency" the bill represented "one of the few efforts made for prevention of the evils whose cure costs the state so much." It was no longer feasible "to let any class live amid conditions that breed disease that endangers the whole community." The debate over the housing bill was, in her view, "simply a question of weighing a little money, belonging to a few people, against the vital interests of all the people of Indiana."[17]

A week later the bill was reported out of committee, and soon after that it passed the House by the astonishing margin of 92 to 1. A reporter who observed Bacon during the final debate and vote wrote that "the sweeping approval of the measure she has worked . . . to place upon the statute books affected her deeply." The *Evansville Press*, which interviewed her soon after her return, praised her efforts by noting that "practically all of Mrs. Bacon's time during the last 12 years has been given to visiting slums and tenement districts and she has lectured in nearly every city in the state in the interest of the bill."[18]

By 1913, Bacon had become a symbol of the housing reform movement as well as an expert in the field. The success of the Indiana campaign increased the requests for her aid from reform groups. Barely a month after her return to Evansville, in the course of a letter of appreciation to the governor for his support, she noted that she had been asked to speak in several midwestern states and to provide advice on securing statewide housing laws. But while she was pleased that Indiana was considered by some to be a model, she was not convinced that the state really was in the lead.

For all the passion it aroused among both supporters and opponents, the 1913 tenement house law was a decidedly limited piece of legislation. Although it was a statewide law, it applied only to incorporated cities; it did not affect small urban places that had not incorporated, suburban tracts outside city corporation boundaries, or the rural areas in which a (slight) majority of the state's residents still lived. In addition, it did not apply to all dwellings but only to tenements. Moreover, the law covered only future tenements or extant buildings converted into multiple dwellings; it did not apply to the many tenement houses already in existence. Finally, in a concession to localism, the law was to be enforced by community building inspectors or boards of health. These officials were not always well qualified and were obviously more susceptible to local pressure than inspectors from the State Board of Health would have been.

Bacon was, of course, aware of the weaknesses in the 1913 law, and she resolved to continue her crusade. Her preference would have been to extend the provisions of the 1913 law to all dwellings, not just multifamily tenements, but she and her advisors soon realized that such a goal was politically unrealistic. So she advanced a more limited bill that aimed to control dwellings deemed "infected and uninhabitable." The measure, as summarized by an Indianapolis newspaper, would "give the state board of health the same power over 'death traps' as the fire marshal now has over fire traps."[19]

The "death trap" bill (as it came to be known) passed the state Senate in 1915 but was defeated in the House. The *Indianapolis Star* reported that opposition revolved around the "drastic powers" given health authorities to condemn unsanitary residences. "It was argued that the bill, if applied literally, would take his home from many a poor man." Understating the case, the paper observed that Bacon "was an interested spectator of the proceedings."[20]

Bacon was, of course, much more than just another interested spectator, and she was deeply disturbed by the failure of the bill. She had previously been neutral (at least publicly) on the issue of women's suffrage, but an Evansville newspaper reported that the 1915 defeat had made her "the latest recruit to the ranks of the suffragists." She reportedly said, "If all men were like some men, the indirect influence of women would be enough and we would not need the ballot. But they are not."[21]

Determined to see the "death trap" bill through, Bacon resolved to try again. In the interim she remained active in housing reform enterprises and maintained a busy lecture schedule. She also had occasion to take her message to an international audience in December 1915, when she made a brief presentation on "The Powers of Darkness—The Housing Problem" to the Women's Auxiliary Conference of the Second Pan-American Scientific Congress. But in January 1917, now as if by habit, she and her allies reintroduced the failed legislation of two years earlier. After the enervating struggles of the previous four assemblies, the 1917 session proved to be almost anticlimactic. A virtual replica of the 1915 "death trap" measure sailed through both chambers of the General Assembly without a single dissenting vote. Bacon, regrettably, was not present, having returned to Evansville for the birth of a grandson. When informed by a reporter for her hometown paper that the measure had passed, she expressed "relief and pleasure" that the decade-long campaign was over and that the state's towns, villages, and rural communities "that had hitherto been unprotected by any kind of housing law, might now be protected from the diseases arising from unfit surroundings."[22]

So the long struggle was over, a struggle that had begun years before when Bacon became convinced that "nothing but a housing law would ever enable us to get relief from the conditions that caused our poor so much misery."[23] As the state and the nation prepared to embark on

another kind of crusade—the First World War—Indiana had two housing statutes in place. The first, the 1913 tenement law, regulated the
construction of multifamily dwellings; the second, the "death trap" law
of 1917, empowered the state's health officers to order corrective action
when any dwelling was deemed to be unfit for human habitation. It is
well to bear in mind that these laws had no claim to originality. While
Bacon was clearly the key personality behind passage of the Indiana
legislation, the content of the statutes owed more to the models prepared and propounded by Veiller. Yet enactment of the two measures
stands as a major accomplishment of Indiana's Progressive-Era social
reformers and marks a signal advance in the state's use of its so-called
police power.

Although 1917 marked the completion of her major work on behalf of "the homes of Indiana," Bacon's interest in housing reform continued. She remained active in the Indiana and national housing
associations, even preparing a pamphlet, *Housing—Its Relation to Social
Work* (1918), for the latter group. As late as the fall of 1931, two years
before her death, she was a delegate to the President's Conference on
Home Building and Home Ownership called by Herbert Hoover. Her
wide-ranging social concerns also manifested themselves in other activities, some of which are detailed here, but it was as a housing reformer that she became and remained well known, in Indiana, the
Midwest, and the nation. In a book published two years after passage of
Indiana's 1917 law, Edith Elmer Wood, one of the country's leading
housing economists, observed that "housing reform in the United States
has produced three magnetic personalities." She identified this trio as
Jacob Riis, "who first made us care how the other half lived"; Lawrence
Veiller, "the high priest of restrictive housing legislation"; and Albion
Fellows Bacon, "who won a housing law for her state by sheer, disinter-
ested persistence."[24]

Bacon's reputation rests principally on her work as a housing reformer, but to describe her as only that is to ignore several other areas of
her activity and accomplishment. As an obituary observed, "her interests were amazing in their catholicity."[25] She played a particularly important role with regard to improving the lives of Indiana's children.
During World War I she headed a child welfare committee (closely al-
lied with the federal Children's Bureau) that was part of the State Council
of Defense. Among other things, Bacon oversaw a drive to assess the
physical development and well-being of preschool children, an effort
that detected correctable health problems in hundreds, perhaps thou-

sands, of cases. Then, when the conflict ended in 1918, she helped transform her small piece of the state's wartime bureaucracy into a private
organization, the Indiana Child Welfare Association.

The next year the state's lawmakers created a 5-member study commission charged with examining child welfare in Indiana, making recommendations for improvements, and drafting possible legislation.
Bacon was appointed to this commission, was an active member of it,
and used her contacts in the Children's Bureau to good effect in crafting
proposed new standards for the state. The 1921 General Assembly enacted several measures based on the commission's recommendations.
First, the legislators revamped the state's system of juvenile probation.
Among other things, they created the position of state juvenile probation officer, along with an Advisory Juvenile Committee to guide
Indiana's juvenile probation operation. Bacon was appointed to this
committee, was elected president of it by her fellow members, and served
in the position from 1921 until her death. Second, and probably the
most important result of the work done by Bacon and the other commissioners, the General Assembly passed a law that codified and revised
previous legislation regarding school attendance and the employment
of minors. This statute strengthened the state's minimum educational
requirements and limitations on child labor, and brought Indiana much
closer to recommended national standards.

While working on behalf of such statewide initiatives as housing
reform and child welfare, Bacon remained very active in efforts for social and cultural betterment in her hometown and county. She served as
either board member or president (sometimes both) of the Vanderburgh
County Tuberculosis Association, the Public Health Nursing Association, the Vanderburgh Child Welfare Association, the Family Welfare
Association, and the Southwestern Indiana Historical Society. Perhaps
most prominently, she became involved in the sometimes contentious
issues of city planning and zoning. In 1921 the mayor appointed her to
the newly created Evansville City Plan Commission, and her colleagues
selected her as the commission's first president. She continued to serve
on the plan commission for the rest of her life and was either president
or vice president throughout the 1920s. Thus, she had a central role in
establishing the agency as an accepted and important part of municipal
government. She was especially influential in lobbying for the city's first
zoning ordinance, which passed in 1925, employing the same medical
metaphors regarding "congestion" that she had often used in her housing reform lectures. And, once again, what began as a local interest led

to state-level activity and visibility. In both 1924 and 1925, Bacon was elected vice president of the Indiana Conference on City Planning; when the group met in Evansville during the latter year, a local newspaper observed that she was considered to be one of the best-known leaders in the state's city planning movement.

In the midst of all her social welfare pursuits, Bacon also found time to write. As noted earlier, she had begun writing poetry as a school-girl; except for the period of her illness in the 1890s, she generally had some sort of literary project under way. Much of what she wrote during her adult years was an outgrowth of her reform efforts, particularly the housing work. She published didactic articles in such local and special-ized journals as the *Indiana Bulletin of Charities and Correction*, but her work also appeared in national forums such as *The American City* and the reform-minded *Survey*. The most significant of her housing-related publications was *Beauty for Ashes* (1914), a book that detailed her pas-sage from "sheltered life" to "municipal housekeeper." (The book's title is a biblical reference, Isaiah 61:2–4, where the prophet explains his mission: "to comfort all that mourn . . . to give unto them beauty for ashes.") She also prepared articles and booklets that proclaimed her re-ligious faith, as well as publishing one volume of children's stories. In addition, she authored program guides for several pageants, including Evansville's state centennial pageant in 1916 and a 1923 *Program for Citizenship Day* prepared for the General Federation of Women's Clubs.

One subject that Bacon did not write about, at least publicly, was women's suffrage. Although involved with numerous social reforms dur-ing the early twentieth century, precisely the time when women's agita-tion for the ballot reached high tide, she was never an active participant in the suffrage crusade. She did not oppose votes for women, as did some of her female contemporaries, and she never missed an opportu-nity to cast a ballot once she had the right to do so. Women's suffrage, however, was not at the top of her priority list. Her public support of the cause came late, about 1915, and was based largely on the belief that women's votes would advance the social welfare reforms that were closer to her heart. But although she was a lukewarm proponent of women's suffrage, the reality of her participation in public affairs had (to borrow a term from historian Nancy Cott) a "feminist aspect" that, even if unintentionally, advanced the cause of women's political equal-ity and provided a role model for future generations.[26]

"Moderation was the hallmark of Indiana's progressive reform," writes a leading student of the state's history, and in many ways Bacon's de facto career supports that contention.[27] There was not much original in the social welfare initiatives she championed and nothing really radical in the methods she used in an effort to secure the reforms she sought. She worked within the strictures of the political system of the day, and she came to rely on the organization and mobilization of voluntary associations to spread information and apply political pressure when necessary. If her willingness to grant the state increased regulatory authority in order to combat social ills did not meet with universal approbation, she nonetheless garnered significant support for that position even in a state described as "conservatively progressive." And while municipal housekeeping brought many women into the public arena for the first time, the movement's rhetoric stressed that they were merely exporting traditional domestic activities from the home to the larger community.

Bacon was unusual, however, in the range of her reform interests, the zeal she brought to them, and the doggedness with which she pursued her goals. Moreover, while she eventually came to rely on the aid of women's voluntary associations, she began her first statewide crusade without such organizational support. Although at first reluctantly, she accepted positions and responsibilities that were highly visible at local, state, and even national levels. Also unusual was the fact that she combined what she once called her "frenzied philanthropy"[28] with prolific authorship in a variety of genres. She did not accomplish all that she wished, either personally or in the realm of public policy; she probably overemphasized environmental causes for urban social pathologies; and she was not immune to the prejudices of her time and place. Still, few Hoosiers of her era expended so much personal time and energy to ensure that all might have, as the title of her book put it, "beauty for ashes."

Notes

1. Vincent P. DeSantis, *The Shaping of Modern America, 1877–1920*, 3d ed. (Wheeling, IL: Harlan Davidson, 2000); Arthur M. Schlesinger, *The Rise of the City, 1878–1898* (New York: Macmillian, 1933).

2. Albion Fellows Bacon, *Beauty for Ashes* (New York: Dodd, Mead and Company, 1914), 3–5.

3. Albion Fellows Bacon, "Autobiography," a 36-page manuscript written in 1926–27 (original in possession of author; photocopy in Willard Library, Evansville, IN), [23–24]; Bacon, *Beauty for Ashes*, 5; Annie Fellows Johnston, *The Land of the Little Colonel: Reminiscence and Autobiography* (Boston: L. C. Page and Company, 1929), 78.

4. Bacon, *Beauty for Ashes*, 5–6.

5. Ibid., 12–13; Johnston, *Land of the Little Colonel*, 38, 40–41.

6. Bacon, *Beauty for Ashes*, 12; Johnston, *Land of the Little Colonel*, 80–81.

7. Bacon, "Autobiography," [24]; Bacon, *Beauty for Ashes*, 14.

8. Bacon, "Autobiography," [25]; Bacon, *Beauty for Ashes*, 15.

9. Anne Firor Scott, *Natural Allies: Women's Associations in American History* (Urbana: University of Illinois Press, 1992), 155, 3.

10. Albion Fellows Bacon, "What the Day's Work Means to Me," *The Bookman* 42 (October 1915): 201.

11. Bacon, *Beauty for Ashes*, 24–28.

12. Ibid., 29–30.

13. Ibid., 188.

14. Ibid., 188–90.

15. Ibid., 257–58.

16. Ibid., 261–65, 281–85.

17. *Indianapolis News*, February 14, 1913.

18. *Indianapolis Star*, February 27, 1913; *Evansville Press*, March 4, 1913.

19. *Indianapolis News*, January 8, 1915.

20. *Indianapolis Star*, February 18, 1915.

21. *Evansville Press*, February 18, 1915.

22. Ibid., February 16, 1917.

23. Bacon, *Beauty for Ashes*, 163.

24. Edith Elmer Wood, *The Housing of the Unskilled Wage Earner: America's Next Problem* (New York: Macmillan, 1919), 287.

25. *Evansville Courier*, December 11, 1933.

26. Nancy Cott, "What's in a Name? The Limits of 'Social Feminism'; or, Expanding the Vocabulary of Women's History," *Journal of American History* 76 (December 1989): 826.

27. James H. Madison, *The Indiana Way: A State History* (Bloomington: Indiana University Press, 1986), 222.

28. Bacon, *Beauty for Ashes*, 154.

Suggested Readings

The best primary source for Albion Fellows Bacon's life, particularly her housing reform work, is her own *Beauty for Ashes* (New York: Dodd, Mead and Company, 1914). Her other works concerning housing reform include: "The Awakening of a State–Indiana," *The Survey* 25 (December 17, 1910): 467–73; *A Tale of the Tenements* (N.p.: Indiana Housing Association, 1912); "Regulation by Law," *The American City* 8 (January 1913): 27–29; and *Housing—Its Relation to Social Work* (New York: National Housing Association, 1918). The intersection of Bacon's religious faith and her social welfare activism is best explicated in "The Divine Call: Follow Me," *The Survey* 29 (October 5, 1912): 37–40; and "What the Day's Work Means to Me," *The Bookman* 42 (October 1915): 201–6.

The first attempt by a historian to essay Bacon's life and de facto career was Roy Lubove, "Albion Fellows Bacon and the Awakening of a State," *Mid-*

west Review (1962): 63–72. The most recent and complete study is Robert G. Barrows, *Albion Fellows Bacon: Indiana's Municipal Housekeeper* (Bloomington: Indiana University Press, 2000).

On the relationship between Albion and her sister, Annie Fellows Johnston, author of the Little Colonel series of children's books, see Mary Boewe, "Annie and Albion: Reformers of Riverville," *Traces of Indiana and Midwestern History* 7 (Winter 1995): 4–11. Valuable for insight into the sisters' childhoods is Annie Fellows Johnston, *The Land of the Little Colonel: Reminiscence and Autobiography* (Boston: L. C. Page and Company, 1929).

For broader treatments of the years and issues in which Bacon was active, see Clarke A. Chambers, *Seedtime of Reform: American Social Service and Social Action, 1918–1933* (Minneapolis: University of Minnesota Press, 1963); Robert M. Crunden, *Ministers of Reform: The Progressives' Achievement in American Civilization, 1889–1920* (New York: Basic Books, 1982); Donald K. Gorrell, *The Age of Social Responsibility: The Social Gospel in the Progressive Era, 1900–1920* (Macon, GA: Mercer University Press, 1988); J. Stanley Lemons, *The Woman Citizen: Social Feminism in the 1920s* (Charlottesville: University Press of Virginia, 1990 [1973]); Kriste Lindenmeyer, *"A Right to Childhood": The U.S. Children's Bureau and Child Welfare, 1912–46* (Urbana: University of Illinois Press, 1997); Robyn Muncy, *Creating a Female Dominion in American Reform, 1890–1935* (New York: Oxford University Press, 1991); and Susan Tiffin, *In Whose Best Interest?: Child Welfare Reform in the Progressive Era* (Westport, CT: Greenwood Press, 1982).

10

Catherine Bauer
The Struggle for Modern Housing in America, 1930–1960

John F. Bauman

The Great Depression brought an abrupt halt to a post–World War I housing boom and left millions of Americans concerned about the loss of their homes as well as their jobs. By 1933 half of the nation's homeowners found themselves in default on their mortgages, and the hallowed American ideal of home ownership seemed genuinely at risk for members of the middle class as well as the working class. Believing that the federal government could no longer maintain a policy of laissez-faire regarding the housing industry, President Franklin D. Roosevelt's administration responded with a series of legislative measures designed to bring immediate relief to the residents of American cities and suburbs. The Home Owners Loan Corporation (HOLC), which refinanced loans at low interest with long-term notes, assumed one-sixth of existing mortgages and by 1937 halved the number of mortgage foreclosures recorded in 1933. The Federal Housing Administration (FHA) insured loans made by banks and other private lending institutions and opened up the possibility of home ownership to a vastly greater population by extending the length of loans, lowering the amounts of down payments, and thereby reducing monthly payments. For the substantial portion of the American people lacking the means to take advantage of HOLC and FHA programs, the New Deal provided a limited number of low-rent units. Section 202(d) of the National Industrial Recovery Act provided for a housing division in the Public Works Administration (PWA) to acquire land and build low-cost housing; by 1937 the PWA had launched construction of 21,800 dwellings in fifty-one public housing projects nationwide.

Exasperated by the generous financial support for HOLC and FHA and the comparatively little attention afforded public housing, a number of architects, planners, labor union officials, and other reformers known collectively as "housers" lobbied strenuously for a permanent federal agency that would subsidize shelter for those Americans unable to compete in the private housing market. Strongly influenced by the modern housing movement in Europe, these housers urged the creation of a state-operated, affordable program based upon modern communitarian housing ideas. They hoped that the government would oversee the construction of housing units arrayed in cohesive neighborhoods with shared community facilities; in short, they sought a housing policy that would serve as a tool for community-building. Catherine Bauer lacked formal training in architecture or planning but nevertheless became the most influential of the housers. An idealistic activist and tireless political lobbyist, she helped shape national housing policy in the mid-twentieth century.

John F. Bauman is professor emeritus of history at California University of Pennsylvania, California, Pennsylvania, and adjunct professor of community planning and development at the Edmund S. Muskie School of Public Service, University of Southern Maine, Portland. He is the author of *Public Housing, Race, and Renewal: Urban Planning in Philadelphia, 1920–1974* (1987) and coeditor of *From Tenements to the Taylor Homes: In Search of an Urban Housing Policy in Twentieth-Century America* (2000).

B etween 1934 and 1964, the year of her death, perhaps no name was more closely linked to housing and housing policy in America than Catherine Bauer's.[1] Coincidentally, a sculpture of Bauer's likeness (created by friend and one-time lover, the Russian-born architect Oscar Stonorov) graces the foyer of the Department of Housing and Urban Development's (HUD's) headquarters in Washington, DC. After all, Bauer supplied much of the political momentum that resulted in the 1937 enactment of the nation's first permanent public housing program. Despite agonizing compromises, the Wagner-Steagall Act captured some of the visionary, European-born, communitarian spirit that Bauer extolled in her landmark 1934 book, *Modern Housing*. Although after World War II she exchanged her persona of the housing activist for the less frenetic life of the academic, Bauer remained a lifelong policy insider, serving on local, state, and national boards and for the United Nations as a planning advisor in India.

Bauer's 1957 article in *Architectural Forum*, "The Dreary Deadlock of Public Housing," a scathing indictment of federal housing policy hurled by a woman deemed the policy's avatar, marked public housing's dénouement. This chapter explores Bauer's odyssey from the architect of modern housing to the messenger of its demise.

In the 1930s, Bauer marched in the vanguard of those American social workers, architects, planners, lawyers, and policy intellectuals who called themselves "housers." These were progressive-minded individuals concerned about the nation's persistent failure to deliver decent, safe, and sanitary housing to working-class families. Bauer's housing ideas reflected in part her association with Lewis Mumford, Henry Wright, Clarence Stein, and the Regional Planning Association of America (RPAA), an intimate body of planners, architects, and intellectuals founded in 1923 by the editor of the *Journal of the American Institute of*

Architects, Charles Whitaker. RPAA members advocated sweeping regional solutions to the problem of congested, substandard urban housing, and espoused the creation of garden cities modeled in part after the ideas of the late nineteenth-century British visionary planner, Ebenezer Howard. Bauer's ideology of modern housing derived from her European travels. She epitomized the cross-fertilization of European and American social welfare ideas that, according to Daniel T. Rodgers, helped shape the institutional framework for social policy in the Atlantic world in the late nineteenth and early twentieth centuries.[2] In fact, to help Lewis Mumford collect data for a series of articles commissioned by *Fortune* magazine, Bauer sailed for Europe in early 1932 to study housing in Amsterdam, Rotterdam, Berlin, London, Munich, and Paris.

This was not the first time the young, modish, liberated Bauer had toured Europe. Born in Elizabeth, New Jersey, on May 11, 1905, Catherine enjoyed a solid middle-class upbringing. The daughter of Jacob L. Bauer, a successful highway engineer, and Alberta Kraus, a schoolteacher, Bauer attended Vail-Deane, a posh private school, before studying art and literature at Vassar. She left Vassar and studied architecture at Cornell, but disillusioned by that discipline's stale traditionalism, she completed her degree at Vassar in 1926. Immediately after graduating, Bauer sailed for Europe, where the rebellious, artsy, and brilliant Vassar graduate found a comfortable niche in the ribald, Bohemian society of post–World War I, jazz-age Europe. She traveled in Italy and Brittany, wrote articles (travel pieces) for *Comet* and the *New York Times*, frequented Paris salons, and developed a taste for European modernism, especially the new functional architecture.

Bauer returned to America in 1927. Twelve months abroad had radicalized her. Europe converted her distaste for traditional "historical" architecture previewed at Cornell into intolerance. She moved to New York's Greenwich Village, a sanctuary for the Art Moderne lifestyle, and dressed conservatively (a style she never abandoned), she found employment, first writing for Butterick Patterns and then for magazines—*Ladies Home Journal*, the *New York Times*, and *Vogue*. Her 1928 *New York Times Magazine* article on "Machine Age Mansions for Ultra Moderns," about Le Corbusier's working-class housing outside Paris, assailed the impractical, "conventional" American chateau- and villa-style dwellings.

However, it was her job with Harcourt-Brace publishers (writing promotional material) that, fortuitously, vaulted the 24-year-old Bauer into housing stardom. Through Harcourt-Brace, Bauer met Lewis

Mumford, who was immediately attracted by her keen intellect, charm, and vibrant, artistic temperament. A lengthy affair ensued, often passionate, frequently tumultuous, but always cerebral. The relationship coincidentally broadened and matured Bauer's understanding of housing and city planning.

With Mumford's blessing and a long list of introductions to the foremost modern architects, Bauer returned to Europe in June 1930 where, in the following months, she metamorphosed from an aesthete to a reformer or, in her words, a "housing expert." Her circuit included Walter Gropius, J. F. Oud, Eric Mendelsohn, Walter C. Behrendt, Bruno Taut, Mies van der Rohe, and Ernst May, the building director of Frankfurt, Germany, who had studied under the British new town planner, Raymond Unwin. In England, Bauer toured the new post–World War I government-subsidized planned housing estates initiated by town councils on London's suburban fringe. Britain cloaked its council housing in traditional architecture; modernism, however, flourished in Weimar Germany, especially in Dessau, where Gropius had his Bauhaus, and in Frankfurt, where Bauer enrolled as the only American in May's course on the *Neues Bauen* (the new buildings). As part of this course, she toured Romerstadt, a *Siedlungen* (settlement) located in the Nidda Valley outside Frankfurt. Romerstadt radiated the functional social modernism that had enthralled Bauer in 1927. It was the centerpiece of Bauer's 1931 article in *Fortune* that won the $1,000 prize for the best essay on the topic "Art in Industry," awarded by Pittsburgh department store tycoon and Frank Lloyd Wright patron, Edgar Kaufmann. Mumford also had submitted an essay, and friction over Bauer's triumph cooled the affair between them.

Along with many cynical postwar literati, Bauer found art incompatible with industrialism. Art was at best a veneer or patina applied after the fact to embellish a product. But Romerstadt, the jewel of May's New Frankfurt, proved the exception. Here in the Nidda Valley was Fordism at its best, abetting not profit but social progress in an area (affordable housing) where, Bauer believed, America had failed horribly. Amid Germany's severe inflation-feuled economic depression, Frankfurt's housing director employed "economy, imagination, large-scale planning and mass production" to produce 16,000 handsome dwellings. May termed combining modern housing architecture with the Ford-pioneered, mass-production economy of scale the *Neuer Sachlichkeit* (the New Reality), and Romerstadt fully embodied it. Like

England's council housing and Vienna's *hof* communities, Romerstadt benefited from the public purchase of land, from rendering housing a public utility, and from breaking what Bauer saw as the speculative stranglehold on real estate. Romerstadt sat outside Frankfurt on the sprawling Nidda River plain. The dazzling concrete, 3-story, white-stucco row buildings (called *Zeilenbau*) faced east, maximizing sunlight and warmth. Every apartment enjoyed a separate kitchen, dining room, sizable living room, toilet (with shower and tub), balcony, and garden plot. While Bauer applauded the generous personal amenities, she most lavishly praised the community facilities—the schools, swimming pool, sports arena, laundries, and cooperative stores, all integral to the plan. Here was art that grew "out of the best modern industrial method, and not . . . [art] applied afterwards as apologetic camouflage." [3]

Bauer forged her "Prize" article about Romerstadt and her months of housing research in 1932 into her signature book, *Modern Housing*. She framed her subject historically, chronicling nineteenth- and early twentieth-century thought about housing and community design. It was in Europe where, in the 1920s, the seminal ideas of Ebenezer Howard and Patrick Geddes coalesced into real "modern housing"—in England's council housing, in Romerstadt, and in Red Vienna's Karl Marx Hoff with its kindergartens, libraries, clinics, and playgrounds. This planned, nonspeculative modern housing contrasted sharply with America's exploitative, wasteful system, which spawned slums and social despair right through the booming 1920s. Indeed, Bauer's book became a primer on how modern planning and architecture might rationally address America's housing dilemma, how the nation could build housing for efficient use rather than for quick profits. Repeatedly, Bauer stressed that housing must become a "public utility"; that "the right to live in a decent dwelling" must take its place among the national minima such as rights to water, sanitation, and paved roads. [4]

Bauer methodically explicated the essential features of the new housing. "Modern housing," asserted Bauer, must be built on the urban rim, not on costly slum land. Espousing Unwin's injunction, "nothing gained by overcrowding," she advocated superblock community design, in which, as at Romerstadt, 2- or 3-story buildings were arranged in parallel rows heliocentrically to capture maximum sunlight. A student of Gropius, Martin Wagner, and the Bauhaus school, she favored modern, functionalist, International Style architecture that embraced dynamic, ornament-free, smooth surfaces. "What remains? Nothing but the real amenities offered by the buildings themselves, light, air, spaciousness, a sense of urgent and pleasant use. Sun, Grass, Color, Form. No meaningless clutter."[5]

Finally, emboldened by the onset of the Great Depression—and undaunted by the deeply embedded tradition of private home ownership—Bauer proposed a radical alteration to housing economics: creating a government-aided, noncommercial, nonspeculative housing sector. She beseeched state subsidies to bridge the gap between market-rate rents and what workers could afford. However, she rejected paternalistic, centralized state control, favoring instead housing programs organized by and administered by worker unions, housing associations, or cooperatives. Government would close the affordability gap by establishing municipal land banks and making low-interest loans to housing associations that would use mass-production techniques to build efficient, affordable communities (the *Siedlungen*) on the urban periphery.

Undoubtedly, Bauer's modern housing ideas influenced Great Depression policy makers, even though her ideas were flawed. Bauer exhibited some naiveté, not only about the strength of the housing movement in Europe (Gropius and Wagner fled Nazi Germany in the early 1930s and Hitler extinguished the modern housing movement shortly thereafter) but also about the general appeal of modern housing to workers themselves. She also underestimated the vast power of the real estate industry in America.[6]

The Great Depression and the Launch of Modern Housing

Catherine Bauer had returned to America in 1931 and was researching community facilities for architect and planner Clarence Stein when the full force of the Great Depression struck. Rampant evictions, foreclosures, and plunging real estate values vindicated the belief of housers like Edith Elmer Wood and Bauer that America's speculative housing marketplace was irreparably flawed. Wood's *Recent Trends in American Housing* (1931) had revealed that despite the "Own Your Own Home" and "Better Homes in America" movement ballyhooed by Washington in the 1920s, one-third or more of Americans were ill-housed; housers chorused that the next third endured, at best, substandard conditions. Reformers like Wood and Bauer rejected restrictive legislation (housing ordinances, code inspection, and zoning), believing that it exacerbated the housing problem by diminishing supply and raising building costs.

In 1931 the depression crisis provoked the champion of the Better Homes movement, President Herbert Hoover, to convene in Washington a Conference on Housing and Home Ownership. While the conference strove to buttress privatism and quell fears, it nevertheless sounded alarms and spurred the creation later of the Federal Home Loan Bank Board, the Home Owners Loan Corporation (HOLC), and the Reconstruction Finance Corporation (RFC), all meant to expand the nation's credit to the thousands of tottering savings and loan banks and to silence the rising demand for direct government intervention. At New York Senator Robert Wagner's behest, the legislation creating the RFC included a provision urged by the National Housing Conference—soon to be the National Public Housing Conference (NPHC)—for government loans to limited-dividend housing corporations.

Housing loomed as a national issue in 1932. Even conservative businessmen confessed the economic benefits of large-scale housing and slum clearance projects. Several organizations, along with the NPHC and the Housing Study Guild, now pressed for a federal housing program. However, the proliferation of housing organizations exposed not only the timeliness but also the divergence of opinion concerning a national housing agenda. Founded by Harold Buttenheim and directed by the New York houser Mary Simkhovitch, NPHC reflected the close linkage in many reformers' minds between slum clearance and housing. The nexus derived from progressivism, which saw bad housing as the cause of crime, disease, and other social and physical pathologies. In progressivists' view, housing was ipso facto a slum problem. Simkhovitch's NPHC echoed not only the social workers' passion for the plight of slum families but also the professions' conviction in 1932 that the job required federal subsidies.

Bauer's and the RPAA's pro-public housing arm, the Housing Study Guild, saw social workers and the NPHC as "do-gooders," and rejected slum clearance. They urged Washington to channel low-interest loans to cooperatives and limited-dividend housing organizations that—as in England and Weimar, Germany—would develop large-scale *Zeilenbau* or garden cities on the urban fringe. As executive secretary of the RPAA in 1932, however, Bauer increasingly found the Housing Study Guild discourse too ethereal and arcane to effect concrete policy changes. Her European trips convinced her that housing reform flowed from political action, an insight that drew her away from Mumford (both philosophically and as a lover) and closer to Cincinnati houser Ernest Bohn, founder in 1933 of the National Association of Housing Officials (NAHO) and dedicated to mobilizing politically on behalf of federal housing programs.

Bauer, in fact, championed the primacy of politics—that to triumph, workers must battle for housing as a "fundamental right." She wrote in 1934, "There will never be any realistic housing movement until the workers and the consumers and the unemployed themselves take a hand in the solution."[7] Workers should demand a permanent housing fund, low-interest loans to housing societies, and the right to large-scale, sun-bathed modern housing communities, with community rooms, pools, and other amenities. Therefore, unlike Wood and Simkhovitch, Bauer soft-pedaled the litany of slum evils and pressed for a nonspeculative, noncommercial housing system. In 1933 the Great Depression plunged the housing market to such depths that her radical ideas had an audience.

Communitarian housers and deslummers alike scorned the new president Franklin D. Roosevelt's first New Deal housing programs, the Home Owners Loan Corporation and the Federal Housing Administration. For housers such as Bauer, the two proposals bailed out risky saving and loan institutions, rescued speculative realtors, and underwrote planless suburbia. Conversely, Bauer and her allies cheered the New Deal's creation of a Housing Division within Secretary of the Interior Harold Ickes's Public Works Administration, believing that it could demonstrate the wisdom of a truly comprehensive modern housing program. The Housing Division inherited from Hoover's RFC plans for six limited-dividend projects, one of them—completed in 1935— Philadelphia's Carl Mackley Homes, a 184-unit housing development sponsored by the American Federation of Full Fashioned Hosiery Workers (AFFFHW).

From start to finish, Mackley evinced Bauer's modern housing. Its authors surveyed hosiery workers about its design. Located in Juniata Park, a Philadelphia neighborhood on the edge of the city's industrialized Northeast, the project featured rectilinear Bauhaus architecture as well as an auditorium, recreation rooms, wading pool, nursery school, and cooperative gas station and grocery store. John Edelman, secretary of the AFFFHW, initiated Mackley and hired Russian-born modernist architect Oscar Stonorov and Alfred Kastner (who, like Bauer, had visited Red Vienna) to design the homes. Radicals all, Edelman, Stonorov, and Kastner intended the Mackley design to nurture working-class solidarity.[8]

At Stonorov's urging, Edelman in 1934 invited the young radical-minded housing activist to become executive secretary of the newly formed Labor Housing Conference (LHC), an organization founded by Edelman and the Pennsylvania State Federation of Labor to mobilize a workers' housing movement. It was exactly what Bauer wanted. From a Greenwich Village polemicist, Bauer now metamorphosed into a tough, fiery union organizer. Bauer and Edelman drafted and then campaigned for a specific labor-housing program. It demanded a cabinet-level Department of Housing and Public Welfare, to administer a $500 million long-term housing program. Significantly, Washington would recognize "workers and consumers" as "responsible public bodies and trustees" for the building and management of government-aided housing. Labor representatives would sit on every housing authority, company housing would be abolished, and demonstration projects would be constructed in every industrial center.[9]

Bauer's labor program differed sharply from the PWA's Housing Division program, especially after Ickes suspended the limited-dividend housing program. Headed initially by the New York architect and RPAA member, Robert Kohn, then by Horatio Hackett, the Housing Division between 1933 and 1937 built fifty-one projects. Many, like Mackley and Hill Creek in Philadelphia, Techwood in Atlanta, and Harlem River (for African Americans) in New York City, were graced with generous light, wading pools, and libraries, and radiated modern housing principles. Nor were these projects poorhouses. Careful tenant selection procedures assured that the "deserving" and "submerged middle class," not the poor, occupied these government-built homes.

Despite the high standards, housers harshly criticized the Housing Division for its slow pace, for Ickes's authoritarian management style, and for the agency's emphasis on slum clearance, its lack of cost controls, and its very impermanence. The idea of a permanent federal housing program gained momentum at the 1934 Baltimore conference sponsored by NAHO and attended by a Who's Who of American housers, including PWA representatives. Determined to rally labor behind a permanent federal housing program, Bauer barnstormed union halls across America and in 1935, at the American Federation of Labor convention in Atlantic City, she won that body's endorsement for the LHC agenda.

Months earlier, Senator Robert Wagner had introduced in Congress a public housing bill written by Simkhovitch and the NPHC. Simkhovitch's bill exposed the rift in the housing movement. Simkhovitch and Bauer agreed on the goal of a permanent national program, but differed sharply on the importance of slum clearance and on the NPHC's desire to lodge a permanent Housing Division in Ickes's Interior Department.

Seeking a sympathetic ear for her ideas about loans to workers' co-operatives and housing societies and for assuring fair wages for union labor engaged in constructing public housing, Bauer turned to Pittsburgh's Congressman Henry Ellenbogen. With Bauer's input, Ellenbogen's bill highlighted planned neighborhoods, housing-management committees, and low-medium-income rental housing, not poverty and slums. Finally, unlike the Simkhovitch legislation, it firmly insisted that government housing be administered by an independent agency—not by Ickes.

In the fall of 1935, fearing that competing bills would undermine the movement, Bauer, Wagner, and Simkhovitch minimized the differences and merged Wagner's and Ellenbogen's proposals into one housing bill. Now a full-time lobbyist and policy insider, Bauer lived in Washington, DC, and worked tirelessly with both Ernest Bohn and Wagner's brilliant assistant, Leon Keyserling, to enact housing legislation. But despite Bauer's energy, the bill foundered, mainly on the Roosevelt administration's lack of full support.

In truth, government-aided low-income housing, unlike Social Security, lacked a broad-based constituency. Bauer, Bohn, Simkhovitch, Charles Abrams (lawyer and housing authority), and the housers produced momentum for the housing issue using, in historian Alexander Von Hoffman's words, "smoke and mirrors" and little else.[10]

Early in 1937, Bauer resumed pressing Wagner and FDR for renewal of the housing bill. Leon Keyserling, along with New Deal economist Warren Vinton and NAHO's Coleman Woodbury, drafted new housing legislation based on Wagner-Ellenbogen. To aid its passage, Roosevelt strategically replaced Ellenbogen as sponsor of the bill, naming instead Alabama Congressman Henry B. Steagall, Chairman of the House Banking and Currency Committee and a vitriolic opponent of public housing. Recasting the legislation once more pitted Ickes's PWA (aligned with the NPHC) against Bauer, labor, and NAHO. Bauer and her cohorts again insisted on an independent federal housing agency uncontrolled by Ickes, the inclusion of demonstration projects, and—to the chagrin of FDR's tightfisted Secretary of the Treasury, Henry Morgenthau—annual federal contributions to keep rents affordable. Bauer's feisty lobbying provoked Ickes to phone AFL chief Bill Green to get that "wild-eyed lady" off Capital Hill. Green never complied.[11]

The two feuding housing blocks, however, ultimately resolved one of the most divisive issues—slum clearance. Bauer adamantly opposed rehousing families in costly slum-cleared sites. She nevertheless compromised, agreeing to call slum clearance important but insisting that the decision on where to relocate slum households be made locally.[12]

In July 1937, FDR signaled his readiness to sign a housing bill. Stung severely by his administration's court-packing fiasco, with the economy slumping, and in need of a legislative success, the president offered Wagner and big labor his support of public housing. Headquartered in Washington's Hay-Adams Hotel and generously aided by Green and labor, Bauer and Boris Shishkin, head of the AFL's Housing Committee, orchestrated a lobbying tour de force. In August the bill moved from Congressional committee chambers into the crucial hearing stage, where conservative real estate interests and others, including the Ickes camp, mounted stiff opposition to the whole bill or to key provisions. Wagner and Bauer ultimately triumphed over Ickes, salvaging the independent agency provision; but the Savings and Loan League, the National Association of Real Estate Boards, and other conservative opponents stripped from the legislation much of what remained of Bauer's modern housing vision.

The Wagner-Steagall Act emerged in 1937 as a job-producing slum clearance measure as much as it was a housing bill. In its defense, Ernest Bohn conceded that, "You could not have sold public housing without the slum."[13] Much to Bauer's and Wood's disappointment, conservatives stamped public housing with the insignia of the poorhouse. Massachusetts congressman David I. Walsh, offended by middle-class families occupying Housing Division projects in Boston, amended the bill to require that for every unit of public housing constructed, a slum dwelling be eliminated. Although Bauer and the housers wrangled an exclusion for cities experiencing serious housing shortages, Walsh's action yoked public housing to slum clearance, protected the real estate industry from a government-created oversupply of affordable rental housing, and left suburbia unscathed.

Next, Virginia's Senator Harry Byrd stripped public housing of its architectural frills and rendered it forever aesthetically mediocre. Byrd's amendment dictated a maximum per dwelling unit spending ceiling of $4,000 ($5,000 in large cities). Conservatives also struck from the bill Bauer's demand for demonstration projects, and likewise (fearful of creeping communism) excised her key provision making housing societies and cooperatives eligible for government funds.

Bauer had desired modern housing, embodying what she believed to be the working class's ambitions for good, well-designed, socially and culturally satisfying communities. She envisioned the advent of a non-commercial housing sector, ushering in a new age wherein society viewed housing as a public utility. The Wagner-Steagall Act fell far short of that vision. Yet Bauer, the political pragmatist and policy insider, rejoiced at the bill's passage in September 1937. She hailed the victory as "radical" and called Wagner-Steagall the "single most important left-wing bill," a "triumph of the left over the right."[14]

As Bauer implied, the Wagner-Steagall bill enunciated a national housing policy: to provide federal aid for the eradication of slums and for "decent, safe, and sanitary dwellings for families of low income . . . for the reduction of unemployment, and the stimulation of business activity, [and] to create a United States Housing Administration and for other purposes."[15] The act provided $500 million in grants to help local housing authorities purchase land and materials. Through an annual contributions contract with local housing authorities, Washington guaranteed payment of up to 90 percent of the local authority's debt and kept project rents low, a key goal of Bauer and the NAHO.

Nathan Straus, the first head of the new U.S. Housing Authority, gave jobs in the organization to Bauer, Keyserling, Jacob Crane, Warren Vinton, and other prime movers behind American public housing. Bauer headed the Division of Research and Information, which enabled her to have an important role in shaping the organization into which she had breathed so much life. Prior to World War II, first as a department chief and later (after resigning her USHA post in 1939) as a consultant and policy insider, Bauer traveled the nation, keenly observing and dutifully chronicling the dawn of public housing. She jabbed critically at times, finding minimum design standards "too rigorous" and some of the early projects "admittedly rather dull." She fretted as well about the "fatal charity smell."[16] She believed that the Wagner-Steagall law, although flawed, compared favorably with Scandinavia's public housing law and especially with British policy, after which it was closely modeled. America, she exhorted, had affirmed the wrongfulness of slums and provided decent, low-rent housing "as a permanent public responsibility."[17]

Bauer praised the decentralization of public housing. She found local housing management to be "business-like and unpaternalistic." Of even greater significance, in 1940, Bauer imagined the fledgling public housing movement gaining strength and ultimately embracing middle-class families who, like their low-income working-class brethren, could benefit from the large-scale planning of modern housing.[18]

The Fate of Modern Housing in Wartime and Postwar America

World War II buttressed Bauer's faith that modern housing could become the centerpiece for what she termed a "balanced civilized life." Wartime housers saw the war as an opportunity to undertake social experimentation in community planning. Toward that end, housers such as Bauer founded the National Committee on the Housing Emergency (NCHE) to promote public housing and community planning via the defense housing program. In 1940, Bauer accepted a visiting professorship at the University of California, Berkeley, where she met and married the modern housing architect William Wurster. In 1942 she accompanied Bill to Harvard, where he earned a master's degree and then accepted deanship of the Massachusetts Institute of Technology's School of Architecture. Meanwhile, Bauer taught at Harvard's Graduate School of Design.

Pearl Harbor spurred the planners' vision of postwar America. As a consultant for the Federal Public Housing Administration (which in 1942 replaced the USHA) and as a member of NCHE, Bauer pressed the cause of public housing and the balanced development of racially diverse, new neighborhoods, cities, and regions. Many of the early Lanham Act defense housing projects (for example, Gropius and Richard Neutra's Aluminum City Terrace in Pittsburgh) encouraged Bauer's belief that World War II afforded America the opportunity to experiment with large-scale, balanced, socially satisfying community forms. Wartime housing projects, in fact, enjoyed a healthy mix of incomes and families and a rich community spirit, producing the kind of vibrant working-class life desired by modern housers like Bauer.

There were ominous signs as well. During World War II resurgent conservative forces crushed upstart wartime modern housing experiments and scattered shabbily built, barracks-like temporary developments across America. With a postwar housing crisis looming, conservatives beat back efforts begun as early as 1944 to restart the public housing program. The housing movement itself waned. Nevertheless, Bauer remained convinced of public housing's critical role in accomplishing urban reconstruction. She battled for passage of the Taft-Ellender-Wagner urban redevelopment legislation in the mid-1940s, and exhorted policymakers to look broadly at the needs of the nation's cities, to explore the function of central cities vis-à-vis the urban region, and to learn how to steer the powerful force of urban decentralization toward the creation of balanced, democratically planned, racially integrated, and livable communities.

The Taft-Ellender-Wagner (T-E-W) Housing Act of 1949, however, reflected urban America's continuing obsession with central-city blight. Although the legislation ordained a decent home in a decent neighborhood for all Americans, Title I provided federal grants underwriting two-thirds of the cost of assembling and clearing central-city land for redevelopment purposes. Yet it shackled public housing to redevelopment, in effect making it—to Bauer's consternation—dependent on slum removal.

T-E-W responded to the varied host of interests intent on "saving the central city," not solving the housing crisis. "Seldom has such a variegated crew of would-be angels tried to sit on the same pin at the same time," wrote Bauer in 1953. Bauer condemned T-E-W's blatant linkage to slum clearance, especially at a time in the 1950s when city slums teemed with people. She branded redevelopment the "Misfit in the Fifties," and charged that it aimed at slum conditions prevalent during the Great Depression, not those currently existing in urban America, where slums were profitable.[19] Such a narrowly conceived view of slum clearance ignored the rampant forces of decentralization and bred at least two great evils: the proliferation of skyscrapers and racial segregation.

Bauer branded the high-rise "indefensible."[20] Not only were those structures "misfits" spatially and socially, they were also potentially undemocratic, strengthening the pattern of discrimination and segregation. Redevelopment, feared Bauer, threatened to deepen the pattern. It vindicated her fears about the disastrous consequences of wedding public housing and slum clearance. Still, in 1953 she harbored some hope for public housing, urging the wisdom of building in the central city some projects to "demonstrate" a "tangible enduring model of really pleasant, well-planned neighborhoods."[21]

Federal officials rebuffed Bauer's pleas for a housing and urban redevelopment policy that was broad, balanced, and regionally based. The 1954 Housing Act more aggressively sacrificed housing need to the development goals of the central city. Historian Arnold Hirsch has observed that in the 1950s, through the Housing and Home Finance Administration (predecessor to HUD), Washington ruthlessly pursued its "two-tiered" policy of warehousing uprooted inner-city families in high-rise public housing, while guaranteeing mortgages for the suburbanizing white middle class.[22]

By the mid-1950s, assailed for its sterile architecture, underfunded by Congress, and attacked by anti-Communist conservatives as subversive, public housing barely limped along. "Problem families"—very poor, often female-headed households, burdened by joblessness, drug addiction, crime, delinquency, and vandalism—increasingly tenanted inner-city projects. It was an exasperated Bauer who in 1957 attacked public housing as a "dreary deadlock." As a driving force in the shaping and enactment of Depression-era public housing legislation, Bauer stung deeply with her bitter language. Symbolically, her words had a death knell quality, for they were untempered by any of the optimism that moderated her earlier harping. "Life in the usual public housing project just is not the way most American families want to live. Nor does it reflect our accepted values. . . ."[23] Bauer's chastisement came from a committed policy insider whose nurturing hand had long shepherded the program, and it had consequences. After 1960, Washington shifted further and further away from the "conventional" government-built public housing policy Bauer helped design toward elderly units, federally subsidized low- and moderate-income housing ventures, and (beginning in the 1970s) the rent certificate program called Section 8. In any case, by 1964, the year Bauer fell to her death while hiking Mount Tamalpais in her beloved Berkeley Hills, public housing was only a shadow of the modern housing she had so fervently espoused in the 1930s.[24]

Bauer's legacy, however, should not be measured by failure of any individual project or piece of legislation. Her real legacy remains her belief in balanced growth; her faith in the vital role of citizen involvement in democratically planned, racially integrated communities; and her support for a noncommercial housing sector and federal subsidies to achieve affordability. These ideals are still viewed as important. Indeed, many Americans in twenty-first century still view them as fundamental to creating sustainable communities.

Notes

1. Catherine Kraus Bauer married the architect William Wurster in 1940. However, throughout this paper, for clarity, we use her maiden name, Bauer.

2. Daniel T. Rodgers, *Atlantic Crossings: Social Politics in a Progressive Age* (Cambridge, MA, 1998).

3. Catherine Bauer, "Prize Essay: Art in Industry," *Fortune* 111, no. 5 (May 1931): 94–110.

4. Catherine Bauer, *Modern Housing* (New York, 1934), 129.

5. Catherine Bauer, "Are Good Houses Un-American?" *New Republic* 70, no. 898 (March 2, 1932): 74.

6. On social politics in Europe, see Rodgers, *Atlantic Crossings*.

7. Bauer, *Modern Housing*, 255.

8. Gail Radford, *Modern Housing for America: Policy Struggles in the New Deal Era* (Chicago, 1996), chap. 5. Note that despite worker input and the carefully planned Modern Housing superblock design, few hosiery workers could ever afford to live there.

9. Timothy L. McDonnell, S.J., *The Wagner Housing Act* (Chicago, 1957), 71.

10. Alexander Von Hoffman, "Vision Limited: The Political Movement for a U.S. Public Housing Program," in *Joint Center for Housing Studies: Working Paper Series*, W96-3 (Boston, 1996), 43–45.

11. Quoted in both H. Peter Oblerlander and Eva Newbrun, *Houser: The Life and Work of Catherine Bauer* (Vancouver, 1999), 296; and McDonnell, *The Wagner Housing Act*, 297.

12. J. Joseph Huthmacher, *Senator Robert F. Wagner and the Rise of Urban Liberalism* (New York, 1971), 226.

13. Radford, *Modern Housing for America*, 190.

14. Catherine Bauer, "Now at Last: Housing: The Meaning of the Wagner-Steagall Act," *New Republic* 92, no. 1188 (September 8, 1937): 119–21.

15. Oberlander and Newbrun, *Houser*, 157.

16. Rodgers, *Atlantic Crossings*, 478.

17. Catherine Bauer, *A Citizen's Guide to Public Housing* (Poughkeepsie, NY, 1940), 24–29.

18. Bauer, *Citizen's Guide*, 38–39.

19. Catherine Bauer, "A Misfit in the Fifties," in Coleman Woodbury, ed., *The Future of Cities and Urban Redevelopment* (Chicago, 1953), 9.

20. Bauer, "A Misfit in the Fifties," 20.

21. Ibid.,19.

22. Arnold R. Hirsch, "Choosing Segregation: Federal Housing Policy between Shelly and Brown," in John F. Bauman, Roger Biles, and Kristin Szylvian, eds., *From Tenements to the Taylor Homes: In Search of an Urban Housing Policy in Twentieth-Century America* (University Park, 2000), 206–26.

23. Catherine Bauer, "The Dreary Deadlock of Public Housing," *Architectural Forum*, 106, no. 5 (May 1957): 141.

24. An avid hiker with failing stamina, Bauer was also a lifelong smoker who, despite efforts to quit, still consumed fifty cigarettes per day in the 1960s.

Suggested Readings

Bauer, Catherine. "Prize Essay: Art in Industry," *Fortune* 111 (May 1931): 94–110.

––––––. *Modern Housing*. New York, 1934.

––––––. "The Dreary Deadlock of Public Housing," *Architectural Forum* 106 (May 1957): 141–42, 219, 212.

Bauman, John F. *Public Housing, Race, and Renewal: Urban Planning in Philadelphia, 1920–1974*. Philadelphia, 1987.

Bauman, John F., Roger Biles, and Kristin Szylvian, eds., *From Tenements to the Taylor Homes: In Search of an Urban Housing Policy in Twentieth-Century America*. University Park, PA, 2000.

Birch, Eugenie L. "An Urban View: Catherine Bauer's Five Questions." In Donald Kreuckeberg, ed., *The American Planner: Biographies and Recollections*. New Brunswick, NJ, 1994.

Huthmacher, J. Joseph. *Senator Robert F. Wagner and the Rise of Urban Liberalism*. New York, 1971.

McDonnell, Timothy L., S. J. *The Wagner Housing Act*. Chicago, 1957.

Oberlander, Peter H., and Eva Newbrun. *Houser: The Life and Work of Catherine Bauer*. Vancouver, 1999.

Radford, Gail. *Modern Housing for America: Policy Struggles in the New Deal Era*. Chicago, 1996.

Von Hoffman, Alexander. "Vision Limited: The Political Movement for a U.S. Public Housing Program." *Joint Center for Housing Studies: Working Paper Series*, W96-3. Boston, 1996.

11

Robert Moses
Relentless Progressive

Joel Schwartz

The industrial American city of the twentieth century presented a host of intractable problems to its residents. Planners, civil engineers, government officials, and reformers grappled with issues involving the provision of adequate housing, transportation, recreation, and other municipal services to a massive, heterogeneous population. Such concerns resonated in all large cities but nowhere more so than in New York City, the nation's busiest port and heart of the sprawling East Coast metropolitan region. After a political consolidation in 1898 merged Manhattan, Brooklyn, Queens, Staten Island, and the Bronx into a single governmental unit, the newly constituted New York City spanned 299 square miles and contained nearly 3.5 million inhabitants. Transportation challenges abounded for a city in which only one of the five boroughs was located on the mainland and, in the age of automobility, the rising number of commuters necessitated the construction of bridges, tunnels, and other public works. Astronomical population densities, the highest in the world on Manhattan Island, and the crumbling of aged, overcrowded tenements raised concerns about the availability of safe and sanitary housing. In New York City the question of how municipal governments could meet the day-to-day needs of so many people in teeming metropolises fell to a powerful and voluble public official, Robert Moses. Gotham's uniqueness notwithstanding, the policy decisions made by Moses served as guideposts for municipal leaders in other large cities, who frequently applied similar solutions to urban problems in their own bailiwicks.

Robert Moses's story is also instructive as a study of politics and governance in the twentieth-century American city. Despite never having been elected to public office, he parlayed a series of appointments to public authorities and commissions into increasing power and autonomy unprecedented in New York City's history. A patrician Republican who served in a series of Democratic mayoral administrations, he proved to be a talented bureaucratic infighter who tailored municipal agencies to his own designs. His ability to shape the New York metropolitan region according to his own vision reminds us of the importance of managerial experts in the modern technocratic society.

Joel Schwartz is professor of history at Montclair State University, Upper Montclair, New Jersey, and adjunct professor in the Graduate Program of Architecture, Planning, and Preservation at Columbia University. His publications include *The New York Approach: Robert Moses, Urban Liberals, and Redevelopment of the Inner City* (1993); *The Development of New Jersey Society* (1997); and *Cities of the Garden State: Essays in the Urban and Suburban History of New Jersey* (1977).

Robert Moses came of age and to the calling of municipal work when America's cities, including its most dynamic, New York, were in the throes of the Progressive Era. Reformers shared an almost Darwinian faith that trained professionals, armed with scientific techniques, could reorder all that was mean and decrepit in metropolitan life. Private philanthropy and public administration, working together in the spirit of systematized advance, would rid cities of slums, tuberculosis, and poverty. Problems that had long plagued urban life could be solved by determined professionals operating with directed intelligence.

Over the following decades, Robert Moses turned that powerful faith into a despotic will with immense consequences for New York. Convinced that the city needed parks and recreation, he gave New Yorkers miles of oceanfront beaches and asphalt playgrounds. Determined to level Gotham's infamous rookeries, he engaged in slum clearance that made way for public housing projects and Title I redevelopments. An ardent believer in superhighways, he rammed 6-lane arterials through the heart of neighborhoods like the Central Bronx. In 1913 he started out a do-gooder in philanthropic service, a Progressive critic of corrupt government. He ended up, by the 1950s, a government unto himself, faithful to his views alone, and relentless in the pursuit of improvements that transformed New York.

Robert Moses was born in New Haven, Connecticut, in 1888, into a family of German-Jewish background. His father owned a local department store, but his ambitious mother moved the household to New York City in 1897, where she took up Fifth Avenue life, including the social teachings at the Ethical Cultural Society and volunteer work at Madison House, the settlement run by Henry Moskowitz. Wanting the best for Robert, she sent him to private tutors and boarding school and then to Yale, where he majored in political science. He pursued advanced studies in jurisprudence at Oxford University, coming under the sway of Graham Wallas, the Fabian Socialist, who stressed modern society's potential for organized purpose. Moses's doctoral thesis, "The Civil Service of Great Britain," was a genteel review of the English bureaucracy, filled with admiration for its "university-bred" public servants and contempt for the "uniform mediocrity" of "ill-educated"

Americans.[1] Back in New York, he rewrote his thesis for a doctoral degree at Columbia University in 1913.

His mother's connections got Moses an apprenticeship with the Bureau of Municipal Research, a private New York agency endowed by reformers to investigate municipal corruption. The Bureau had joined the good-government war against Tammany Hall being waged by Mayor John Purroy Mitchel, a high-toned Democrat, who expected city employees to observe a stopwatch efficiency. As a Bureau staffer, Moses devised performance ratings for the New York City Civil Service Commission, whose chairman, Henry Moskowitz, wished to use them to measure the productivity of city employees. Moses found that Bureau "field work" made investigators feel like "busy bodies," whom city workers told to "mind their own business."[2] His discomfort did not last long. With America's entry into World War I, Mayor Mitchel's hectoring was overtaken by the roughneck patriotism of Tammany candidate John F. "Red Mike" Hylan, who won the 1917 mayoral election. Having joined Bureau "goo-goos," activists for good government, young Dr. Moses was out of a job.

Moses was rescued by Henry Moskowitz's wife, Belle Israels Moskowitz, shrewd wire-puller and political adviser to another Tammany man, New York State Assembly leader Alfred E. Smith. Running for governor in 1918, Smith forged a coalition of Tammany Irish-Catholic and Socialist Jewish voters on the Lower East Side. After Smith's narrow victory, Mrs. Moskowitz brought the bookish Ph.D., a Republican and reformer, into the governor's circle. Smith understood that he needed to enlarge his voter base to include nonpartisans and moderate Republicans. The means emerged in late 1918 as public attention focused on the issue of "reconstruction," the range of programs intended to tackle the dislocations brought by total war. Across the state, the Great War had left crowded cities with jammed harbors, broken-down transit systems, and scandalous housing near arsenals and shipyards. Experts predicted postwar turbulence and unemployment, and already bitter strikes had overtaken the September influenza epidemic as the scourge of New York. Mrs. Moskowitz suggested that Governor Smith sponsor a commission to examine the challenges of postwar readjustment.

In January 1919, Smith appointed a Reconstruction Commission composed of Tammany Democrats, Reform Jews, and broad-minded Republicans. At Mrs. Moskowitz's suggestion, he chose Moses as chief of staff. Moses coordinated the research effort, which produced position papers advocating regional planning, a New York port authority, public works as an employment stabilizer, and municipal public housing. Moses contributed a plan for executive reorganization to provide the governor with a strong cabinet and an "executive budget." The Commission would have given New York gubernatorial direction and bureaucracy, what political theorists today call capacity to create the modern welfare state. Looking forward to Smith's 1920 reelection campaign, Moses helped to coordinate efforts to realize the Commission's blueprints, particularly focusing on the constitutional amendments and enabling bills for submission to the state legislature. But the entire program (except for the port authority), along with Smith's own reelection hopes, was buried by the Harding landslide.

Moses's reputation, however, landed him a position as secretary of the New York State Association, a new reform watchdog. He edited the association's pronouncements on Albany legislation and in 1922 authored its pamphlet, "A Park Plan for New York," advocating a state system funded by a public bond issue. When Al Smith regained the governorship in 1922, he brought Moses back as a liaison to the reform community. By all accounts, the two men got along, despite differences in age and political perspective. Moses became a regular at the governor's mansion, filling Smith's appetite for facts. His uncanny grasp of the bill-writing process dovetailed with Smith's intricate knowledge of the legislative process. While neither had gone to law school, they had become expert in the essentials of drafting reform legislation: the preamble to justify application of the constitutional "police power" to sway skeptical judges, and operative authority that was "sufficiently elastic," Moses once blandly put it, "to meet unforseen developments."[3] In April 1923, Smith urged the legislature to adopt the bill Moses had drafted to create a system of state parks.

Parks were dear to Governor Smith's heart. He never forgot how poor kids, like himself, dove off the docks into the polluted East River. But he also saw parks as a vast potential for state construction and patronage, an opportunity for inner-city Democrats (like Tammany) in the regional hinterlands. Moses's bill was a deft amalgam of shared authority. Regional park commissions would acquire land by donation or by eminent domain (condemnation), develop regional plans, and call upon local governments for supportive funds. Statewide policy would be coordinated by a council appointed by the governor. After the legislature's enactment of the Moses bill in 1924, Smith promptly appointed Moses president of one of eleven local bodies, the Long Island

State Park Commission (LISPC), as well as chairman of the State Council of Parks.

The parks ideal had not changed much since advocates like Frederick Law Olmsted artfully arranged nature in the 1860s. Parks were conceived as islands of repose apart from the hustle and bustle of the city and, for all the rhetoric from Olmsted and others about how parks rejuvenated the soul and set the imagination free, they were terrains of authority and control. Moses instinctively understood this premise, but with an important difference. As an official who answered to Al Smith, he knew that state parks must also be arranged for the masses. Consequently, the typical Moses park combined a steely authority with mass, sometimes vulgar, taste. As president of the LISPC, he set his staff to work on recreation areas at Sunken Meadows, Fire Island, and Montauk Point. He made headlines overriding "a little group of wealthy men" to condemn hundreds of acres on Long Island's south shore for Jones Beach State Park, Moses's earliest and best-known creation. Jones Beach mixed authoritarian control with crass details such as a Venetian campanile straight out of the Italian Renaissance with trash receptacles disguised to look like steamship funnels. While Olmsted trained park-goers to keep off the grass and observe nature from a distance, Moses's Long Island parks welcomed the motor-age masses. (Jones Beach alone was designed for 300,000 daily visitors.)

Moses's parks had another important feature—the parkways that connected them. They were an old idea, dating back to the emerald necklace that Olmsted proposed along the Fenway for the Boston park system. Designed as ribbons of repose for walkers, cyclists, and upper-class horse riders, the parkways were carefully landscaped, generously wide, and zoned against commercial intrusions. By the 1920s they were championed by visionaries of regional planning like Benton MacKaye, who called them "townless highways," greenways to draw harried city dwellers into the countryside. On the LISPC in the late 1920s, Moses pushed for green 300-foot-wide ribbons, the Northern and Southern State parkways, and a north-south connector, the Sagtikos. At the time, advocates of regional planning considered motorways a crucial part of their blueprints for the deconcentration of the metropolis. The corporate and banking interests, which had launched the Regional Plan of New York and Its Environs, recommended a radial system of railroads and highways, along with land-use controls, for the tri-state area. Vigorous opponents, led by Benton MacKaye, socialist Stuart Chase, and urban critic Lewis Mumford, had organized a rival rostrum, the Regional Planning Association of America, which dreamed of drawing congested New York into small planned towns embedded in leafy "green belts." But Moses trumped them all with parkways that promised healthy recreation and weekends in the sun to millions.

The promise was staggered by the 1929 stock market crash, but hard times and mass unemployment only reinforced Moses's hold on the metropolitan tomorrow. In 1933, Governor Herbert H. Lehman turned to Moses to head the State Emergency Public Works Commission, which drew up New York's wish list of projects funded by the U.S. Reconstruction Finance Corporation (RFC). They included toll bridges such as the span at Bear Mountain and parkways such as the Taconic, which would be self-liquidating (toll collections would pay off the RFC debt) and built quickly with maximum use of unemployed labor. The list also included limited-dividend housing projects (so called because philanthropic investors accepted a limited return on their capital investment) such as the Hillside Houses in the Bronx and Knickerbocker Village on the Lower East Side.

The emergency work not only drew the federal government into the cause of slum clearance, it also brought Moses back to New York City. In 1934, Mayor Fiorello H. La Guardia, a reformer whom Moses had supported for election, appointed Moses commissioner of the New York City Park Department. (He served without salary, which rendered moot the civil service rules against holding multiple public offices.) Taking advantage of Franklin D. Roosevelt's New Deal, Moses organized the park department to use millions of federal dollars to employ thousands on emergency make-work. As the money poured in from the U.S. Civil Works Administration and, ultimately, the Works Progress Administration (WPA), Moses's workforce built and refurbished 255 playgrounds, scores of basketball courts, and ten giant community pools. He also parlayed federal funds into an extensive network of parkways, notably an inspired circumference, the Belt Parkway, around Brooklyn and Queens to speed city dwellers (trucks forbidden) to beaches and parks on Long Island's south shore.

The frenzied accomplishment gained Moses a national reputation as New York's can-do public servant, even as close observers began to regard him with uneasiness. The public applauded his park achievements during a decade that was convinced that big cities stifled residents' lives and Hollywood films like *Dead End* (1937) depicted slums as child-destroyers. Moses's park department offered jungle gyms, basketball courts, and model airplane fields to help build sturdy bodies and young citizens. Park enthusiasts were troubled by his penchant for enclosing greenery with asphalt and Cyclone fences—and stung by his icy ridicule of their views. But they excused Moses's nasty attacks as the outbursts of a busy public servant trying to do the people's business. The reaction was more muted among the politicians, who feared Moses's growing power. He transformed the park department into the city's largest WPA workforce and helped New York City capture, by 1936, one-seventh of the country's entire WPA budget. It was a success that made Mayor La Guardia and Governor Lehman grudging allies. For his part, President Roosevelt worried about the public works empire that Moses was building in New York. But Moses kept the dirt flying and helped to anchor the Empire State for the New Deal.

That growing sense of Moses's indispensability made possible his appointment by Mayor La Guardia to chair the Triborough Bridge Authority, the most powerful of the city's independent authorities. The Triborough was modeled on the Port Authority of New York, a public corporation that could issue bonds financed by revenues from piers and other cargo facilities. After a shaky start, Port Authority debt had achieved a blue-chip rating with investors, particularly the National City Bank. In 1934 the Triborough was launched to build a $51 million bridge to connect Manhattan and two outer boroughs, the Bronx and Queens. Funded by a down payment from the New Deal's Public Works Authority (PWA) and flotations of Triborough bonds, the immense debt would be liquidated by 25-cent tolls charged to motorists. La Guardia had acted on the perception that Moses had the unimpeachable honesty and drive to bolster the confidence of the PWA and Triborough bondholders.

The Triborough proved of immense importance to New York and Robert Moses. A creature of the motor age, it planted connective tissue across the middle of the city and virtually begged for further tributaries—across the Bronx to meet with the George Washington Bridge, across Queens, and perhaps across Manhattan itself. More significant for Moses's power base, the Triborough's burgeoning tolls handed Moses a revenue stream to support a bureaucracy of planners, lawyers, and engineers to devise more revenue-producing bridges and toll roads. In expanding the Triborough's domain, Moses merely followed the logic of the era that spawned him. The public wanted routes for the motor age and applauded the selfless bureaucrat who supplied them. Few questioned the priorities of an authority whose independent board was far removed from public review. According to good Progressive doctrine, it took a meritocratic bureaucracy, shielded from political influence, to served democracy's needs. And Triborough bondholders insisted that nothing less would ensure the safety of their investment.

Public works for the jobless, public demand for motorways, and public trust in the man who got things done all combined to support more Moses projects. He pushed for an expressway across Gowanus Creek in Brooklyn and called for a harbor bridge to connect Brooklyn with the Battery at Manhattan. (Moses had to settle for a tunnel built by an enlarged Triborough Authority.) He laid out the Grand Central, Interboro, and Laurelton Parkways, which opened in 1936. With Triborough funds, he added another bridge at Whitestone, Queens, and completed the Belt system around Brooklyn by 1940. For the largest project of all, Manhattan's West Side Improvement, Moses corralled federal, state, and city funds to build Riverside Park over railroad tracks and extend a parkway, the Henry Hudson, to connect with the Saw Mill in Westchester County. Friends of Riverside Park were shocked that Moses's highway cut through a charming, wooded area, but the Triborough's glossy brochures of cars speeding down the West Side Improvement reminded the public how Moses was moving New York into the motor age. By 1940 the city had more expressways than Chicago, Philadelphia, Detroit, Los Angeles, and Cleveland put together. Moses became the prophet for highway builders in other cities, including New Orleans, Baltimore, and Pittsburgh, where he put forth his usual formula of belt parkways, radial spurs, and parking garages to make central business districts accommodate the automobile. His international following among urban theorists included Belgian architect Le Corbusier and German Bauhaus champion Sigfried Giedion, who enthused that Moses's parkways captured "the space-time feeling of our period."[4]

Meanwhile, Moses made a foray into the areas of public housing and city planning. He took up the mantra "housing and recreation"— the need to build projects alongside playgrounds—to bolster his request that Mayor La Guardia give him influence over the New York City Housing Authority (NYCHA). La Guardia turned him down, but during a tough reelection campaign in 1941 he appointed Moses to the City Planning Commission. Its chairman, Rexford G. Tugwell, that visionary New Dealer, had proposed shifting New York's congested population into planned communities along "greenbelts" in the outer boroughs. Moses called Tugwell's greenbelts a "preposterous" dreamscape, telling La Guardia it was the sort of nonsense that made planning "odious to sensible people."[5] Hounding Tugwell off the commission, Moses went after NYCHA chairman Alfred Rheinstein, belittling his policies and conspiring behind his back with NYCHA underlings. Rheinstein thought Moses would listen to reason and pointed out that sites for low-income housing should accord with "neighborhood tradition, loyalty, commerce, capital investment, and social activities." Moses formally replied, "I don't know what the hell you are talking about," and made sure everyone in City Hall learned of the humiliating exchange.[6]

Moses remained on the edge of housing policy until World War II, when New York's economy turned to war production. Fearing massive housing congestion and traffic jams, La Guardia called upon Planning Commissioner Moses to sketch additional arterials and to expedite NYCHA projects near the Brooklyn Navy Yard and other industrial centers. Moses was also asked to coordinate La Guardia's wish list for the postwar metropolis. La Guardia's motives were understandably mixed. Like many of his generation, the mayor was an unabashed modernist. He delighted in sleek planes and air terminals, admired bridges and motorways, and thought New Yorkers deserved schools and hospitals of tile glass, granular brick, and stainless steel. But La Guardia also shared the anxiety of wartime liberals that victory might bring renewal of depression joblessness unless government developed a shelf of construction projects to act as an employment stabilizer.

For all these reasons, the mayor in 1943 made Moses coordinator of the city's demands for postwar construction. With that, Moses set his Triborough staff to work on the master list of schools, hospitals, libraries, playgrounds, and swimming pools. Because Moses controlled access to the list and pressed his formula "housing and recreation," he finally obtained a grip on the project decisions of the Housing Authority. At the time, housing advocates called for replacing slum tenements with "superblocks" of buildings that included community facilities for the needs of low-income residents. Who would question Moses's arguments that he was coordinating the location of low-rent projects with an eye toward the libraries, schools, health clinics, and other facilities that the city intended to build after the war?

La Guardia also handed Moses the responsibility for dealing with the state officials and life insurance giants, who completed the legal details that conferred the power of eminent domain on life insurance companies that established limited-dividend housing corporations. This formula for urban redevelopment resulted in Stuyvesant Town, a massive slum clearance project on the Lower East Side begun by Metropolitan Life in 1945. Stuyvesant Town embodied many of the necessary cruelties that Moses had exhibited in his park and highway projects. The middle-class project would erase a community of working-class tenements—a scale of removals that Moses and La Guardia justified as helping the city retain its valued middle class. But another issue erupted when Metropolitan Life announced that Stuyvesant Town was for whites only. At the height of the war against Hitler's racism—and only months after the 1943 Harlem Riot (in part against crowded ghetto housing)— Met Life had decreed Jim-Crow-as-usual.

While he had become the most powerful voice behind plans for postwar New York, Robert Moses was indifferent to the social forces driving them forward. He refused to respond to the racial issue at Stuyvesant Town, even when liberals recommended that city policies aim at dispersal of the Harlem ghetto. Moses dismissed the idea as an absurd ploy by his critics to block slum clearance. And he was blind to the future of Long Island, a place he assuredly shaped but scarcely understood. He never foresaw that the island would develop a commercial future, even while his Long Island State Park Commission worked on the parkways that took workers to defense plants like Sperry Gyroscope. In early 1946, Moses opined for the *Rotarian* magazine, "On many of the great mass-production areas the workers are folding their tents and silently stealing away, leaving their houses permanent or temporary, jerry built or sound, to the natives."[7] Never anticipating the postwar housing boom, let alone the vast suburban trek, Moses remained a good Progressive, who continued to think of Long Island as New York City's recreation center—a Sunday retreat, not a residential place.

How did Moses impose his will over so many aspects of the city's development? The answer must start with his undeniable intelligence and ferocious energies. He impressed everyone with his braininess, his ability to exhaust the essentials of a subject with a quick review of memos or a scan of blueprints. A workaholic, he used his limousine as an office (the man who rammed expressways through the city never learned to drive), dictating to secretaries, who mimeoed septuplicate copies for files that supplied ready reference to hundreds of projects. The staff consisted of scores of "Moses men" (and some women) plucked from the LISPC, the city park department, the Triborough, and other scattered agencies—dozens of lawyers, engineers, landscape architects, draftsmen, and general flunkies, all doing the boss's bidding. Moses handled so much public works construction that he came to know every major architectural partnership and every major construction firm, not to mention the heads of every building trades union. All soon learned that with Moses their jobs were on the line, and to cross him meant jeopardizing their careers. Moses's ultimate weapon, first used in the late 1930s against La Guardia and Lehman, was his threat to resign if he did not get his way. During the depths of the depression and the war, few politicians dared call his bluff, for fear of having to explain to voters why they "forced out" the man who got things done.

By 1947, La Guardia's successor, Mayor William O'Dwyer, formally centralized Moses's scattered ad hoc authority. He appointed the Park Commissioner, City Planning Commissioner, Triborough Bridge and Tunnel Authority chairman, Long Island State Park Commission president, and chairman of the State Council on Parks to the new post of City Construction Coordinator. One of Moses's first acts was to push blueprints for new arterials across the outer boroughs to complete connections with the beaches and parks on Long Island, join the Bronx and Queens with more crossings, and even mark expressways across Manhattan. Most of the routes, like the Cross Bronx and completion of the Belt system around Queens, replicated those proposed by the Regional Plan in the 1920s. The Manhattan arterials were also advocated by modernist planners, who argued that the only way to relieve traffic congestion was to run separate interstate highways across and around the city. Moses pursued the idea with a vengeance, producing expressways like the Van Wyck, which split apart a neighborhood of homes on its way to Idlewild (Kennedy) Airport, and the infamous Cross Bronx, a concrete gash through an apartment district.

At the same time, Moses drove the NYCHA bulldozers, insisting that new housing had to be pursued on existing slum sites and not, as in Tugwell's old dream, in the outer boroughs. Moses's decision had two crucial consequences. First, it compounded the already difficult business of relocating slum populations. At Stuyvesant Town, Moses had relocated some 3,000 families off 72 acres. The NYCHA clearance involved scores of thousands more, mostly African Americans and Puerto Ricans, who could not find decent rehousing in the Jim Crow city. Nevertheless, Moses rejected as "the most stupid thing in the world" the idea, advocated by Charles Abrams and other critics, that NYCHA should construct projects in the outer boroughs before it embarked on slum clearance.[8] It would evade city responsibility, Moses said, and leave "the slums in worse condition than they were before." Instead he concocted an alternative scheme, "including moving houses and even apartment houses, paying tenants to move, rehabilitating boarded-up structures, building half or one-third of a project at a time," and the like.[9] This scenario for a vast, continuous churning of neighborhoods would affect some 170,000 people between 1946 and 1953. Second, NYCHA projects on cleared slum sites meant recycling some of the most expensive land in the inner city at the same time that the federal government limited construction grants for public housing construction and housing authorities had to keep project rents within the budgets of the poor. With the cost squeeze, NYCHA had no choice but to build up, constructing projects of towers fourteen to eighteen stories tall. Spartan warehouses for the low-income population soon became alienating, crime-ridden warrens. But Moses insisted that high-rises were the most efficient way to rid New York of slums.

Moses's work with Metropolitan Life also made him the city's inevitable man to deal with the federal program of urban redevelopment under Title I of the Housing Act of 1949. In theory, Title I required the city to work with local communities to choose the sites to be cleared and turned over to private sponsors for the construction of middle-class housing. After Mayor O'Dwyer appointed Moses chairman of the Committee on Slum Clearance Plans, he proceeded to make decisions *for* neighborhoods rather than *with* them. Regarding community advisory groups as "letterhead organizations" that lacked "the broader aspects of city government," Moses met privately with sponsors to pick Title I sites.[10] As a result, the program skipped over the worst slums to attack housing blight that endangered the central business district and valued educational and medical institutions. Moses approved just one slum redevelopment—a project in Central Harlem—along with a host of Title I projects to help New York University to reclaim Greenwich Village, Columbia University to defend Morningside Heights from encroaching African Americans, and NYU Medical School-Bellevue Hospital to build the "medical capital of the world." Moses's crown jewel, the redevelopment at Lincoln Square, created the huge civic plaza, Lincoln Center for the Performing Arts, with enough middle-class housing nearby to make the Title I designation plausible.

While critics claimed that Moses's projects were developed to remove blacks and Puerto Ricans from certain areas, their real aim was to cordon off urban blight that endangered downtown civic and commercial centers such as Brooklyn Heights and Lincoln Square. Clearance, in fact, shoved aside as many whites as blacks, particularly in Lincoln Square, the South Village, and the West Thirties. Like many of his generation, Moses looked askance at any dissolute inhabitants who threatened the fragile revival of postwar cities. Critics estimated that during the heyday of Moses's improvements, from 1954 to 1957, nearly 75,000 housing units (each with 3.2 human beings) were displaced for all the improvements under Moses's sway. The chaos that this inflicted on minority neighborhoods such as East Harlem, the South Bronx, and Brownsville was nearly unfathomable. The NYCHA and Title I operations created whole populations of urban nomads, refugees from one clearance site huddled in decrepit tenements waiting the next round of demolitions. By 1956 dissidents on the City Planning Commission tried to convince Mayor Robert F. Wagner Jr. to end the havoc by ordering projects for the refugees in the outer boroughs. But Moses would have none of it. Most whites, he pointed out, resisted having blacks and Hispanics as their neighbors. He dared the critics to take the issue up with the mayor, rubbing their noses in New York's dirty little secret by asking, "Why don't you say frankly that such opposition has official recognition and tell more about it?"[11]

By the late 1950s, however, Moses managed to gather a host of enemies in white, upscale Manhattan, where residents cared more about parks and community values than about race. His projects for Manhattan expressways along 34th Street and Broome Street enraged neighborhood activists. But for many, the last straw was his betrayal as Park Commissioner: his plan to run Fifth Avenue as a highway through Washington Square Park and put more asphalt parking lots in Central Park. Those proposals produced redoubtable enemies, notably Mrs. Eleanor Roosevelt and the Greenwich Village activist and architectural writer, Jane Jacobs. Moses's superblocks and arterials had helped stir a values revolution across New York for neighborhood planning districts, brownstone preservation, and small-scale community life. Mayor Wagner, heretofore one of Moses's genuflecting admirers, dropped his pilot from the Mayor's Committee on Slum Clearance Plans and the City Planning Commission. Another powerful enemy, Governor Nelson A. Rockefeller, detached Moses from the Triborough Bridge and Tunnel Authority. For all intents and purposes, Moses's nearly forty years of public service had ended.

The 30-year debate about the meaning of Moses's career that went on before and after his death at the age of 88, in 1981, was jumpstarted by Jane Jacobs's book, *The Death and Life of Great American Cities* (1961), which attacked everything that Moses stood for: high-rise public housing, large plazas like Lincoln Center, and highways that cut through neighborhoods. The 1974 publication of Robert A. Caro's biography, *The Power Broker*, pulled away the mask of Moses the selfless, incorruptible public servant to depict a monster corrupted by the will to power. In 1,100 pitiless pages, Caro detailed how Moses bulldozed East Harlem and Brownsville and seemed to relish the business of Negro removal. Sociologists and political scientists broadened the analysis to argue that corporate interests used public servants like Moses to prepare downtowns for postindustrial expansion. By the late 1980s a postrevisionism set in, highlighted by New Yorkers engaged in Moses nostalgia who wondered whether the city could get things done in the face of tiresome veto groups and not-in-my-backyard politics. We need another Moses, some cried, who could override niggling protests and create the buildings, bridges, and tunnels that New York deserved.

From the perspective of the new century, Robert Moses's willfulness seems the product of his remarkable generation, its utter confidence and sense of matchless opportunity. Moses was shaped by the fierce conviction, based on late nineteenth-century Darwinian thought, scientific positivism, and Progressive reform, that the great problems of urban civilization were susceptible to scientific analysis and brick-and-mortar solutions. While not a planner nor architect nor engineer, Moses fashioned powerful government administrations, armed with fact finders and technical personnel, to weave the fabric of Progressive ambition. That ambition only grew larger with the involvement of the New Deal as the source of funds for revitalizing urban America. The best bill drafter in Albany became the best project deviser, the best expeditor of plans and specifications. When effective liberal government really meant the accumulation of bureaucratic staff, Moses gathered the best team around and drove it relentlessly.

In the last analysis, Moses could not have driven these policies so far without the people's will behind him: the people's faith that at Jones Beach and at Stuyvesant Town, on slum clearance sites across New York and in public housing projects for the black and Hispanic poor, brick-and-mortar idealism was making a modern New York. Progress was splendid as well as inevitable. This unassailable faith gave Robert Moses his career.

Notes

1. Robert Moses, *The Civil Service of Great Britain*, submitted for the Ph.D. in Faculty of Political Science, Columbia University (New York, 1914), 9, 7, 119.

2. Ibid., 263.

3. "Pattern for Parks," *Architectural Forum* 65 (December 1936): 498.

4. Sigfried Giedion, *Space, Time, and Architecture: The Growth of a New Tradition* (Cambridge: Harvard University Press, 1941; 5th ed., 1967), 826.

5. Robert Moses to Rexford G. Tugwell, July 5, 1939, Box 102429; and Moses to Fiorello H. La Guardia, December 4, 1940, Box 102519, both in Park Department Records, New York City Municipal Archives and Records Center (hereafter cited as Park Department Records).

6. Alfred Rheinstein to Moses, September 15, 1939; and Moses to Rheinstein, September 18, 1939, both in Box 97, Robert Moses Papers, Rare Books and Manuscripts Division, New York Public Library (hereafter cited as Moses Papers).

7. Robert Moses, "Housing Headaches," *Rotarian* 68 (March 1946): 18.

8. Moses to Maxwell H. Tretter, June 13, 1946, Box 102741, Park Department Records.

9. Moses to William Charney Vladeck, November 10, 1948, Box 102845, Park Department Records.

10. Moses to Robert F. Wagner Jr., July 11, 1949, Box 102834, Park Department Records.

11. Moses to James Felt, August 20, 1956, Box 116, Moses Papers.

Suggested Readings

The best introduction to Robert Moses's career is his writings, which were invariably pungent and caustic about his achievements and the people who got in the way of them. His books include *Public Works: A Dangerous Trade* (New York: McGraw-Hill, 1970); and *Working for the People: Promise and Performance in Public Service* (New York: Harper, 1956). Among his magazine pieces, one can consult "Hordes from the City," *Saturday Evening Post* 204 (October 31, 1931): 14–15; "Mr. Moses Dissects the 'Long-Haired Planners,' " *New York Times Magazine* (June 25, 1944): 16; and "The Changing City," *Architectural Forum* 72 (March 1940): 142–55. The best studies of his career are Robert A. Caro, *The Power Broker: Robert Moses and the Fall of New York* (New York: Alfred A. Knopf, 1974), the scathing biography that won a Pulitzer Prize; Cleveland Rodgers, *Robert Moses, Builder for Democracy* (New York: Holt, 1952), a work of sheer idolatry; and Joel Schwartz, *The New York Approach: Robert Moses, Urban Liberals, and Redevelopment of the Inner City* (Columbus: Ohio State University Press, 1993), which looks at the liberals' embrace of his policies.

Moses's park work in New York City is admired in "Pattern for Parks," *Architectural Forum* 65 (December 1936): 491–510; and grudgingly praised in Roy Rosenzweig and Elizabeth Blackmar, *The Park and the People* (Ithaca, NY: Cornell University Press, 1992). Jo Ann Krieg, ed., *Robert Moses: Single-Minded Genius*, Long Island Studies (Interlaken, NY: Heart of the Lakes Publishing, 1989), includes several essays on his role as a park developer and environmentalist. The world of the public authorities such as the Triborough Bridge Authority can be glimpsed in Ann Marie Hauck Walsh, *The Public's Business: The Politics and Practices of Government Corporations*, A Twentieth-Century Fund Study (Cambridge, MA: MIT Press, 1978); and Julius Henry Cohen, *They*

Builded Better Than They Knew (New York: Julian Messner, 1946). For the Clarence Stein–Lewis Mumford regional ideas that Moses regularly ridiculed, see State of New York, *Report of the Commission of Housing and Regional Planning to Governor Alfred E. Smith . . . May 7, 1926* (Albany, 1926); articles by Stein, Mumford, MacKaye, and others in "The Regional Plan Number," *Survey Graphic* 7 (May 1925); and Edward K. Spann, *Designing Modern America: The Regional Plan Association and Its Members* (Columbus: Ohio State University Press, 1996). Mark I. Gelfand, *A Nation of Cities* (New York: Oxford University Press, 1975); Sigfried Giedion, *Space, Time, and Architecture; the Growth of a New Tradition* (Cambridge: Harvard University Press, 1941; 5th ed., 1967); and Jane Jacobs, *The Death and Life of Great American Cities* (New York: Random House, 1961), put Moses's career in larger perspective.

Moses's highway obsession should be judged within the context of postwar proposals, such as Holden et al., "A Redevelopment Project for New York," *Architectural Forum* 79 (October 1943), which was part of the series, "Planned Neighborhoods for 194X," featured in *Architectural Forum* during 1943 and 1944. Besides the Caro and Schwartz volumes already mentioned, the huge literature on public housing and urban redevelopment includes John H. Mollenkopf, *The Contested City* (Princeton: Princeton University Press, 1983); Arnold Hirsch, *Making the Second Ghetto: Race and Housing in Chicago, 1940–1960* (New York: Cambridge University Press, 1983); Chester Hartman, *The Transformation of San Francisco* (Totowa, NJ: Rowman & Allanheld, 1984); and Susan S. Fainstein et al., *Restructuring the City: The Political Ecomony of Urban Redevelopment* (New York: Longman, 1983). A. Scott Henderson, *Housing and the Democratic Ideal: The Life and Thought of Charles Abrams* (New York: Columbia University Press, 2000), is a welcome study of the outspoken opponent of Moses's housing and Title I policies.

12

Coleman A. Young
Race and the Reshaping of Postwar Urban Politics

Heather Thompson

From the earliest days, blacks played an extremely limited role in the political life of the nation's cities. In great measure this low level of participation owed not only to the relatively small number of blacks living in urban areas but also to the franchise restrictions imposed in state constitutions and municipal statutes. With the exception of Tennessee, all southern states entering the Union after 1789 denied African Americans suffrage. In the early nineteenth century, several states disfranchised blacks, beginning with Maryland in 1810 and including Indiana as late as 1851. Early city charters prohibited blacks from voting as well. Disfranchisement came in the 1820s for New York City and Providence, Rhode Island, and in the 1830s for Philadelphia and Pittsburgh. Among the nation's leading cities, only in Boston could blacks vote without restriction in the first half of the nineteenth century, and then only about 40 percent of them (approximately 350) actually did so.

The passage of the Reconstruction Acts and the Fifteenth Amendment enfranchised freedmen in the South, and blacks won election to municipal offices in significant numbers. As long as federal troops patrolled the South, blacks enjoyed unprecedented political freedom, but the return to power by white conservatives signaled the restoration of more restrictive policies. Although some African Americans served on city councils in Nashville and Jackson, Mississippi, until the 1880s, in Richmond and Raleigh until the 1890s, and in Jacksonville, Florida, after the turn of the century, the passage of disfranchising Jim Crow laws throughout the South effectively removed black office holders and emasculated the black vote in the cities. Except in a few locations—principally in the Upper South areas of Tennessee and North Carolina—poll taxes, white primaries, and other devices restored politics to its antebellum white-only status.

A previous version of this chapter appeared in David R. Colburn and Jeffrey S. Adler, eds., *African-American Mayors: Race, Politics, and the American City* (Urbana: University of Illinois Press, 2001).

In the much larger, more heavily industrialized cities of the North, no such systematic legal framework existed in the late nineteenth century to keep blacks from voting. In the days before the Great Migration of southern blacks to northern cities, however, nonwhite populations were small and politically insignificant in places such as New York City, Chicago, and Philadelphia. The leaders of local political organizations saw no reason to slate or support black office-seekers when larger ethnic groups could produce more votes and deserved to be rewarded for past performance at the polls. The problem of racial discrimination aside, African Americans simply lacked the votes to compete in the political arena.

In the last decades of the twentieth century, African Americans began exerting significant influence in local politics and electing some of their own as mayors of the nation's largest cities. White flight to the suburbs left large cities with sizable black populations that comprised a larger percentage of the electorate. In the decade of the 1960s alone, the black population of central cities increased by more than 35 percent while the white population decreased by 9 percent. Also by the mid-1960s, the black masses enjoyed new legal protections, allowing them to vote in greater numbers. The passage of civil rights legislation in 1957, 1960, 1964, 1965, and 1975 (especially the Voting Rights Act of 1965) greatly increased voter turnout in urban America. In 1967 big-city electorates chose two black men as mayors—Carl Stokes in Cleveland, Ohio, and Richard Hatcher in Gary, Indiana—and in subsequent years, the number of African American mayors mushroomed. In this chapter, Heather Thompson tells the story of a member of the first generation of black mayors, Coleman Young of Detroit.

Heather Thompson received a Ph.D. degree from Princeton University and is currently assistant professor of history at the University of North Carolina at Charlotte. She is the author of *Whose Detroit? Politics, Race, and Labor in a Modern American City* (2001).

B y the mid-1970s numerous African Americans had risen to key positions of political power in urban centers across the United States. In fact, American inner cities witnessed the most dramatic black political ascendancy of the entire twentieth century after 1970, with 316 black mayors in charge of major urban enclaves and countless African Americans holding other positions of significant civic authority by 1990.[1] Because the overwhelming majority of new black civic leaders were deeply committed to the Democratic Party as well as to the programs and ideology of postwar (and particularly Great Society) liberalism, and because they made civil rights activism an integral part of their leadership agenda, their rise to power reveals much about urban American politics more broadly after the tumultuous 1960s had passed.

Coleman Alexander Young, southern migrant, union activist, state politician, and civil rights champion, became the first African American mayor of Detroit, Michigan, in 1974. Although Young's rise to power was bitterly contested, he went on to enjoy a remarkable 20-year career as leader of the Motor City. By touching on the dramatic events that set the stage for Young's election and by closely examining his mayoralty, we can illuminate the broader political significance of black rule in the mid to late twentieth century. In sum, African American politicians such as Young won office during the 1970s specifically because they supported liberal programs to effect greater equality. Clearly, even while the postwar liberal agenda was being rejected by those who moved in growing numbers to the nation's suburbs and into the Republican Party, urban America continued to raise powerful voices for racial and economic parity. In analyzing Young's rise to power in Detroit, we will see clearly that the support base of sixties-style liberalism did not fully collapse in the wake of the turbulent 1960s, as so many would have it, but rather that it had noticeably changed color and had become almost exclusively urban.

Coleman Alexander Young was born in Tuscaloosa, Alabama, on May 28, 1918, and like many southern African Americans, he moved to Detroit with his family in 1923. Significantly, the Great Migration that brought the Young family to the Motor City after World War I was followed, both during and after World War II, by another massive exodus of southern African Americans.[2] As a result of these dramatic demographic shifts, by the mid-1960s the Motor City was more than 40 percent African American. And yet, despite their growing presence in the population, black migrants new to Detroit quickly realized that racial discrimination existed there in ways ominously similar to the southern cities from which they had fled.

Black Detroiters refused to allow their dreams of equality and opportunity to be further deferred, and by the 1960s they had mobilized a powerful civil rights presence in the Motor City through organizations such as the NAACP, the Urban League, and the Trade Union Leadership Council (TULC). Through these groups, urban blacks hoped to effect greater racial equity in housing and education as well as employment, and in 1961 their determined efforts appeared to bear fruit. That year, black Detroiters joined forces with racially progressive white city residents to elect a liberal mayor named Jerome Cavanagh who promised to end the discrimination that plagued Detroit.

Sadly, however, despite the efforts of the Cavanagh administration to work closely with local black leaders and to implement many liberal programs of the Great Society after 1964, housing segregation and work-place discrimination continued to flourish in Detroit. While numerous city whites supported Cavanagh's efforts to improve race relations in the city, many others did not. Ultimately their virulent commitment to civic segregation managed to thwart virtually every racially progressive effort emanating from city hall. Notably, the actions of Detroit's virtually all-white and highly discriminatory police force soon transformed what initially was the black community's dismay at administration ineffectiveness into outright hostility.[3] And although Cavanagh could see that his best efforts to reform the Detroit Police Department (DPD) were failing, he steadfastly refused to rethink his strategic course. The ultimate result of this situation was that city blacks felt utterly betrayed by civic liberals, and in 1967 not a few of them expressed their frustration in an ugly urban uprising.

In late July 1967, after yet another confrontation between the all-white police department and poor African Americans, numerous disenchanted urbanites took to the streets and soon engulfed Detroit in flames. Cavanagh watched in horror as his administration's hopes of greater civic harmony went up in the smoke of those fires. Clearly, this dramatic event reflected the degree to which ordinary African American citizens had become fed up with the mayor's plans for dealing with conservative whites who were so resistant to sharing power and opportunity in the city. Just as significantly, however, it also indicated that many city blacks had lost faith in the formal political process itself.

Well aware that their pre- and post-riot efforts to better Detroit no longer resonated with community blacks, in 1969 liberal city leaders made the surprising decision to support the candidacy of a local African American liberal named Richard Austin in the upcoming mayoral election. Their desire was that Austin, a moderate liberal firmly within the Lyndon Johnson fold, would bridge the growing gap between leadership liberals and the black community at large and thus defeat a conservative white law enforcement candidate by the name of Roman Gribbs. But because racially conservative white Detroiters mobilized very effectively, on November 4, 1969, Roman Gribbs became mayor of Detroit with 257,312 votes to Austin's 250,000, in what scholars have deemed the "closest political contest in the city's history."[4]

If conservative voters had hoped that the ousting of a liberal mayor with civil rights sympathies would restore the racial status quo or discourage greater black activism, events that took place in the city between 1969 and 1973 indicated that they were quite mistaken. Indeed, the combination of Gribbs's strict law enforcement platform and Austin's defeat not only led poor and working-class blacks to become even more politically active, but it spurred a key minority of African Americans throughout the city to form militant black organizations that advocated far more radical avenues for challenging the racial inequities in Detroit.[5] The vocal presence of these new radical organizations in the city virtually ensured that between 1969 and 1973 battles over representation and equality would rage in Detroit's neighborhoods, schools, workplaces, churches, and courtrooms with unmitigated intensity.

Notably, it was once again the actions of the DPD that brought an increased sense of urgency to the battles being waged among radicals, conservatives, and liberals within the Motor City after 1969. When Mayor Gribbs had encouraged police officials to form a special undercover decoy unit called STRESS (which stood for "Stop the Robberies, Enjoy Safe Streets") in January 1971, the already severely strained relationship between the police and the black community deteriorated further. By the police department's own admission, by October 1971 ten suspects had died at the hands of STRESS officers and thirty-eight had been injured.[6]

Although few Detroiters thought the situation in the city could become more tense than it had been during the July insurrection of 1967, the formation of STRESS seriously heightened civic conflict.[7] But it was when a series of controversial legal battles came to trial between 1969 and 1973, distinct cases in which city blacks were charged with killing whites (such as a number of police officers and plant foremen), that the conflict in Detroit not only changed venue but led directly, albeit quite unintentionally, to the election of Detroit's first black mayor.

During the course of these trials, the now decades-old African American struggle for equality came to engulf Detroit's legal arena. The courtroom became both a new site in which African Americans could air long-held grievances about racial discrimination and a place that racially conservative white Detroiters were convinced was being used to promote a wholly pro-black and liberal agenda. As seeming confirmation of this view, in each of these contentious proceedings jurors resoundingly acquitted every black defendant who stood trial.[8] In essence, radical defense attorneys had managed to shift the critical gaze of jurors from the black accused to their white accusers, with little resistance from the presiding liberal judges. Indeed, it was STRESS, not a defendant, most often in the hot seat as these trials unfolded.

Detroit's black and white liberal leaders themselves saw these trials as direct evidence of justice being color-blind and of urban conflict being resolved peacefully and rationally. Both because they feared the rise of black militancy and because they sought to regain legitimacy in the eyes of city blacks, liberal city leaders actively took credit for facilitating the dramatic legal outcomes between 1969 and 1973, and thus they changed the course of Detroit's political history. In short, city liberals' success in claiming the courtroom victories of radical blacks as their own served to renew city blacks' faith in liberalism and in working "through the system" for change. At the same time, it undercut the community appeal of the black radicals and fueled the fires of conservative reaction in Detroit. Thus, by 1973, with black radicals no longer contenders for Detroit's destiny and with white conservatives newly determined to take power, the local political spectrum became divided in a new way altogether. In that pivotal election year, white liberals once again sought to lead Detroit in coalition with blacks, racially conservative whites demanded an overhaul of city government along even more rigorous law enforcement lines, and the liberally reoriented black community had come to decide that only an African American could really be trusted to lead the city into the future. Significantly, each of these groups had a candidate ready and waiting to reshape Detroit in its image.

Determined by 1973 that Detroit would be governed not only by a liberal mayor but specifically by an African American, the black middle class in the city chose its candidate carefully. Sensing the desire in the larger black community for a political figure more daring than Austin had been, it decided that the fiery figure, Coleman Alexander Young, would fit the bill perfectly. Indeed, Young had been in the public eye throughout the 1950s and 1960s but unlike Austin, he had been a highly controversial figure for most of those years. For example, in 1937, when the UAW was engaged in its most bitter battles for union recognition, Young was an organizer for this militant labor organization. And though he had served in the Air Corps during World War II, his outspoken criticism of racial discrimination in the military as well as his vocal support of Henry Wallace by 1948 netted him a reputation as a troublemaker.

Throughout the decade of the 1950s, Young's choice of friends and his organizational affiliations caused many to view him not only as a rabble-rouser but also, more seriously, as a subversive. Young certainly did have close relationships with several politically controversial figures, such as W. E. B. DuBois and Paul Robeson. During these years, he also lent his hearty support to groups such as the National Negro Labor Council, which by 1951 had been deemed a subversive organization by none other than U.S. Attorney General Herbert Brownell.[9] Although Young stated publicly on numerous occasions that "I am not now and never have been a member of any organization that was subversive or whose design was to overthrow the United States in any way," many nevertheless considered him to be too far on the left of the political spectrum. In 1954, for example, the head of the Detroit office of the FBI wrote to J. Edgar Hoover, noting that "this man is a dangerous individual and should be one of the first to be picked up in an emergency and one of the first to be considered for future prosecution."[10]

However, as the 1950s drew to a close, Young's political reputation began to change. In 1959 he decided to run for a seat on Detroit's City Council and, though he lost, during his candidacy he became a popular figure among many working-class black Detroiters on the East Side of the city. In Young they saw a man they could relate to and admire. Never a member of the black bourgeoisie in Detroit, Young was familiar as one who worked numerous menial jobs and thus could understand the needs of ordinary city residents. Grassroots admiration of Young eventually translated into votes, and in 1961 Detroiters elected him as a Democratic candidate for the state constitutional convention. Three years later he won a seat in the Michigan State Senate representing the East Side district of Detroit, and in 1968 he became one of the first black members of the Democratic National Committee. Throughout the 1960s, Young also played a prominent role in the NAACP and the American Civil Liberties Union, and he worked aggressively to secure a state open-housing law as well as to create the Michigan Civil Rights Commission.

Because Young and Jerome Cavanagh shared a deep commitment to civil rights, Young stood firmly behind the white liberal when Detroiters elected him mayor in 1961. But by 1968, Young's support of the Cavanagh administration had become qualified. As Young put it, "I've been for Jerry [Cavanagh] until recently. . . . But the one thing I've got against him is he has been capitulating to the police."[11] Needless to say, as white liberals geared up for the election of 1969, such pointed remarks made Young less attractive than Austin as a potential candidate. But Young was not to be deterred from speaking out critically. As the Cavanagh administration gave way to the Gribbs administration and as police brutality escalated, State Senator Young became even more vocal about the need to rein in the police department. By the early 1970s, Young was not only speaking out against police power, but he also was arguing publicly that blacks needed a stronger voice within the local liberal coalition. Because Young was firmly within the liberal Democratic fold and also was a passionate orator who was deeply committed to reforming the police department, he was an obvious choice for a candidate to many in 1973. As Young noted many times, he was "a Negro first and a Democrat second."[12]

While middle-class black liberals mobilized the poor and working-class African American community to support Young, Detroit's white racial conservatives were initiating their own dramatic effort to keep a law enforcement advocate in the mayor's office. Soon they approached none other than Detroit's own police commissioner, John F. Nichols, to run for office. After the 1967 riot, while Young spoke in favor of establishing a civilian review board for the police department, then-superintendent Nichols argued vehemently that the department must have the right to oversee its own affairs.[13] Indeed, it was Nichols's vocal protection of the police department in the face of mounting community criticism, as well as his no-nonsense approach to the maintenance of law and order, that made him Detroit's police commissioner in 1969 and the architect of STRESS in 1971. Even though Nichols had never run for political office and despite the widespread unpopularity of his STRESS unit in the black community of the city, the *Detroit News* opined on October 8, 1973, that "if white voters follow their usual pattern of higher turnout than black voters . . . Nichols will be the next tenant in the Manoogian Mansion."[14]

As the 1973 campaign unfolded, it was Young, not Nichols, who most defined the election issues and worked them to his advantage. Although Young campaigned for housing reform, educational reform, and other issues that had long been central to blacks and to white racial progressives alike, his primary pledge to Detroiters was to create a "people's police department."[15] Before long, police–community relations in Detroit became the defining issue in the 1973 campaign. By making law enforcement the central issue, Young ran the risk that Nichols would use the bogeyman of "escalating black crime" and the pervasive argument that only a stronger police force could combat such crime, to win needed votes.

In a surprising move, Young immediately went on the offense and challenged Nichols to explain why the level of crime in Detroit was so high, which in turn forced Nichols to defend his own track record as

police commissioner. To do this, Nichols routinely cited statistics showing that, in fact, "Detroit had been controlling crime and that it had
dropped over the last years."[16] Ironically, it was the law enforcement
candidate in 1973 who was forced into arguing that any voter preoccu-
pation with urban crime was simply unfounded. Young clearly stole
Nichols's thunder and successfully persuaded many voters who were on
the fence that, while STRESS had contributed immeasurably to the racial tension in the city, it had not solved its crime problem.[17]

As the 1973 election approached, its outcome remained quite difficult to predict. Both Young's and Nichols's chances depended on how
many blacks turned out to vote, on how many liberal whites would in
fact vote for Young, and on how many black votes Nichols could win
from Young. In the September primary, Young had won fewer white
votes than had black candidate Austin in the 1969 race, which did not
bode well for his chances. On the other hand, Nichols could not rely
solely upon there being more registered white voters in the city than
black to secure his bid for power, as his predecessor Gribbs had done. In
fact, by election day the city had 79,624 more registered voters than in
1969 when voters put Gribbs into office, and the bulk of these new
registrants were African Americans.[18] When the final ballots were tal-
lied on November 6, 1973, it was Coleman Young who managed to
capture these new votes, becoming Detroit's first black mayor with
233,674 votes to John Nichols's 216,933.[19]

Young had won by a very slim margin—3.7 percent of all votes
cast—which meant that he faced many critics from the moment that he
took office. As they well knew, Young had been a staunch supporter of
the Great Society's most controversial economic and racial initiatives
long before he became mayor. For example, Young had routinely and
unapologetically voiced the opinion that "all welfare assistance should
be extended and received AS A MATTER OF SOCIAL RIGHT. . . ."[20]
While in the state senate, not only did Young support a controversial
bill designed to raise benefits to families under Aid to Dependent Children (ADC), but he also played a vital role in enacting Michigan's abor-
tion law.[21] Likewise, Young had made his support of broad-scale
integration initiatives equally clear early on in his career by arguing that
"segregation in the schools can never be eliminated while segregated
housing is allowed to exist."[22]

To the dismay of city as well as suburban white conservatives, Young
did not waver from these sixties-style liberal views even when the national political context in which he was trying to promote them grew

increasingly inhospitable. For example, Young tackled the thorny issue of deteriorating police–community relations with the weapon of integration even when affirmative action was coming under severe attack elsewhere in the country.[23] The mayor's notion that integration must be used to better police–community relations stemmed from the fact that as late as 1972, the 5,558-member DPD was still only 15 percent nonwhite, and it was his administration's belief that "when the police department is fully integrated, all segments of the community will have a chance to feel more directly involved in the department because their sons and friends will be a part of the force."[24] Gradually, Young achieved a far more integrated police department than had any mayor before him. By 1981 a total of 1,126 out of 5,013 police officers were African American, and ten of the twenty police commanders were black as well. The number of women on the force also increased after Young became mayor. Whereas women comprised only 2 percent of the department in 1967, by 1987 they made up 20 percent of the police force and, in addition, there were three female commanders and one female deputy chief.[25] While desegregating law enforcement in the Motor City, Young also paved the way for countless African Americans to become heads of key city agencies as well as to staff these units in unprecedented numbers. Furthermore, Young "set a national record for awarding contracts to minority firms."[26]

That Young largely succeeded in his attempts to integrate positions of power in Detroit and also to bolster several Great Society initiatives for the city's poor only affirmed the conviction of his supporters that liberalism was still a sound political philosophy. Indeed, even though the federal government was busily dismantling Great Society programs like Model Cities throughout the 1970s and 1980s, Detroiters' decision to give Young four additional terms in office (by comfortable and sometimes by spectacular margins) indicates that they were still optimistic that liberalism would prove the salvation of urban America.[27] Several new projects designed to revitalize the city's economy and improve its image helped to fuel this citizen optimism. Young built many new parks and erected recreation centers, low-income housing units, and even a downtown civic center. In 1976, Young also proudly unveiled a huge hotel, office, and shopping complex on the city's riverfront, which he intended to draw both tourists and new businesses into Detroit.

Unfortunately for the Young administration and thus for the city of Detroit itself, the mayor's ambitious urban renewal projects never offset conservative white hostility toward his rule. As scholar Wilbur Rich has noted, many such whites "believed that Young would treat them like second-class citizens. This misconception among whites came from the belief that a black mayor cannot be evenhanded in his approach to racial issues."[28] Clearly, Young did not remove whites from important positions of civic power. Nevertheless, as Young's tenure as mayor unfolded, the hostility of white racial conservatives continued to grow, and their ongoing exodus from the city reached its zenith during his years in office. According to data collected by the city, whereas there had been 891,000 whites in Detroit in 1969, by 1976 only 543,000 remained.[29] As a result of the massive outmigration of urban whites, the percentage of blacks in Detroit rose from 44.5 to 78.4 percent between 1970 and 1990, giving the Motor City one of the largest African American populations in the urban North.[30]

In fact, no accomplishment of the Young administration ever stemmed the tide of white flight, and the effect of this exodus was to bring severe economic distress to the Motor City. When Detroit lost much of its white population, it also lost a significant portion of its economic base. As social geographers Bryan Thompson and Robert Sinclair have pointed out, when white Detroiters left the inner city, they took "the majority of the important service, professional, and leadership activities of the Detroit Metropolitan system" with them.[31] Soon it was no longer inner-city Detroit but the surrounding suburbs that housed the core of the region's auto industry. And, not surprisingly, as Detroit became more impoverished after 1973, its suburbs grew ever wealthier.[32] For example, by 1980 the median income in Detroit was $17,033, whereas in bordering suburb Grosse Pointe Woods it was $35,673.[33] That same year in Detroit, 27 percent of blacks and 6.8 percent of whites in the city were receiving some type of public assistance, and 25 percent of blacks and 7 percent of whites lived below the poverty level.[34] By 1983, "the $11,685 gap in average household income between the overall region of Metropolitan Detroit ($33,241) and Detroit City ($21,556) . . . was the widest of the 33 largest metropolitan areas in the United States."[35]

To be sure, the urban renaissance that Mayor Young and his supporters had dreamed of was not thwarted simply by white flight. When Young took office, the nation as a whole was heading into a major economic recession induced by an oil shortage. As a result of this national downturn, in 1975, Detroit experienced "its worst fiscal crisis since the Great Depression."[36] That year, the city had to lay off more than 4,000 employees, and in time Chrysler's Jefferson Avenue plant (one of the city's largest factories) closed its doors. By 1977 the city had lost 56,400 jobs, and Detroiters were clearly suffering.[37] As Young put it, "No city in America has been harder hit by the national economic recession. Detroit's unemployment rate is three times the national average."[38] Indeed, black unemployment reached a full 25 percent in 1977 as the mayor prepared for another term in office.[39]

Even though the national recession clearly hindered the Young administration's ambitious revitalization goals, hard times alone cannot explain the economic evisceration of Detroit.[40] While every major industrial city in the urban North suffered the recession of the 1970s, few suffered to the extent that Detroit did. It was when Detroit lost most of its white population, tax base, and political support that its future was severely compromised.[41] Not coincidentally, while Detroit had lost 56,400 jobs by 1977, its suburbs had gained 36,500 jobs.[42] As the city grew poorer, its social deterioration escalated, setting in motion a vicious cycle of greater suburban antipathy toward the inner city and, in turn, greater social malaise there. As the longtime NAACP leader and former Deputy Superintendent of the Detroit Public School System, Arthur Johnson, opined bitterly in 1990, "Whites don't know a god damned thing about what's gone wrong here . . . It's Apartheid. They rape the city and then they come and say, 'look what these niggers did to the city' as if they were guiltless."[43]

Despite the social and economic deterioration of the Motor City, Detroit's black community and many of the white liberals still residing there remained fiercely loyal to Coleman Young and his plans to save the city. As perhaps the most striking evidence of this, at the mayor's request in 1981, Detroiters voted themselves a hefty tax increase while city unions simultaneously agreed to wage concessions in order to help out with the deepening fiscal crisis at hand. And even when it became clear that Detroit was losing ground in its War on Poverty, city residents continued to believe that Young was still their best bet. With him, at least, their long-held goals of integration and greater racial equality were finally being tackled head-on. In the end, it would seem, Detroiters tended to gauge the success of Young's liberal leadership primarily in racial, rather than economic, terms.[44]

When Mayor Young finally stepped down from office in 1994 and when he was eulogized following his death in 1997, it became quite clear that his legacy as one of the nation's first African American mayors would be as bitterly contested as his original election had been. Suburban whites, and much of America for that matter, saw the dramatic post-1970s economic disintegration of Detroit as Young's ultimate legacy. To them, the fact that Detroit had declined from a prosperous industrial mecca to an economic wasteland was irrefutable evidence that Mayor Young's election, the politics of liberalism, and the programs of the Great Society in particular had been a terrible social and economic mistake. Even after Young left office, most metro-area suburbanites still wanted nothing to do with the Motor City. As far as much of white America was concerned, Detroit had become too black, too decayed, too crime-ridden—the epitome of all that had gone wrong with the politics of liberalism after LBJ. In short, Detroit was still not a place one wanted to call home.

However, many in the Motor City remained proud to claim Detroit as their home in the 1990s and to them, Young's legacy was more positive. To be sure, many a Detroiter had sharp criticism for how Young had handled the economic crisis that beset their city after 1974. Nevertheless, these inner-city residents overwhelmingly continued to believe that Young's lifelong goal of combating racial discrimination and economic inequality and eschewing the politics of the Reagan Right was something to be proud of and to take into the future.

While a noticeable white disengagement from America's inner cities and from the premises of postwar liberalism is indeed a remarkable chapter in postwar urban and political history, so is the rise to power of numerous self-consciously liberal black mayors in these same inner cities. Indeed, by not grappling sufficiently with the significance of African American political ascendancy in urban centers across the United States, scholars have been too quick to pronounce the irrelevancy of inner cities as well as the death of liberalism as a potent force in American politics.

Specifically, scholarly overemphasis on disaffected and hostile whites has obscured the facts that inner-city blacks and white racial progressives were an equal part of the nation's political equation. The actions of the latter group would determine the viability of social welfare and civil rights liberalism in the United States. Indeed, when whites chose to abandon Detroit in the 1970s and to vote for Ronald Reagan in 1980, they did so as losers, not as victors of the political battle to lead urban America into the future. As important as it was for the contours of America that many whites chose to abandon inner-city living and liberalism after the politically tumultuous and racially rancorous 1960s, it was equally important that urban centers across the United States in the

1970s witnessed the most dramatic increase in black liberal political power ever seen in American history, as a result of the same tumult and rancor. Much white support for inner cities and the politics of liberalism did disappear after 1980, but clearly a biracial faith in the promises of urban living and in liberal prescriptions for effecting social and racial equality thrived well past that year.

Notes

1. Frank McCoy, "Black Power in City Hall," *Black Enterprise* (August 1990): 148–52.

2. For a great deal of interesting information on the African American migration from the South to the North, as well as many U.S. census statistics on migration, see Marcus E. Jones, *Black Migration in the United States, with Emphasis on Selected Central Cities* (Saratoga, CA: Century Twenty-One Publishers, 1980); and National Advisory Commission on Civil Disorders, *The Kerner Report: The 1968 Report of the National Advisory Commission on Civil Disorders* (New York: Pantheon Books, 1988 ed.), 12. See also Joseph Darden et al., *Detroit: Race and Uneven Development* (Philadelphia: Temple University Press, 1987), 69.

3. Leaders of the prestigious black social organization, the Cotillion Club, put the problem of continuing police brutality most pointedly when they wrote directly to Cavanagh in 1965. As they noted, "Records available to you and the police commissioner show that between May of 1961 and February 1964, more than 1,000 citizens sustained physical injuries at the hands of Detroit policemen. Over 600 of these were Negro. . . ." See Cotillion Club to Mayor Jerome P. Cavanagh, January 22, 1965, Part 2, Box 24-3, NAACP Collection, Reuther Library, Detroit.

4. Darden et al., *Detroit: Race and Uneven Development*, 209.

5. By 1969 black radical activism had taken off in Detroit in various grassroots community organizations, labor organizations, and Black Nationalist religious organizations. For more on these groups, see Dan Georgakas and Marvin Surkin, *Detroit: I Do Mind Dying* (New York: St. Martin's Press, 1975); and Heather Thompson, *Whose Detroit? Politics, Race, and Labor in a Modern American City* (Ithaca: Cornell University Press, 2001).

6. Statement by Commissioner John F. Nichols to Common Council, October 4, 1971, Part 3, Box 66, Detroit Commission on Community Relations Collection, Reuther Library, Detroit.

7. Because liberal leaders in Detroit sincerely felt that the police department had to be monitored, racially conservative whites became even more certain that these liberals did not represent their interests, and because virtually every liberal monitoring effort was wholly ineffective, black radicals felt equally unrepresented.

8. Space constraints prevent me from detailing these cases here, but needless to say, in each of them, both city whites and blacks knew that liberal judges, hearing referees, and juries had afforded the defendants unprecedented leeway. For more on this topic, see Thompson, *Whose Detroit?*.

9. Wilbur C. Rich, *Coleman Young and Detroit Politics: From Social Activist to Power Broker* (Detroit: Wayne State University Press, 1989), 71; Darden et al., *Detroit: Race and Uneven Development*, 213.

10. See interview with Young in the *Detroit News*, August 15, 1973, and FBI memo printed in the *Detroit News*, January 27, 1985, in the Young Biographical File, Reuther Library, Detroit.

11. *Detroit News*, November 8, 1968.

12. *Detroit Free Press*, September, 22, 1968.

13. Radio and TV Reports, Inc., April 14, 1972, WWJ-TV, News 4, Box 3, Charter Revision Commission Collection, Burton Historical Collection, Detroit Public Library, Detroit.

14. *Detroit News*, October 8, 1973.

15. Ibid., July 11, 1973.

16. Ibid., October 20, 1973.

17. Young's tactic of pointing to high crime figures was ironic because the police department had inflated those numbers in a bid for federal funding years earlier. See Gebhard Long et al., "The Detroit Police Department—A Research Report on Previous Studies; Criminal Statistics; and Police Technology, Productivity, and Competence," May 1970, Box 37, Kenneth Cockrel/Sheila Murphy Cockrel Collection, Reuther Library, Detroit.

18. Desmond Brandy, Elections Specialist, City of Detroit to author, November 14, 1990.

19. Detroit Election Commission, "Official Canvas of Votes 1953–1978," Vertical Files, Sociology and Economics Department, Detroit Public Library, Detroit.

20. " 'I Take My Stand'—Coleman A. Young for Common Council," Campaign Brochure, Young Biographical File.

21. Public Act No. 370, State of Michigan.

22. "I Take My Stand," Young Biographical File.

23. Mayor's Office Press Release. February 13, 1974, Box 11, Cockrel/Murphy Collection.

24. "Turn Around in the Seventies," The Detroit Police Department and Michigan Office of Criminal Justice Programs, 1973 Booklet, Part 3, Box 68-19, Detroit Commission on Community Relations Collection. Also see: WJR Editorial by Denise Lewis of the Detroit Commission on Community Relations, Part 3, Box 68-19, Detroit Commission on Community Relations Collection.

25. B. J. Widick, *Detroit: City of Race and Class Violence* (Chicago: Quadrangle Books, 1972), 24.

26. *Detroit Free Press*, December 5, 1997.

27. No matter how many hard times befell Detroit, Motor City residents stood by Young and his liberal agenda in election after election. Note the voter returns from the mayoral elections of 1977, 1981, 1985, and 1989:

1977	Young: 164,626	Browne: 63,626
1981	Young: 176,710	Koslowski: 91,245
1985	Young: 141,551	Barrow: 90,907
1989	Young: 138,312	Barrow: 107,073

Figures are courtesy of the Department of Sociology and Economics, Detroit Public Library, Detroit.

28. Rich, *Coleman Young and Detroit Politics*, 266.

29. See City of Detroit Department of Heath Data Book: 1969, 1973, 1976, City of Detroit Municipal Library, Detroit City County Building, Detroit.

30. U.S. Bureau of the Census, *Summary Characteristics for Government Units and Standard Metropolitan Statistical Areas—Michigan* (Washington, DC: U.S. Department of Commerce, Bureau of the Census, 1970, 1990).

31. Bryan Thompson and Robert Sinclair, *Metropolitan Detroit: An Anatomy of Social Change* (Cambridge: Ballinger, 1977), 14.

32. Thompson and Sinclair, *Metropolitan Detroit*, 54.

33. Darden et al., *Detroit: Race and Uneven Development*, 101.

34. Ibid, 70.

35. Ibid, 100.

36. Rich, *Coleman Young and Detroit Politics*, 112.

37. Sheldon Friedman and Leon Potok, "Detroit and the Auto Industry: An Historical Overview," UAW Research Department, International UAW, December 1981.

38. Coleman Young, Mayoral Press Release, April 10, 1975, Box 38, Cockrel/Murphy Collection.

39. Darden et al., *Detroit: Race and Uneven Development*, 217.

40. *New York Times*, January 22, 1975.

41. For an examination of how conservative white hostility to black mayors compromised the viability of inner cities other than Detroit, see Jack White, "The Limits of Black Power," *Time*, May 11, 1992.

42. Friedman and Potok, "Detroit and the Auto Industry."

43. Z'ev Chafets, "The Tragedy of Detroit," *New York Times Magazine*, July 29, 1990.

44. "An Evening with . . . Coleman A. Young," Detroit Chapter of the National Negro Labor Coalition, Pamphlet, August 13, 1994, Young Biographical File.

Suggested Readings

The background literature on the city that Coleman Young came to rule and the material specifically on Young's life is quite rich. For some of the best books on Detroit during the 1940s and 1950s, see Thomas Sugrue, *The Origins of the Urban Crisis: Race and Inequality in Postwar Detroit* (Princeton: Princeton University Press, 1996); and June Manning Thomas, *Redevelopment and Race: Planning a Finer City in Postwar Detroit* (Baltimore: Johns Hopkins University Press, 1997). For more on Detroit during the tumultuous 1960s and early 1970s, see Joseph Darden et al., *Detroit: Race and Uneven Development* (Philadelphia: Temple University Press, 1987); James Geschwender, *Class, Race, and Worker Insurgency: The League of Revolutionary Black Workers* (New York: Cambridge University Press, 1977); Dan Georgakas and Marvin Surkin, *Detroit: I Do Mind Dying* (New York: St. Martin's Press, 1975); B. J. Widick, *Detroit: City of Race and Class Violence* (Chicago: Quadrangle Books, 1972); and Suzanne Smith, *Dancing in the Streets* (Cambridge: Harvard University Press, 2000). For more on Detroit's labor past, see Steve Babson, *Working Detroit: The Making of a Union Town* (New York: Adama Books, 1984); Kevin Boyle, *The UAW in the Heyday of American Liberalism, 1945–1968* (Ithaca:

Cornell University Press, 1989); and Nelson Lichtenstein, *Labor's War at Home: The CIO in World War II* (New York: Cambridge University Press, 1982). For a more contemporary view of how Detroiters assess the Young legacy, see John Hartigan, *Racial Situations: Class Predicaments of Whiteness in Detroit* (Princeton: Princeton University Press, 1999); and Richard Mast, *Detroit Lives* (Philadelphia: Temple University Press, 1994). Finally, for more on Young's life, see Wilbur C. Rich, *Coleman Young and Detroit Politics: From Social Activist to Power Broker* (Detroit: Wayne State University Press, 1989); and Young's autobiography written with Lonnie Wheeler, *Hard Stuff: The Autobiography of Coleman Young* (New York: Viking, 1994).

13

Elizabeth Virrick
The "Concrete Monsters" and
Housing Reform in Postwar Miami

Raymond A. Mohl

In the aftermath of World War II, plans surfaced for the reconstruction of America's aging cities. Crumbling inner-city housing built generations earlier had turned into squalid slums, and narrow roadways designed for pedestrians, horse-drawn streetcars, and electric trolleys had proved incapable of handling traffic in the age of automobility. Population growth and demographic reshuffling—most notably, the massive migration of southern African Americans to industrial centers in other areas of the country and the relocation of much of the white population to sprawling suburban tracts—altered the composition of urban populations. At the same time, the accelerated flight of industry and retail from central cities to outlying areas in metropolitan regions transformed the economic character of the cities.

The pace of urban change accelerated significantly in postwar decades. A severe postwar housing shortage, the tireless proselytizing of housers such as Catherine Bauer, and the unrelenting efforts of labor unions and organizations such as the National Association of Housing Officials led to the passage of the Taft-Ellender-Wagner Housing Act in 1949. Title II of the 1949 law set a national housing goal of a "decent home and a suitable living environment for every American family" and established a six-year target of 810,000 units of new public housing (135,000 units per year). Title I appropriated $1.5 billion to enable local authorities to clear and redevelop city slums. Unfortunately for housing reformers, however, the law's slum clearance and urban redevelopment provisions took precedence under the skillful direction of private developers who used Title I to condemn blighted housing areas for the construction of shopping centers, high-income rental properties, office buildings, and other lucrative investments. The Housing Act of 1954 substituted the term "urban renewal" for "urban redevelopment" and enhanced money-making opportunities for eager entrepreneurs. Urban renewal demolished aging housing units to make way for expanding universities and hospitals, convention centers, and downtown shopping malls. Because low-income African American communities often fell before the wrecker's ball, urban renewal became known as "Negro renewal" and "Negro removal."

Just as they lambasted federal housing laws for their disastrous effects on inner-city residents, so did reformers denounce the impact of the 1956 Highway Act. The new freeways and expressways built as part of the interstate highway system opened up the possibility of high-speed commuting and thereby enhanced the attractiveness of suburbia. Even worse to housing reformers and neighborhood activists, the construction of multilane thoroughfares and massive cloverleaf exchanges necessitated the leveling of existing homes and the displacement of thousands of residents. Again, African American communities most often became the targets for urban "improvements." Local activists such as Elizabeth Virrick questioned whether viable neighborhoods needed to be sacrificed in the name of progress.

Raymond A. Mohl received a Ph.D. degree from New York University and is currently professor of history and chair of the department of history at the University of Alabama at Birmingham. He is the author, editor, or coeditor of ten books, including *The New City: Urban America in the Industrial Age, 1860–1920* (1985); *Urban Policy in Twentieth-Century America* (1993); and *The New African American Urban History* (1996). He is the founding editor of the *Journal of Urban History* and in 1998 served as the president of the Urban History Association.

T o the casual visitor, postwar Miami had all the appearances of a dreamlike tropical paradise. This glitzy resort capital of the nation seemed perpetually bathed in warm sunshine and gentle ocean breezes, an urban landscape buried in lush foliage and tall, stately palms. Its beautiful beaches, fishing and sailing waters, golf courses, country clubs, racetracks, and illegal gambling casinos attracted the rich and famous each winter season. Endless promotional extravaganzas and intense national media attention kept the public spotlight focused on Miami well into the 1950s and after.

Beneath this façade, there was trouble in this winter paradise, stemming from Miami's Deep South racial divide. From Miami's origins in the 1890s, the city's African American population had been subjected to second-class citizenship, denied equal educational and job opportunities, and confined residentially to a few segregated areas of mostly rundown rental housing controlled by politically powerful slumlords. As Miami's Mayor Perrine Palmer put it in a 1947 speech on Miami's low-cost housing needs, "Even though Miami is the youngest of the metropolitan cities, it is already rotting at the core, like the older ones."[1] It was a shocking admission, coming from the leading public official of America's number-one tourist and recreational playground. At the time, Mayor Palmer was pushing for Congressional passage of the hotly debated Taft-Ellender-Wagner bill, which provided federal funds for slum clearance, public housing, and urban redevelopment. Congress eventually approved the legislation, known as the federal Housing Act of 1949, but its full implementation remained problematic, especially in southern cities such as Miami.

In the late 1940s, Mayor Palmer and other Miami advocates of public housing and urban redevelopment found an unlikely ally in a citizen's movement for housing reform led by a diminutive, middle-class, middle-aged white woman named Elizabeth Virrick. By the early 1950s, when she had become Miami's "number-one slum fighter," community organizer, and housing advocate, Virrick was a force to be reckoned with in the city's highly contested political landscape. Throughout the postwar era, she fought the slumlords and the speculative builders who were squeezing tremendous profits from what Virrick called the "concrete monsters"—the newly built 2- and 3-story apartments that densely covered Miami's inner-city black ghetto. She challenged the implementation of urban renewal programs that benefited landowners and developers but ignored low-income housing needs. In the late 1950s and the 1960s, when inner-city expressways threatened to decimate Miami's black neighborhoods, Virrick launched a virtual one-woman antifreeway movement. By the 1960s, Virrick was deeply involved in Great Society fair housing, job opportunity, and social service programs. Most Miamians generally agreed that for their city, Virrick "fired the first shots in the war on poverty."[2] Urban change is generally a slow and tedious process, but through her relentless social activism over four decades, Virrick demonstrated that human agency could make a difference in urban policy, municipal politics, and community life.

A native of Winchester, Kentucky, and the daughter of an attorney, Elizabeth Landsberg was born in 1897. She attended the University of Wisconsin and then Columbia University in New York City, where she studied architecture but never graduated. At Columbia she met Vladimir E. Virrick, a young architect from Russia who had been serving in the Russian Embassy in Washington, DC, when the Revolution broke out in 1917. He never returned to his native country and soon went on to the Columbia University School of Architecture. The Virricks married in 1925 and traveled to Miami on their honeymoon. At the time, Miami and Miami Beach were in the midst of the astonishing but short-lived South Florida real estate and housing boom. It must have seemed a promising time and place for a young architect to begin building a professional career, and the Virricks never left South Florida. Vladimir established an architectural practice in Miami while Elizabeth kept house, raised a daughter, and for several years ran a stenography business in Miami Beach. The family lived in Haiti for a time in the early 1940s, when Vladimir worked as the chief architect for the Société Haitienne Américaine de Développement Agricole, but otherwise their life in Miami remained uneventful until Elizabeth's conversion to housing reform and political activism.

Virrick's political awakening took place in 1948. The instigating issue seemed less than momentous at the time. The place was Coconut Grove, one of the oldest communities in Miami. A self-contained village within the city, Coconut Grove had expensive waterfront villas, neat blocks of white-owned middle-class homes, and a sizable black community. Black immigrants from the Bahamas and their descendants made up most of the residents of black Coconut Grove. White landlords owned a large portion of the black Grove's tiny wood-frame homes and small apartment buildings. A compact and badly overcrowded area of about forty blocks, heavily planted with gardens and fruit trees, black Coconut Grove suffered from inadequate municipal ·services, and few houses had both running water and indoor toilets. The one large tract of empty land that still remained in the black Grove—the so-called St. Albans tract of about 17 acres—had recently been purchased by two well-known Miami speculative builders, John Bouvier and Malcolm Wiseheart. Already active in Miami's black housing market, Bouvier and Wiseheart saw potential profit in Coconut Grove and planned to build apartments and duplexes on the St. Albans tract. These development plans stirred passions in the Coconut Grove community.

Enter Elizabeth Virrick. She and her husband had just invested in a small, newly constructed apartment building in a white section of Coconut Grove. When the lily-white Coconut Grove Civic Club held a public meeting in August 1948 to protest the Bouvier-Wiseheart plan to put multiple units of black housing on the St. Albans tract, Virrick attended to see what all the commotion was about. Also invited to attend was the Reverend Theodore Gibson, a black Episcopal priest from the Grove, who gave an electrifying speech about the desperate living conditions in the black community. A deep-voiced and stirring orator with roots in the Bahamas, Gibson proclaimed that "My people are living seven deep."[3] He demanded better enforcement of housing and sanitation codes and condemned the activities of slumlords. It was a transforming event for Virrick, who felt at the time that Gibson spoke directly to her. As she later remembered in a set of autobiographical notes, Virrick went to see Gibson at his church the next day, asking what could be done. Consequently, they organized a second meeting, this one focused on conditions in black Coconut Grove and attended by over 200 people, both blacks and whites, which in itself was a remarkable event in deeply segregated Miami. A quick convert to grassroots activism, Virrick came to the meeting with a reform agenda and a plan of action. One observer reported what happened: "Father Gibson spoke. Mrs. Virrick spoke. Some people spoke who seemed aroused only by a fear of Negro encroachment. But there were many others who were shocked into action for improvement."[4] This memorable mass meeting ended with the formation of the Coconut Grove Citizens Committee for Slum Clearance, with Elizabeth Virrick as chairman.

With her newly formed institutional base, Virrick became a human dynamo, devoting her energies toward social reform and social action. She appointed subcommittees on sanitation, rezoning, and exorbitant rents. She convinced the Miami City Commission to conduct a survey of sanitation and public health in Coconut Grove. She persuaded the city to collect garbage regularly and prompted the local water company to extend water mains to every street in the black Grove. Virrick successfully used her contacts in the press and local radio to publicly pressure Grove landlords to reduce rents to the same level paid by white families for comparable housing. Despite opposition from slumlords such as Luther L. Brooks, who managed a large rent collection agency for apartment owners, the Citizens Committee prevailed upon the Miami City Commission to enact ordinances in October 1948 requiring every Coconut Grove residence to have running water, flush toilets, and septic tanks, replacing widely used outdoor wells and privies. When some landlords refused to comply with the new rules, the Citizens Committee got the city health department to initiate legal action. A low-interest loan fund was created to help black homeowners comply with the new ordinance. Successful passage of the city sanitation ordinances seemingly empowered Virrick and her reform colleagues.

The Citizens Committee soon initiated a variety of other programs and reforms. A new system of block clubs in the Grove led to a massive clean-up campaign, complete with parades, bands, speeches, and prizes for the best home improvements. Neighbors banded together to clean up and transform empty lots into small parks and playgrounds. Plans for a community center, a health clinic, adult education programs, and a day nursery were implemented. The health department began a campaign of rat, fly, and mosquito extermination. For the first time, the city hired black policemen to patrol the Grove area. Within a year, through persistent local action, Virrick's Citizens Committee had sparked a remarkable transformation of black Coconut Grove.

These early achievements of the Coconut Grove Citizens Committee represented a modest beginning. Coconut Grove, after all, was a small neighborhood. The slumlords still owned most of the rental housing. Little had been accomplished on the issue of rezoning black Coconut Grove from commercial and industrial to single-family residential use. Speculative builders had already begun putting up some new apartment blocks in the black Grove. The slumlords, represented by Brooks and apartment builders such as Bouvier and Wiseheart, had much to lose and were more intransigent on the zoning issue, and they used their collective influence to stave off city commission action. The rezoning issue became Elizabeth Virrick's next big battle for urban reform.

The rezoning campaign pitted the increasingly relentless Virrick and the Citizens Committee against the locally powerful real estate lobby and their political allies. Virrick's group pushed a new zoning plan that would retain the primarily small-home, single-family character of the neighborhood. However, early in 1949, despite much debate, numerous public hearings, and vigorous lobbying, the Citizens Committee zoning proposals were rejected by Miami planning officials and city commissioners. In numerous editorials, the *Miami Daily News* lashed out at recalcitrant public officials as "willing tools" of land speculators and ghetto builders. But the builders and landlords came away from the political debate over zoning with a free hand to put up their "concrete monsters," as Virrick began calling the planned multiple-apartment units.[5]

The Coconut Grove reformers did not give up. They continued to press for zoning reform, this time using the petition and referendum process. In November 1949, apparently swayed by Virrick's reformist vision of better housing for all, Miami voters approved the rezoning plan by a large majority. It was the first time in Florida history that the initiative and referendum method had been implemented successfully. In the aftermath of the successful 2-year Coconut Grove struggle, Virrick received local and national recognition for her community work, including the Dade County "Woman of the Year" award.

For Elizabeth Virrick, the Coconut Grove zoning battle of the late 1940s turned out to be a mere beginning. In the months and years that followed, the Citizens Committee carefully monitored activities of the city planning board, which had the authority to approve zoning variances. Miami planning officials and city commissioners, not to mention the builders and slumlords, remained hostile to housing reform even after passage of the National Housing Act of 1949, which promised federal assistance to cities for slum clearance and public housing. Many southern cities and states rejected federal assistance of any kind because of a narrowly held conception of states' rights. Such views were still powerful in Miami in the 1950s, when federal support for public housing seemed to many an opening wedge to take control of local programs. Moreover, the real estate lobby, nationally and in southern Florida, portrayed public housing as dangerously un-American and socialistic. At the same time, they soon recognized the huge profit potential in slum clearance and urban redevelopment activity. Virrick's next big battle sought to secure, against powerful opposition, local implementation of the public housing provisions of the Housing Act of 1949. She also began shifting her focus from the small and compact neighborhood of Coconut Grove to the larger and more complex arena of metropolitan Miami.

The reformers sparked a protracted struggle in early 1950, a struggle that lasted more than a decade, after the Miami City Commission by a 3 to 2 vote rejected federal funding for slum clearance and public housing. The Housing Act of 1949 had authorized 810,000 units of public housing and provided the mechanism for a widespread program of slum clearance and urban redevelopment. The trouble, as might be expected, lay in local implementation of the new legislation. Miami's civic leaders held differing positions on public housing, with some adamantly opposed to any federal funding and others willing to use federal funds to maintain racial separation. Miami City Commission meetings became a battleground between housing reformers and the real estate owners and their attorneys, as well as among the commissioners themselves.

Politically charged conceptions of free enterprise lay at the heart of the Miami housing debate. In April 1950 the city commission enacted a slum clearance ordinance of its own, one that did not rely on federal funding. The new ordinance required more rigorous self-enforcement of sanitation and building codes by the slum landlords themselves. Parrying the public housers, city officials contended that the local private housing industry could build all the low-income housing that was needed, which is what the builders themselves maintained. Political leaders claimed to be interested in slum clearance and better housing, but they argued that the private real estate industry was best positioned to achieve these goals.

Virrick publicly scoffed at these claims. The city's housing plan, she wrote, was "merely a patchwork job of slum perpetuation." The new Miami slum clearance ordinance "had no more chance of accomplishing this end than a jack rabbit." She also linked city commissioners to local real estate interests, saying, "this ordinance was dreamed up by the opponents of public housing as a panacea" and then put into place by the politicians.[6] The *Miami Herald* agreed with Virrick, editorializing in March 1950 that "Free enterprise has nothing to do with the issue. Yet it has been the slogan which has been used as the sandbag to beat to its knees every slum clearance proposal which has dared to show its head to the public in the last twenty years."[7] The landlords and builders waved the flag of Americanism and free enterprise to advance their financial interests, and the politicians went along. It was a carefully calculated strategy in 1950, in the midst of the anti-Communist crusade we have come to know as McCarthyism.

The feisty Virrick ominously noted that "the storm clouds [are] now gathering," but she did not shy away from another fight.[8] During 1950 and 1951 housing reformers resurrected the initiative and referendum process that had worked so well in Coconut Grove, hoping in this way to implement a city ordinance on slum clearance and public housing. Reformers established an ad hoc Miami Citizens Housing Improvement Committee, with Virrick and Abe Aronovitz, a local attorney, playing major roles, to challenge the Miami commission's rejection of federally financed public housing. The new housing reform committee launched the petition campaign in early April at a mass public rally at Miami's downtown Bayfront Park that drew over 2,000 people. Aronovitz made an impassioned pro-housing speech, sarcastically attacking the "big-bellied builders."[9] Over the next two months, Virrick, Aronovitz, and other housing advocates spoke at innumerable gatherings, including at least one meeting of unfriendly real estate brokers and builders. Debates were held at local club and association meetings as well as on Miami radio and television shows. As with the earlier Coconut Grove campaign, the reformers sought to engage the public on housing issues.

With profits at stake, the builders and landlords defended their position aggressively. They formed the Committee Against Socialized Housing, with the appropriate acronym of CASH, in response to Miami's public housers. The group had the backing of the Miami Board of Realtors, several leading bankers, and top politicians, including Miami's new mayor, William Wolfarth. CASH distributed printed leaflets, brochures, pamphlets, and cartoons against public housing. These materials had been sent to Miami by the national real estate lobby, composed of the National Association of Real Estate Boards, the Mortgage Bankers Association, the National Association of Home Builders, and the U.S. Savings and Loan League. Full-page newspaper ads trumpeted the builders' and landlords' position. Public housing, CASH contended, represented the first "step toward the socialistic state."[10] One CASH newspaper ad suggested that the reformers' expressions of concern about "poor slum dwellers [was] a mere sentimental smoke screen to close the eyes of the sympathetic American people, while socialism takes over this country."[11] Similar battles against public housing were under way in other cities, using, as Virrick noted, "the same slogans, the same billboards, the same distorted and untruthful arguments."[12]

Thanks to Virrick's earlier work in Coconut Grove, public consciousness on housing issues had been raised substantially in Miami by 1950. Consequently, opponents of housing reform often found themselves on the defensive. Newspaper columnists attacked the builders and landlords as heartless, selfish, and greedy, seeking only to maximize profits from building and renting in the slums. *Miami News* columnist Bill Baggs, a big supporter of Virrick's movement (he fondly called Virrick "my ol' Kentucky babe"), labeled CASH "an outrageously stupid and dangerous group."[13] In several columns, he hinted at collusion and payoffs between the real estate people and some city commissioners. Columnist Jack Bell of the *Miami Herald* considered as laughable the builders' claim that they would supply all the needed low-income housing and accept lower profits: "altruism isn't exactly running rampant among that group," Bell wrote in a column dripping with sarcasm.[14] Investigative reporter Luther Voltz of the *Herald* demonstrated that the builders' private redevelopment plan was simply "rebuilding" new slums, replacing older shotgun shacks with multiple-unit concrete apartment houses that quickly became overcrowded but that also produced greater income.[15] Leaders from the black community similarly condemned CASH's motives. Typically, the Reverend Edward Graham, Miami's leading black Baptist minister, attacked opponents of public housing as "persons seeking to profit from their own rental units at the expense of human misery."[16] Harry Simonhoff, editor of the *Jewish Floridian*, strongly endorsed public housing but also blasted Miami's white establishment, writing, "The treatment accorded to Negroes in metropolitan Miami is a blot upon American civilization."[17]

The petition campaign of 1950 led to a positive outcome, at least temporarily. With more than enough signatures, reformers forced a referendum on slum clearance and public housing. Voters approved the proposal by a substantial majority. However, subsequent legal challenges by housing opponents forced a second referendum in 1951, which supported housing reform by an even greater majority. The same election put a pro-housing majority on the city commission as well.

Virrick's initiative and referendum victories between 1949 and 1951 demonstrated that Miami's voters were ready for housing reform. Unexpectedly, more legal wrangling soon prevented any immediate public action on urban redevelopment. In August 1952, Miami's housing and redevelopment plans were thrown into disarray by a Florida Supreme Court decision in the case of *Adams v. Housing Authority of the City of Daytona Beach, Florida*. The ruling declared that using the eminent domain process for federally funded redevelopment was unconstitutional in Florida. This legal decision delayed redevelopment and urban renewal programs in Miami for more than a decade.

Virrick spent a good part of the 1950s trying to get an amendment to the Florida constitution through the legislature that would authorize urban renewal. Failing that, she actively promoted four separate efforts to put legislation enabling urban renewal on the Florida statute books. She sponsored public forums to educate the public but also denounced the Florida legislature at every opportunity. As Virrick told a Miami reporter, "We have officials who are supposed to be leaders, but who don't have any common sense. They talk about sin and motherhood, but everything they utter shows they don't know anything about urban renewal."[18] Not until 1959, when the state supreme court upheld a Tampa redevelopment law, did Florida join other states in accepting urban renewal funds from the federal government. Political and jurisdictional disputes in the early 1960s between the city of Miami and the newly established Dade County metropolitan government, known as Metro, delayed implementation of urban renewal still further.

There were other battles in the years and decades to come. Throughout the 1950s, Virrick hammered away on the issues of slum clearance, public housing, and building and zoning controls in Miami's expanding black neighborhoods. However, none of these housing reforms did anything to diminish racial segregation in Miami neighborhoods or public housing projects. Dating to the early twentieth century, racial zoning policies maintained physical distance between blacks and whites, even though that practice had been outlawed by the U.S. Supreme Court in the case of *Buchanan v. Warley* in 1917. Miami's housing reformers accepted residential segregation as a given in the 1950s, but sought better housing for blacks and expansion areas for new black housing developments. Miami's black civil rights leaders at the time, notably preachers Theodore Gibson and Edward Graham, also worked for housing reform within the context of a racially segregated society. Elizabeth Virrick was not a civil rights activist, but instead sought to expand housing availability through public housing and urban renewal. Influenced by the emerging black freedom struggle, Virrick later came to recognize that ending slums depended on ending racial segregation. "It is a plain hard fact," she contended in 1960, "that we will never get rid of slums if we have segregation, and vice versa, if we did not have segregation, we could get rid of slums."[19]

Maintaining the status quo seemed to be the official watchword throughout the 1950s. Federal redevelopment funding was banned at the time, but city and county officials failed to come up with alternative slum clearance plans. Miami established a Department of Slum Clearance and Rehabilitation in 1952 after Virrick packed city commission meetings with hundreds of supporters, but eventually the new department came to be headed by an ally of the slumlords. Building codes went unenforced for years; landlords ignored repair notices and condemnations. The Miami Housing Authority, controlled for a time by anti-housing appointees, made little progress on new public housing until the mid-1950s, when a single new project was completed. Minimal as this effort was, given the city's need for low-cost housing, the Miami Board of Realtors went to court to halt construction. In the late 1950s, Miami city commissioners continued to undermine the efforts of the Miami Housing Authority. As Virrick put it in 1958, "The opposition to any change in the status quo here is unbelievable and is carried on by the very influential and wealthy so-called respectable people who own the extensive and profitable Negro slums." Not only did the slumlords have friends in government, but as Virrick bitterly suggested, "Almost none of our officials [seem] to be interested in anything from which they cannot profit."[20]

During the 1950s and 1960s, Virrick engaged in a long-running battle with Miami builders, realtors, and slumlords. Most of Miami's housing problems, Virrick sarcastically noted in 1958, could be attributed to "the number of real estate people to the square inch."[21] These were the people who reshaped Miami's residential landscape in a major way in the 1950s. Even during Virrick's petition drives, residential transitions were already under way as white neighborhoods gave way to African Americans seeking better housing. Segments of the local real estate industry facilitated the process of neighborhood turnover. The idea of maintaining residential segregation remained a powerful imperative in Miami. And in Miami's black ghetto, slumlords were moving quickly to replace thousands of small, wooden houses with the much larger and ultimately more lucrative concrete monsters.

Despite Virrick's persistent warnings about the spread of slum conditions to new areas, things seemed to get worse in the 1960s. In August 1965 the *Miami Herald* reported on a wave of new apartment house construction all over metropolitan Miami, a trend fostered by inadequate zoning laws and the weakness of planning controls. "Big blockbusters wedged on tiny plots of ground and surrounded by asphalt are cropping out all over," reporter Juanita Greene noted. Greene traced this construction pattern back to the mid-1950s, when the city of Miami began granting more building permits for apartments than for single-family houses or duplexes. By 1963, the movement had "engulfed" all of Dade County. Up to that point, the concrete monsters had been mostly confined to the inner-city black community. But, Greene went on, "in the past three years the monster has migrated from his original habitat."[22] Virrick had been throwing out caution signs about the multiple-unit apartments since the late 1940s, but the ghetto builders had continued and mostly prevailed.

Luther Brooks, owner of the Bonded Collection Agency and Miami's chief slumlord, emerged as the special target of Virrick's scorn during these years. By the late 1950s, Brooks's company collected rents from over 10,000 rental units in Miami, making it one of the largest rental firms in the country. Politically connected, Brooks was said to be "chummy" with four of the five Miami city commissioners. Press reports in 1958 and a subsequent grand jury investigation linked Brooks to city officials charged with enforcing building and sanitation codes. Records on over 500 already condemned Brooks properties were somehow "lost" by Frank A. Kelly, Brooks's friend and head of Miami's Department of Slum Clearance and Rehabilitation.[23] Reported violations in hundreds of other Brooks properties were never followed up.

An outspoken opponent of public housing, Brooks cleverly manipulated the furor over slum clearance to benefit the slumlords, and his own company as well. Using the slogan of "free enterprise," Brooks took the lead in encouraging property owners to replace aging wooden slum houses with new concrete monsters. In so doing, he argued that the private real estate sector was able to provide for the housing needs of low-income families. Later, when urban renewal and expressway building destroyed thousands of inner-city rental units, Brooks essentially managed the process of blockbusting by which displaced blacks moved into transitional white neighborhoods. Trading barbs at city commission meetings, in the newspapers, and in radio debates, Virrick and Brooks engaged in a bitter sparring match that lasted more than two decades.

Although a consistent advocate of public housing, Virrick eventually became a hard-edged critic of urban renewal in the 1960s. The Housing Act of 1954, by using eminent domain to assemble large land parcels for private developers, had become nothing but a massive "real estate promotion." The program, she said, was "rigged in favor of the slum owners," who profited from government purchase of their rental properties. The builders and developers "eat a rich meal and we grab the check and pay it," she wrote, with her typical flair for the dramatic phrase. Unless revisions were made to urban renewal legislation in Florida, the program would simply create more permanent slums. Virrick asked vehemently, "Why should there be a profit for anybody in clearing slums? Why should a sugar tit be given to the slum owners or the real estate and home builder people to pacify them so they will permit us to clear our slums?"[24] She wanted safeguards built into Miami's urban renewal plan that would provide decent, low-income housing and that would guarantee appropriate relocation provisions for those dislocated by redevelopment. Equally important, she promoted the idea that all urban renewal housing should be built by philanthropic or nonprofit organizations—a means of insulating urban renewal from the real estate speculators and slumlords.

Virrick enjoyed word games and had a habit of writing clever, doggerel verse, which she often recited at meetings. One such piece, titled simply "Housing," skewered urban renewal.

Said Congressman Botch to Congressman Bungle,
"Let's give a thought to the darn slum jungle;
Previous bills gained their authors fame
And there are votes galore to be had from same."

So off with their notebooks went Bungle and Botch
To speech-make and hand-shake, to pry and to watch.
Their erudite study of five days or so
Conclusively proved that the slums had to go.

The Congressmen thrilled to the challenge before them;
The bills and amendments would surely restore them
To office again when their terms had expired.
With campaign hopes high, they worked and perspired.

Bill number X was proposed forthwith
To care for poor people and all their kith.
Filibustering went from morn till night
And they finally agreed that right was right.

Just as success seemed forthcoming at last,
From the town's leading hostess, they felt a cold blast.
To her gala occasions they weren't asked to come.
The reason uncovered was: she owned a slum.

The real estate lobby howled with rage
And the bill went into amendment stage.
"All right," said Bungle, so gay and witty,
"We'll let them have their hands in the kitty.

"We'll buy up the slums with taxpayers' dough
And sell it for less than it costs us, you know.
Then enterprise private will grab at the deal
Because it has a big business appeal."

So they wrote and rewrote until finally they had
A masterful bill that made nobody mad.
After all this ado, is it naughty to wonder
If the whole blessed thing has been one great, big blunder?

'Cause people who need housing are left in the lurch,
Going hither and yon in search of a perch.
They haven't the money to pay the high cost
So the cause of the people seems dismally lost.

Is it possible, really, in this day and age
That we haven't the people sufficiently sage
To solve this slum problem that gnaws at our core
And spreads in our vitals, a cancerous sore?

It takes courage and vision and thinking it through
And not caring a whit what the lobbyists do.
No, Botch, and no, Bungle, you have not succeeded
In giving the people the housing that's needed.[25]

By the mid- to late 1950s, expansive plans for interstate highway construction in downtown Miami complicated Virrick's campaign for housing reform. Interstate planning called for an expressway that traversed the heart of black Miami. A contemplated downtown interchange eventually leveled twenty square blocks, including densely populated black housing and the entire black business district. As these expressway plans became public in 1956 and 1957, Virrick immediately recognized the devastating consequences for black Miami. As she wrote to Wilbur Jones, director of the Florida State Road Department, "the pathway of the new expressway will cause great hardship to the Negroes in the Central Negro area, both home owners and tenants, who will be displaced." She urged the creation of a relocation agency that would provide assistance to those displaced by expressway construction. Without such relocation assistance, Virrick argued, black population densities would rise rapidly, "aggravating the miserable slum conditions that already exist."[26]

Virrick did not get very far with the state road department, because the business of that agency was highway building, not relocation housing. In fact, the Florida road department provided only a 30-day eviction notice to those in the path of the Miami expressway. This policy conformed to federal Bureau of Public Roads guidelines on housing relocation. Federal policy required relocation assistance for those displaced by urban renewal activities but not by interstate highway construction.

Construction of the south leg of the Miami expressway through the black community and into the central business district began in 1964. Influenced by the writings of urban critic Jane Jacobs, Virrick intensified her attack on the highway builders. As Virrick framed the issue, "the helter-skelter spewing out of expressways without proper forethought and planning" would destroy the urban fabric. In a series of hard-hitting articles in her monthly newsletter, *Ink: The Journal of Civic Affairs*, she mounted an assault on a new type of monster—the inner-city expressways (she called them "great Frankensteinian monsters") that destroyed neighborhoods and parks, disfigured the city, and created new slums. Miami, she wrote, was suffering badly from "bulldozitis followed rapidly by asphaltitis." As Virrick phrased it with typical sarcasm, "The theme appears to be: never mind about anything, but Woodman, spare those twelve lanes for the automobile!" Echoing the national outcry against urban expressways that had emerged by the early 1960s, Virrick pleaded often for "a fresh evaluation of the entire expressway system."[27]

Throughout the expressway-building era, Elizabeth Virrick was a lonely but publicly respected voice speaking out on the necessity of linking highway construction with public housing and relocation programs. But it was not to be. Virrick was the closest thing Miami had to an anti-expressway movement, but a one-woman crusade was not enough. The Miami expressway system was completed by the late 1960s, at the cost of uprooting most of Miami's inner-city black community, leaving behind a rubble-strewn urban wasteland in the shadows of an elevated expressway.

By the end of the 1950s, Elizabeth Virrick had become an expert on housing issues. She kept up with housing issues in cities around the country and developed extensive correspondence with the nationwide community of housing officials and reformers. She attended meetings of the National Housing Conference and the National Association of Housing and Redevelopment Officials, published articles in the public housers' *Journal of Housing*, contributed chapters to scholarly books on housing, and toured European cities with others investigating alternative models of housing reform. With her friend Marjory Stoneman Douglas, she began researching and writing a book on slums and housing in American cities—a project left unfinished. In the mid-1950s she began publishing her own Miami housing and slum clearance newsletter, *Ink: The Journal of Civil Affairs*, which became an influential vehicle for her monthly critique of city officials, housing bureaucrats, slumlords, and the local real estate industry. In the mid-1960s the Coconut Grove Citizens Committee became the Dade County Conference on Civic Affairs, reflecting Virrick's wider urban interests and involvement. She became something of an institution in Miami, and she seemed to be everywhere, serving on over a dozen advisory boards and committees from the 1950s through the 1970s. Serving on the Dade County Community Relations Board in the 1960s, for instance, put Virrick at the center of an emerging conflict between Miami's African Americans and the growing community of Cuban exiles. Her work on the board of directors of Miami's antipoverty agency, Economic Opportunity Program, Inc., drew upon her years of activism for housing reform.

Virrick demonstrated her political savvy in three successful initiative and referendum campaigns. Her appeals to blacks and whites and across social and economic boundaries reflected extremely effective interpersonal and organizational skills. She quickly developed persuasive powers as an articulate and impassioned speaker, soft-spoken but confident and powerful nevertheless. Her writings for local newspapers and later for her own newsletter were hard-hitting, known for impatient criticism and biting sarcasm but also for sensible analysis and carefully crafted policy prescriptions. Her ability to connect with powerful voices in the media, especially local newspaper columnists and radio and television news reporters, cemented her position as Miami's trusted voice on housing matters.

Virrick was the gadfly, the crusader, the militant watchdog, operating outside the official power structure, badgering city commissioners and planning and housing officials into action. Politicians learned that to cross swords with Virrick might shorten their careers in office. Slumlords, builders, and attorneys for the local real estate lobby hated to see her show up at hearings and meetings. She often made public officials squirm at those open forums, as she demanded full public accountability. As one observer put it, "No one could storm into city commission meetings and lay 'em low so effectively with invective."[28] Her opponents called her a Communist for advocating public housing, but Virrick easily turned that argument around, often making the case that "slums are the most fertile soil for the seed of communism."[29] She was knowledgeable, unintimidated, impatient, tenacious, witty, and sarcastic— and she made good press copy. "She mostly battles in the open," one scribe reported, "but if the need arises, she doesn't hesitate to play a cloak and dagger role."[30] Perhaps most of all, Virrick's role was one of educating the public about urban renewal and housing issues. On these matters, Virrick wrote, "Miamians need educating, and I am the teacher."[31]

By the late 1960s, twenty years of community organizing and reform militancy had taken its toll. Now in her seventies, Virrick cut back on her activism, retreating to the arena she knew best—Coconut Grove. Reflecting this shift in priorities, by 1970 the Dade County Conference on Civic Affairs took on the new name of Coconut Grove Cares. The new organization engaged in various social service functions in the black Grove, but Virrick was most proud of the Elizabeth Virrick Boxing Gym, a former Coast Guard seaplane hangar transformed into an athletic facility for Miami teenage boys aspiring to Golden Gloves fame. In the late 1980s, Virrick still came to work every day, sitting at her desk and keeping an eye on things at Coconut Grove Cares. When she died in 1990 at the age of ninety-three, Virrick left a lasting legacy of urban commitment and accomplishment. Given the social and cultural constraints imposed on southern women in the 1940s and 1950s, Virrick established a remarkable public career. For the Miami metropolitan area and its citizens, Virrick and her reform activism made a difference at a time of dramatic urban change.

Postwar urban policy on many issues emanated from Washington, DC, but implementation took place at the local level under the direction of mayors, city councils, city and county commissioners, and local agency bureaucrats. Consequently, a full understanding of late twentieth-century urban history and urban change requires an examination of the decision makers and opinion shapers in cities across the nation—the activists and gadflies as well as the mayors and public officials. In Miami, Elizabeth Virrick confronted local power, appealed to a larger public, and often forced the resolution of conflict on housing and urban reform issues. Every city had such individuals: women and men who made a difference. Virrick's public career puts a human face on American urban history, demonstrating the ways in which individual action mediated, moderated, and shaped the larger patterns of postwar urban change.

Notes

1. Perrine Palmer Jr., "What the Taft-Ellender-Wagner Bill Means to Miami," undated typescript, c. 1947, in Elizabeth Virrick Papers, Historical Association of Southern Florida, Miami, Florida (hereafter cited as Virrick Papers).

2. William Tucker, "She's No. 1 Slum Fighter," undated clipping, c. 1958, Virrick Papers; "Elizabeth Virrick: She Fired the First Shots in the War on Poverty," *Village Post: The Magazine of Miami* 13 (March 1967): 1.

3. Elizabeth Virrick, Autobiographical Notes, undated typescript, Virrick Papers.

4. Marjory Stoneman Douglas, "Slum Clearance, Community Style," undated typescript, c. 1953, Virrick Papers, 4.

5. Stephen B. Harris, "St. Albans Developers Win Commission's Vote," *Miami Daily News*, February 4, 1949.

6. Elizabeth Virrick, "History of the Site Selection for Public Housing," undated typescript, c. 1954, Virrick Papers, 5.

7. "Same Story with Same Sad Ending," *Miami Herald*, March 17, 1950.

8. Virrick, "History of the Site Selection for Public Housing," Virrick Papers, 6.

9. Lawrence Thompson, "Heated Slums Debate Draws 2000," *Miami Herald*, undated clipping, c. March 1950, Virrick Papers.

10. Committee Against Socialized Housing, "Can You Afford to Pay Somebody Else's Rent?" undated newspaper ad, c. March 1950, Virrick Papers.

11. Jack Kofoed, "Ads Opposing Federal Housing Termed Ridiculous Propaganda," *Miami Herald*, April 18, 1950.

12. Virrick, "History of the Site Selection for Public Housing," Virrick Papers, 7.

13. Bill Baggs, "In the Bag," *Miami Daily News*, undated clipping, c. June 1950, Virrick Papers; Bill Baggs to Elizabeth Virrick, October 8, 1968, Bill Baggs Papers, Richter Library, University of Miami, Coral Gables, Florida.

14. Jack Bell, "Letter to Mayor Wolfarth," *Miami Herald*, undated clipping, c. March 1950, Virrick Papers.

15. Luther Voltz, "Rebuilding of Slums Under Way," *Miami Herald*, undated clipping, c. March 1950, Virrick Papers.

16. "Slum Clearance Group Asks Action on Housing Project," *Miami Herald*, March 14, 1950.

17. Harry Simonhoff, "Low Rent Housing and Negro Segregation," *Jewish Floridian*, March 31, 1950.

18. Tucker, "She's No. 1 Slum Fighter," Verrick Papers.

19. Maxine Phyllis Harris, "Coconut Grove Citizens Committee for Slum Clearance, Inc.," unpublished typescript, 1960, Virrick Papers, 17.

20. Elizabeth Virrick to Arthur Field, March 14, 1958, Correspondence Files, Virrick Papers; Elizabeth Virrick to Marion Mason, August 31, 1958, Correspondence Files, Virrick Papers.

21. Elizabeth Virrick to Dorothy S. Montgomery, April 23, 1958, Correspondence Files, Virrick Papers.

22. Juanita Greene, "Booming New Slums Blight Miami Scene," *Miami Herald*, August 23, 1965.

23. Morty Freedman, "Slum Agent Has Right Friends," *Miami Herald*, March 17, 1958; Morty Freedman, " 'Dead File' Saves Slums: 500 Condemned Hovels 'Lost,' " *Miami Herald*, March 16, 1958.

24. Elizabeth Virrick to Joe O. Eaton, March 26, 1957, Correspondence Files, Virrick Papers; Elizabeth Virrick to Frederic Sherman, December 5, 1960, Correspondence Files, Virrick Papers; Draft Letter on Redevelopment, undated typescript, c. March 1957, Virrick Papers; Untitled Article Draft on Housing and Redevelopment, undated typescript, c. late 1950s, Virrick Papers.

25. Elizabeth Virrick, "Housing," typescript poem, c. early 1960s, Virrick Papers.

26. Elizabeth Virrick to Wilbur Jones, May 9, 1957, Correspondence Files, Virrick Papers.

27. Elizabeth Virrick, "Expressways: Boon or Blight," *Ink Newsletter* 16 (April 1964), 2–3; Elizabeth Virrick, "Expressways," *Ink: The Journal of Civic Affairs* 16 (November 1964), 3–4; Elizabeth Virrick, "Is This Planning?" *Ink: The Journal of Civic Affairs* 17 (January 1966), 6.

28. Ian Glass, "Little Battler against Slums to Get Honor," *Miami News*, May 25, 1967.

29. Elizabeth Virrick, Untitled Position Statement on Public Housing, undated typescript, c. 1950, Virrick Papers.

30. Tucker, "She's No. 1 Slum Fighter," Virrick Papers.

31. Elizabeth Virrick, "Biographical Information," typescript, 1974, Virrick Papers.

Suggested Readings

Bauman, John F., et al. *From Tenements to the Taylor Homes: In Search of an Urban Housing Policy in Twentieth-Century America.* University Park: Pennsylvania State University Press, 2000.

Gelfand, Mark. *A Nation of Cities: The Federal Government and Urban America, 1933–1965.* New York: Oxford University Press, 1975.

Mohl, Raymond A. "Making the Second Ghetto in Metropolitan Miami, 1940–1960." *Journal of Urban History* 21 (March 1995): 395–427.

———. "Race and Space in the Modern City: Interstate 95 and the Black Community in Miami." In *Urban Policy in Twentieth-Century America*, edited by Arnold R. Hirsch and Raymond A. Mohl, 100–58. New Brunswick, NJ: Rutgers University Press, 1993.

———. "Whitening Miami: Race, Housing, and Government Policy in Twentieth-Century Dade County." *Florida Historical Quarterly* 79 (Winter 2001): 319–45.

Teaford, Jon C. *The Rough Road to Renaissance: Urban Revitalization in America, 1940–1985.* Baltimore: Johns Hopkins University Press, 1990.

Virrick, Elizabeth. "New Housing for Negroes in Dade County, Florida." In *Studies in Housing and Minority Groups*, edited by Nathan Glazer and Davis McEntire, 135–43. Berkeley: University of California Press, 1960.

Index